0

INCOME and WEALTH

from

SELF-DIRECTED

INVESTING

2019

IAN DUNCAN

MACDONALD

Informus Inc, Publishing Division

Library and Archives Canada Cataloguing in Publication

MacDonald, Ian D., author

INCOME AND WEALTH FROM SELF-DIRECTED INVESTING 2019 / Ian Duncan MacDonald

Issued in print and electronic formats

ISBN 978-1-9991-980-0-8 (paperback).

1.Stocks 2. Dividends I Title. II Income and Wealth from Self-directed Investing 2019

Published by

Informus Inc, Publishing Division,

2 Vista Humber Drive, Toronto, Ontario, Canada, M9p 3R7

www.informus.ca

tel. 929-800-2397

Publisher: Ian D. MacDonald / Cover Design: Ian D. MacDonald

This book is for all those who sought help with their investments and could find no one they could trust.

A special acknowledgment to J. G. Peter King, artist, inventor, computer scientist and friend of forty years, he died before I finished this book. His encouragement and assistance in the writing of this and all my books is not forgotten.

A special thanks to Ms. Innocence, Carmen MacDonald, Allan Swartz and Ivana Tupone for their encouragement, words of wisdom and for going through the book searching for errors. They wanted this book to be the best it could be, because they thought its message was important and needed to be heard.

I worked on this book for years. It not only reflects what I have learned about investing through trial and error, but what I personally experienced and observed about business and life. I am sure there are some who will question my insights and conclusions. I hope they will take the time to bring their concerns to my attention so I can address them in future editions.

Ian D. MacDonald

CONTENTS

(A final word and invitation to read Ian Duncan MacDonald's 3 novels)

CHAPTER 1

Greed & Ignorance

Invest for security, wealth and for the freedom of a reliable dividend income. Despite the honeyed words of financial advisers, keep total control of your investments.

It is critical that you know what you are investing in, why you are investing in it and what each investment transaction is costing you. If you don't, your dream of financial freedom may remain just a dream. Unfortunately, it is not the inclination of investment advisers to educate you about investing. They want you to accept the plans they have for your money without questioning them. My objective is to remove any naivete you have about investing and to make you a "street smart" investor.

This book describes a method of investing that can provide you with a safe, reliable, dividend income equal to at least 6 % of the value of the 20 stocks, that you will choose for your stock portfolio. A portfolio whose value will grow, year-after-year, with ever increasing dividend pay outs. Your fears of outliving your money; inflation depleting your portfolio or surviving a stock market crash, will cease to be a concern.

My method of investing comes from the forty years I spent as a senior executive in the commercial risk information industry. In 1991 several clients requested that I analyze two million business records and create a risk score that would sort businesses from the highest to lowest credit risk. My clients were manufacturers, wholesalers, banks and insurance companies. I created this scoring system at a time when it was not known if such a score was possible. A major bank thoroughly tested the scoring system and declared that it was "amazingly predictive" in anticipating commercial failures. It is still being used daily by thousands of corporations.

When my employer was acquired in 1996 by a much larger corporation, I received a large settlement in lieu of a pension. I knew nothing about investing. Control of that money was given to an investment adviser. By 2000, the money had lost half its value.

 I took back control of my portfolio-and created a stock scoring matrix. I quickly recognized that investment decisions were not dissimilar to the business risk decisions that my commercial credit scoring system had solved. With little effort, this stock scoring system guides the selection and management of my stock portfolio. That portfolio has grown by 300% since the year 2000. Its ever-growing dividends now provide me with an income greater than what I earned as a Senior Vice President in a large international corporation.

Initially, I wrote this book thinking that those with hundreds of thousands, or even millions of dollars, to invest would benefit most from it. However, I have since come to realize that even those who are $200 away from insolvency, could also benefit by reading it.

I can identify with those who live pay cheque to pay cheque. When I was twenty-four, after a car accident, I needed to borrow $100, at a high rate of interest, from a finance company to pay my insurance deductible. Unpredicted expenses do occur. Financial independence would never have crossed my mind at that age. Reading this book would have opened my eyes to the benefits and importance of investing. Some of you may want to share the book with your children.

When I was twenty-four, I was oblivious to the reality that I was skirting on the edge of insolvency. It was only the new need to provide for a wife and child that drove me to make a career change, hoping it would bring more income and security. Much to my surprise, I was a success in my new job. I doubled my income in a year. It released my ambition. I learned that if you are stuck in a financial rut, to gain wealth, you must make changes that are outside your comfort zone.

A concern for my wife and my children's ability to manage the stock portfolio that they will inherit, was also a major motivator in writing this book. A sense of responsibility requires preparing for all possible events.

I wanted to warn investors of the financial adviser sharks who always come to feed on naive investors - just like they came to feed on me. The greed of these sharks forced me to learn how to build and manage a self-directed investment portfolio that would provide a reliable income.

This book will accomplish two things:

(1) It will negate any fears of being destined to out live your money and living your final years in abject poverty.

(2) It will give you the confidence to make your own investment decisions for the greatest, safest returns.

Perhaps, my children may squander the inheritance. However, let it never be said that I did not try to prepare them for surviving in an investment jungle that feeds on the innocent, the trusting and the ignorant. If they follow the method laid out in this book, their inheritance will be safe. Their portfolios will grow, and they too will live as comfortably as I have.

Upon hearing that my next book was going to be about investing, several worried people approached me. They told me how stressed they were with their investments because they really did not understand whether their investments were good or bad. Their portfolios were shrinking. When questioned their advisers responded with jargon and a condescending attitude. They were made to feel stupid, intimidated and unsure about the safety of their investments. I was urged to finish this book quickly so they could see a safe path for their investments.

What these investors were seeking was someone who would answer their basic questions about investing the way a friend would. A friend, who was bluntly honest and had nothing to gain from their investments. Someone who had learned to invest successfully and would patiently explain in detail how it was done. They wanted to understand WHAT they should invest in; WHY they should invest in it; WHERE to find these investments; HOW to acquire them and HOW to monitor them.

I am that friend. I am not an investment adviser. I do not have a long list of impressive investment credentials on my business card. All I have is my investment experience and decades of in-depth business knowledge, gained designing systems that predicted the success or failure of millions of businesses

In Chapter 13 you will find a list of 654 companies traded on the Toronto Stock Exchange sorted from best to worse by my IDM score (*all those buying this book can request a free copy of a computer program for their personal computer to instantly score the stock of any company traded on a stock exchange. The matrix that was used to develop the program is available in Chapter 12, for those who wish to calculate scores manually).* These 654 met my method's first criteria, which was paying an annual dividend of at least 3.5% of their stock price. From these 654, I recommend that you pick the 20 best stocks to give you a reliable passive income in an ever-growing portfolio. In Chapter 6 you will learn how I found 20 desirable stocks in the list of 654. In Chapter 9 you will see how easy it is to buy the stocks you have chosen for your portfolio.

You do not need to be a mathematical genius to invest well. Nor, do you need to spend more than five minutes a day monitoring your portfolio once it is established. You do need to have the self discipline to avoid impulsive, unresearched investment decisions and to stick with the decisions your careful analysis has revealed. Patience is important. Stock prices never move in a straight line. The price of good stocks improves over time, but they do it slowly.

 No one can accurately predict the future. You can't guarantee anyone's future financial success. What I guarantee is that you will understand why you chose to invest in the common shares of a publicly traded company and why that company's shares are most likely to increase in price and pay you a good dividend.

For tax reasons and to avoid foreign exchange complications, I invest in Canadian companies. However, anyone, in any country, who wants to buy shares in "good" companies traded on their local stock exchanges can benefit from reading this book. On-line, self-directed investment services are available around the world.

To use the self-directed investment services of a Canadian bank, I had understood that you must be resident in Canada. This may no longer be true. I read a Toronto-Dominion Bank advertisement in Bermuda's Royal Gazette newspaper offering access to self-directed investment services in US and Canadian stocks.

I do not recommend the investment services of one bank over another. They strive to match each other's services. I am sure many offer a satisfactory self-directed investment service.

My self-directed investment method is as far away from speculative investing as you can get. It is not a get-rich-quick method that would excite speculators.

Investing is not an exciting game. It is a serious business. Your future happiness is contingent upon the informed decisions you make for your investment portfolio.

Not long ago, a woman, let us call her Ms. Innocence, sought my help. She was frightened that her future financial health was in jeopardy. Answering her questions and concerns proved to me that my method of investing could work for anyone, no matter how old they were or how little they knew about investing.

I met her when I was involved in a grass roots organization fighting to stop a billion-dollar development. Ms. Innocence was one of the volunteers who assisted me in this battle. She was the resident of a senior's apartment building.

English was not her first language, but she writes and speaks it extremely well. Despite the many challenges she has faced in her life, she has not only survived but flourished. Four years earlier she had sold a successful business. This sale left her with a very impressive sum to invest.

While working together on a community project, we talked about investing. I mentioned the investment book I was writing. Despite her business experience, she said that her knowledge of investing had been restricted to bank savings accounts and government bonds. An investment adviser was managing her wealth. It was her sole source of income. Her investment portfolio had lost $300,000. She now feared that she would outlive her investment and become penniless. The dream of passing an inheritance on to her children and grandchildren seemed in jeopardy.

An investment adviser had managed her portfolio for twenty years. Upon retiring she told him that she now wished to withdraw a modest income of $3,500 per month from her portfolio. The investment adviser assured her that such an amount would present allow her income for a lifetime.

Ms. Innocence asked me if it was normal for an investment portfolio to shrink every year and whether her modest income would really continue into her nineties. I looked at her monthly statements and informed her that there was no reason a large portfolio should be shrinking so quickly. Also, she should have been able to withdraw double the monthly amount without affecting the value of the portfolio.

I asked her why the investment adviser had put most of her money into low interest bonds, preferred shares and mutual funds? She did not know and had never paid attention to what he was doing with her money. All she had ever looked at was the total amount in her portfolio. Her only concern had been receiving $3,500 every month. She said that she would now look more closely at her portfolio.

A few days later, she reported that the investment adviser's annual fee of 1% of her portfolio's value was, on closer inspection, almost 2%. She had not realized that she was paying additional transaction fees every month. Her investment portfolio was experiencing more investment transactions in a month than I would probably put through in ten years. These transactions were generating thousands of dollars annually for the bank's investment service.

In Chapter 4, an extract from a bank's full-service contract appears. It describes all the fees that a client agrees to upon signing. The original is written in the smallest font and displayed in such a compressed format making it almost impossible to read. Could it be they do not want you to read it?

Ms. Innocence, who had been living very frugally, regretted not looking more closely at her portfolio. I told her of my similar experience in 2000 that had caused me to sever the relationship with my investment adviser and open a self-directed investment account. My huge financial loss at that time motivated me to learn how to select stocks that would give a safe income and increase my portfolio's value year-after-year.

Ms. Innocence sought help with her portfolio. Since she had assisted me with the community project, I felt obliged to help her. Thus, began the education of Ms. Innocence.

I quickly realized that her knowledge of investing was very limited. Despite her business background, she understood little about finance. It made me realize that there are many, like her, who need to be shown how to protect and grow their wealth. If my method of investing could remove Ms. Innocence's fear of managing her own money, then I knew it could help thousands.

Many of her questions were so basic that I would never have thought of addressing them. She made this a better book by giving me insight into who needed investment help. Until then, I had only considered, those receiving large inheritances, winning lotteries, signing multi-million-dollar contracts or accepting large legal settlements.

Ms. Innocence told me of the many widows in her senior's apartment building who, from a lifetime of saving and the sale of their homes, had a net worth of hundreds of thousands of dollars. Most of these women had only an elementary education. Unable to comprehend the bank's investment advice, their pride prevented them from revealing their ignorance. They too needed help.

Existing self-directed websites assume a level of investment knowledge that thousands of potential investors do not have. While the banks may write sophisticated instructional material in a scholarly manner, they fail to provide the easy to understand, basic investment information that thousands of unsophisticated investors require.

Ms. Innocence revealed that many of these widows had never written a cheque until forced to do so after their husbands died. Their husbands had done them no favour in taking care of all the family's money matters. Since they were suspicious of anyone prying into their financial affairs, these women had parked their wealth in savings accounts. Here, it was being depleted by living expenses and inflation. Over the last 25 years, while inflation has been running at an average of 1.83%, the major Canadian banks were paying as little as 0.05% interest in savings accounts.

These widows really do face the possibility of outliving their savings

After four months of answering Ms. Innocence's questions, she sent me an email in which she stated, *"in the last day or so I realized that the stress I lived with, is slowly dissipating and my face is relaxing. It is almost impossible to actually believe that I can feel safe. That I can trust my own judgment, though in all fairness you did help even with that. The decisions were mine, of course but I had to be discerning, learning all the time why I took a specific stock and invested in it.*

I am one of possibly millions of people who are discovering the Self Directing Investment and the alternative to using a Private Financial Advisor. And most of us had not been directly involved in managing our money. I might not have been as unusual or naïve, when I let him manage my investments, because at that particular point and in those years, he knew far more than I did. A lot of us ignorant people have jobs or are busy with their lives and it is easier to have an adviser who will manage our savings. So, when you then discover the alternative and learn about Self Direct Investing, you are not only learning the strategies or lessons. You are not only learning about stocks and dividends, but you are entering a totally different way of life. With total control of your financial life, you start to regain your pride and self confidence."

Over the four months, Ms. Innocence's questions were those   of a proud, intelligent woman. Questions, she had been too intimidated to ask her investment adviser. All she wanted was for someone to come down to her level and carefully explain the investment options to her. Polite timidity and pride made her easy prey for an investment adviser.

Too many investment advisers seem to prefer that investors be ignorant and timid. Often, they seem to discourage questions regarding the handling of your money. Some seem to be unable to resist manipulating a client's account to their own financial advantage. Too many, behave like sharks. You are the prey. Buyer beware.

The investment industry has conditioned millions to believe that only qualified investment advisers can make intelligent investment choices. That anyone, after reading this book, could generate greater capital gains and realize more income without their assistance, raises the question as to what are they do to earn the thousands of dollars they charge their clients?

Why don't investment advisers see educating clients in investing as their primary responsibility? If clients are unable to distinguish between a good investment and a bad investment, why do they see that as the client's problem instead of their problem?

The 1 or 2 percent of their portfolio's value that clients pay their advisors each year, may seem like a small amount. However, over twenty years, a client could pay hundreds of thousands of dollars for an investment adviser's service. They continue to pay it whether the value of the portfolio increases or decreases. These fees represent hundreds of thousands of dollars that could have provided additional dividend income.

I stressed with Ms. Innocence that the stock market is not a casino. She should not equate investing with gambling. The wealth of our economy increases when its citizens invest in the common shares of companies. It creates true value. A publicly traded company traded on a stock market is like a living organism. It competes, develops new products, builds an infrastructure and improves the lives of employees, customers and society. A stock represents ownership in a company. It gives the investor a claim to a portion of a company's assets and a share in its profits. This is something not immediately grasped by new investors.

Ms. Innocence pointed out an obvious problem that had not occurred to me. Self-directed investing requires access to a computer and the internet. To self-invest you need to be comfortable with computers (fortunately Ms. Innocence was quite computer literate). You need to do simple things like gaining access to your trading account, finding good stocks, researching stock purchases and doing your banking. These are the first basic skills you need to acquire for self-directed investing. In addition, you need to invest a few hundred dollars in a personal computer. Instructions in basic computer skills are available from many free or inexpensive sources. Libraries, high schools and others often conduct such courses.

I explained to Ms. Innocence that her objective was to find the 20 best dividend stocks among the 4,000 stocks traded on the Toronto Stock Exchange. This sounds intimidating, but all the tools to quickly and easily do so are available, free of charge. While you may not now be able to tell the difference between the stock you want, and a stock that you should ignore, you soon will.

CHAPTER 2

Value Investors & Speculators

To be a self-directed value investor, you need to first establish a self-directed trading account which will take a few hours. Chapter 6 walks you through this process. Once, this portfolio is established, you will only need to spend a few minutes each day confirming that it is performing as expected. Perhaps every six months you may want to spend a few hours doing a thorough review of your 20 stocks.

Why 20 stocks? Why not 50 or 500?

The larger the number of stocks, the more time you must devote to managing your portfolio. Twenty is an optimum number. For safety's sake, only 5% of your wealth should be invested in any one stock (no matter how wonderful you think one stock might be) 5% X 20 stocks = 100% of the cash that you wish to invest. You should buy stocks that you expect to own for the rest of your life.

Inevitably one or two of these carefully selected stocks will show a temporary loss in value and may be worth less than what you paid for them. However, this loss will be offset by the 18 other stocks in your portfolio that will show a gain in value. When one stock that was down bounces back, another one of the 20 will probably decline. To have all 20 as gainers at the same time would be unusual, no matter how carefully you have chosen your portfolio. Therefore, the emphasis should be on the total value of the portfolio, not on the status of an individual stock. It would be unusual if a carefully chosen portfolio did not grow.

Anticipate that your dividend income will exceed what you need to live on. You may add this surplus income to the 20 stocks in your portfolio.

I recognized that there are some who love the thrill of "gambling" in the stock market. They are "speculators". To maximize quick profits, they will risk every cent, or even borrow money, to buy a single stock. They are certain, it is going to skyrocket and deliver great wealth. As soon as the stock has reached, what they think, is its highest price, they sell it. To realize a profit there must be a buyer, someone who is convinced the stock has not achieved its highest price. One of them is wrong. Having sold the stock, the seller must now search for another *hot* stock whose price is undervalued. Speculators repeat this game over and over.

Since speculative stocks do not usually pay dividends, speculators generate income by selling shares in their portfolio. With less capital to invest, they take greater risks to compensate for their shrunken portfolio. Unlike speculators, value investors realize income by buying shares in well-run, profitable, dividend paying companies which have prospered for years and will continue to prosper.

Laws exist that require public companies to make their audited, financial statements available to the public. This financial data makes it possible to identify profitable companies paying dividends year-after-year. You are unlikely to see a dividend paid by a company that is not profitable.

The reason you invest in several companies is that some companies are in favour, while others are out of favour. Stock prices fluctuate based on facts, emotions and rumours. Of my shares in 20 good solid companies, I may have one to three that are below the share price at which I bought them. Since even these out-of-favour stocks are in good solid companies, they almost always recover and show an increase over the price I paid originally for them.

The price gains in my other stocks make up for those that are down. Almost all the stocks that I have bought over the last 20 years are still in my portfolio, generating a steady income while the share prices grow and increase my wealth.

Perhaps two or three times in a lifetime, an investor will pass through a period where large numbers of investors lose confidence in the stock market and sell their shares. It is surprising how quickly the value of a portfolio can drop when this happens. Within weeks the value of your portfolio could be worth half of what it once was. However, while the stock price has dropped in several of your stocks (but not all), you still own the same number of shares you have always owned in those companies.

Since you have invested in solid profitable companies, you will find that they will most likely continue to pay the same amount in dividends that they were paying before the drop. Why? Because even in times of economic decline, people still buy food, keep money in a bank, pay rent, etc. Companies still make sales and profits. It is unlikely that your dividend income will show any significant decrease as you wait for the share prices to rebound. A stock market downturn is not the end of the world. It is a pause, a period of adjustment in the economy. You are not a speculator. You wait it out. If you look at a hundred-year chart, you will see significant setbacks perhaps every 5 to 10 years but the stock market over decades shows an ever-increasing value.

Speculators often sell at the first sign of a major stock market downturn and take their losses. They will sit with their cash looking for safe investments. This is the time when some will invest in solid companies paying dividends because they know that the share prices of these companies are the first to recover. As soon as speculators think the market has recovered, they will sell their dividend-paying stocks. This cash is needed to invest in the next *hot* speculative stock, certain to make them super rich.

My long career in the commercial risk information industry taught me the benefits of being a value investor. Research showed me that every year 20% of businesses cease to operate. A similar number of new businesses appear to replace them. Businesses fail because of competition, new technology and poor management. Their removal from the marketplace is of benefit to competitors who acquire the failed company's clients.

Over a period of twenty years I researched commercial success and failure, in a data base of 2,000,000 businesses. I learned that companies, like human beings, establish a unique "character". These patterns of successful behaviour are passed on to future generations of employees. Profitable companies that pay dividends, year-after year, reveal the successful behaviour value investors seek.

The only thing consistent in life is change. Value investors need to consult the Canadian business press daily online editions of the Financial Post, The Globe & Mail's Report On Business; watch Business News Network on television, etc.). They know mergers, acquisitions, changes in laws, departures of key executives and new technologies can wipe out profits. In anticipation of significant changes in a few companies in their portfolio, no more than 5% should be invested in any one stock.

Speculators don't look for such patterns. I admire their bravery even if I do not understand it. One of my close friends, a speculator, buys hundreds of thousands, even millions of shares in a company, for a few cents. Sometimes, the penny share price rises, over a few months, to be worth more than a dollar. He can realize a profit of several hundred thousand dollars. However, to realize this gain the shares must be sold and taxes paid on the capital gain.

A few times he was fortunate to sell a penny stock at its height, just before the public learned that the stock was a fraud. Million were lost by those investors whose late entry and exit timing were not as fortuitous.

My research of his speculative stock purchases revealed that all were new companies with a share price below one dollar, unprofitable and having problems marketing their services. My friend told me stories of being a victim of "pump and dump" investments. This occurs when a stock promoter "pumps" (talks up) the tremendous potential of a penny stock, as if it were the next Apple or the next Microsoft. Gullible speculators jump in and bid up the limited number of penny shares to dizzying heights. When the stock's promoter, a major share holder, thinks the price has peaked, he "dumps" (sells) his shares. The price of this worthless stock then drops back to a few cents.

Some late entry speculators, who put all their money into what they thought was a "sure thing", when the share price was quickly rising, lose their life's savings. Usually they learn nothing from this loss. As soon as they have saved more money, they start looking for the next big "opportunity" to become rich and recoup their previous losses.

Speculators, who at various times, appear to be wealthy, do not seem to live happier or more fulfilled lives than value investors. They check their penny stock every few hours to see whether it has gone up or down by a penny. A rise of a few pennies can make them joyful. The decline of the stock price by a few pennies can make them fear that they are about to become paupers. They are constantly waging a battle of indecision. Has the stock reached its peak? Have I made a bad decision on this stock? Is it ever going to rise? Should I sell or should I hold?

As a value investor, I can go for months without looking closely at all the stocks that I manage. I carefully choose stocks for their value. My sole concern is the growth of the total diversified portfolio, not just one stock in it. From time to time, the share price of some of my stocks will go down temporarily, but almost all my shares are well above the price that I first bought them. Some have tripled in value. The most value a stock can lose is the price you paid for it but there is no limit as to how high the share price of a well-chosen value stock can rise.

CHAPTER 3

Sudden Wealth

Those receiving large sums of unexpected money have no natural constraints on how to invest. Those who struggle to save $5,000 must make careful investment decisions.

Some acquire sudden wealth through inheritance. Others win lotteries. Some receive large settlements. Many are successful athletes, artists, authors or entertainers who sign multi-million-dollar-contracts. When this sudden wealth appears, they need to be prepared. It is so easy to run through a fortune if you think you could never spend it all. Therefore, before the sharks descend and bite off much of the newly acquired riches, it is critical that the suddenly affluent learn how to both preserve and grow their wealth.

When I graduated from university and moved to the big city, with all my possessions in one small suitcase, I took the first job offered. It was with an international corporation that paid me less than what I had earned in my summer jobs working as a labourer in a mine. Without that summer income, I would never have been able to pay for my education. The habit, I acquired in carefully managing that summer money, is something that has never left me.

$20,000 in my bank account seemed more than enough to meet all my needs. I was a senior executive with a large salary, working for a profitable, long-established company. Almost my entire income was being spent to maintain a nice lifestyle. Investing or in saving money was never a serious consideration. My rich lifestyle was supposed to continue right into my retirement, at which time I was to receive an indexed pension, equivalent to 80% of my salary.

Man plans. Gods laughs. A generous indexed pension fund was not to be. A large settlement was substituted for that pension when the company was suddenly sold. Investing it seemed to be my next step. Despite decades of business experience, I had no investment experience. Protecting myself from future poverty was suddenly a priority.

I contacted a friend who owned a small investment company. He had always displayed all the trappings of wealth. This even included a private resort on a large island where he entertained dozens of clients every summer. Surely, he must have become successful by providing excellent investment advice to his clients.

I visited his office in the heart of the financial district. He asked one of his employees to recommend where my fortune should be invested. In less than ten minutes, I was handed a short list of mutual funds to approve. What he had selected meant nothing to me. I asked no questions then or when I was presented with a contract which I signed without reading. A cheque was made out to my "trusted friend's" company for the largest amount I had ever written in my life.

Now, with both my money and my approval, my "friend" smiled and told me that my retirement was now secure. When I retired, each year I was expected to sell enough units of the mutual fund to live on.

My "friend" assured me that the only investment cost I would incur would be an annual fee of a few thousand dollars to cover his advisory duties and preparation of my income tax return. It would be such a small percentage of the portfolio that he doubted that I would even notice the deduction, in what would be an ever-increasing portfolio. I remember thinking how fortunate I was to have such a good "friend".

Since I now worked for the conglomerate that had acquired my previous employer, I was able to ignore my investment portfolio's very existence. It was going to be more than a decade before I would retire and need to draw on these funds.

Every month, I received a statement. It was a jumble of numbers that meant little to me. It seemed to indicate that the portfolio was increasing in value. I had no idea what my mutual funds were invested in, nor did I care. I vaguely understood that the purpose of a mutual fund was to diversify your investments and protect you from the disasters that investing in a single stock might encounter.

Every summer my "friend" now invited me to his private resort to be wined and dined. What a fine fellow, so generous. Nothing but the best of wine was served. It had been won, at the rare wine auctions he attended. He loved to brag about his clever bidding. I am sure he wrote off the cost of the resort (and the rare wine) as a business expense. It never occurred to me that I was paying for my vacation. There is no such thing as a free lunch.

One day, in the year 2000, at a time when dotcom companies were all the rage, my investment adviser took me to lunch. He was not a happy man. Angrily he ranted about some foolish client who had liquidated a portfolio of a few million dollars because this fool thought that all stock prices were over valued and about to collapse. The fool feared his portfolio would be wiped out. My "friend", who had been an investment adviser for four decades, scoffed at the client's negative crystal ball gazing.

In 2000, hundreds of small internet companies were listing themselves on stock exchanges. They were known as "dotcom" companies. The internet was something new and exciting. Ownership of a dotcom company's shares were believed to be an investor's ticket to great wealth. Many newly formed dotcoms quickly had stock market valuations worth billions of dollars. These were often corporations who had yet to realize more than a few million dollars in sales and had never shown a profit.

Traditional investors, who scoffed at the ballooning dotcom valuations were told by promoters that a dotcom's lack of sales and profits could be ignored because this was a new era. The conventional ways of evaluating an investment were no longer relevant. Dotcom companies had to be judged "differently" than stodgy, profitable companies that had been trading on the stock exchange for decades.

Within a month, after our lunch, speculators panicked and sold their shares in dotcom companies. The stock market collapsed. I, and millions of others, lost half of our wealth. I suddenly realized that my investment adviser, despite his experience, obviously had no clearer insight as to where stock market values were going than I did. I was in trouble. Any plans I had for an early retirement had vanished. This disaster taught me that no one can accurately predict the future and that there are none so blind as those who choose to be. I was now motivated to find a better safer way to invest what remained.

Meanwhile my "friend" was searching for new sources of revenue to replace the lost commissions from his clients' shrunken portfolios. He asked me to give him a letter that would turn over complete control of my diminished portfolio to him. I took this as confirmation that it was now time for me to learn how to manage my own money.

No longer naïve, I had become aware that in addition to the thousands of dollars I was being charged for his advice, he was also receiving a commission of 2%, or more, annually from the mutual fund companies where he had invested my money. If shares, on average, gain 6% on a stock exchange annually, I had probably been giving away half of my portfolio's gain.

Fortunately, I did learn how to invest safely and wisely. Even after living off my dividend income for the last 15 years, my portfolio is still three times larger, and growing, than when I began to self-direct my investments. I now have more disposable income than when I earned an executive salary. Much less of it is being eaten up by income tax. **This is due to a lower tax rate charged on dividend income than on salaried income**.

Recently a teacher in his fifties asked me if I expected to run out of money before I died. I assured him that I saw no reason why my wealth would not grow until the day I met my maker.

Receiving a large amount of money that has no specific destination, is seductively easy to spend. I recommend that you adopt the attitude that this is not really your money. All you are is this generation's steward, responsible for preserving wealth for the next generation. Hopefully, you will be able to teach the next generation how to manage it with a similar attitude.

Have you found yourself with unexpected wealth? Read this book. It can prepare you to counter the onslaught of those who will be eager to get their sticky fingers on as much of your wealth as they can elicit.

In addition to the sharks, you have the government wanting to take its tax bite. A smart chartered accountant will ensure that the government gets no more than what it is entitled. Pay your taxes, if the government comes after you for unpaid taxes, the money in your investment accounts and whatever other assets they can find will be seized. They will not be satisfied until they have everything to which, they believe they are entitled. Getting disputed money back from the government is time consuming and difficult.

How to achieve financial independence or even having it as a goal is not taught in school. Our educational system is geared to turning out workers who are expected to toil away for 40 years. The idea that we were not born to be worker bees is foreign to most of us. Sooner than you think, you can, if you choose, live very well without being employed, just by changing your attitude towards money. Such an idea may seem subversive, but it is possible.

This book was initially going to be directed to only those few who had suddenly received a fortune, however, there are millions who have slowly acquired wealth and stored it in savings accounts and similar low yielding havens devoid of capital gains. For these people, their intolerance of risk makes them open to the benefits of value investing, as described in this book. Safe, self-directed stock investments will protect their future far better than the meagre interest rates they are now receiving. Their wealth is being depleted by inflation, year-after-year. They really could outlive their money.

You may have sufficient cash in your bank savings account to shield you from unforeseen setbacks. However, a retirement, that could go on for decades, needs investments that will generate steady capital gains. Growing your lifetime savings faster than you have been doing, may not now seem possible, but it can be done. In Chapter 11 read my tips on how you can direct more of your cash to investments. You may be surprised how quickly, with a few changes in habits and attitude, how much more income can be generated. The objective is to live as well on your invested income as you are now living on your employment income.

 How do you go from living pay-cheque-to-pay-cheque, to saving $5,000? Chapter 11 provides ways to save money. Suppose, you did save $5,000 to invest in a stock. That $5,000 would be more precious to you than $500,000 would be to a millionaire. You would want to find a stock to invest in that was safe, paid a high dividend with great potential for growth. This book will show you how to find that stock.

After the establishment of your initial $5,000 portfolio, you can now start saving towards buying the next $5,000 worth of stocks. It will be a little easier to save for the second $5,000 because you will now be receiving a minimum of $30 in dividends every month from the initial $5,000 stock purchase. The grand objective is to acquire $5,000 worth of shares in 20 carefully chosen dividend paying companies. The shares of all 20 companies, added together would give you a safe, substantial, diversified portfolio worth $100,000.

Depending on the length of time invested the 20 shares worth $100,000 could grow at a rate of 10% a year to eventually be worth a million dollars. If you also bought more shares, in the twenty companies, with the dividend income being realized from all 20 shares, a million dollars could be realized more quickly. Out living your money and being ravaged by inflation would cease to be a concern.

CHAPTER 4
Why Self-Directed Investing?

It is very important that you understand with whom you are dealing when you enter a bank and encounter the employees selling the bank's investment services.

Is the first loyalty a financial adviser has to the bank that employs him? Like all employees an adviser's responsibility to contribute to their employer's profits. The fees you pay are not going to the adviser, they are going to the bank. Advisers have varied compensation plans, but I suspect that the bank, not the adviser, gets the greatest percentage of any fees charged. Otherwise the bank would be unprofitable and go out of business. The bank would most likely deserve the bigger share because it gives the financial adviser credibility and access to millions of potential customers. To maximize profits, it would seem reasonable that the bank would wants the financial adviser to sell you investments that generate the most profit for the bank. If those investments also generate a safe income for you that may only be coincidental.

If the bank is paid a 5% commission when it sells one mutual fund versus another mutual fund that is only paying a 4% commission, which one is most likely to appear in your portfolio? Customers rarely question their investment advisors. They do not normally ask why one mutual fund is being recommended over the thousands that are available? If questioned by a client, the advisor would likely respond with a jargon-filled explanation that would be both confusing and intimidating.

Financial advisors are commissioned salespeople. I have managed large sales forces of both commissioned and salaried salespeople. The friction, disputes and in-fighting between salesmen, their managers and their customers was ten times greater with a commissioned sales force than a salaried sales force. I used to spend a third of my time arbitrating disputes about who should or should not have received a commission from a sale. Commissions do not bring out the best in people. **They encourage greed and ruthlessness.**

Salesmen are measured by their ability to convince people to sign binding contracts. If, in a month, a salesman's income can double by how much he can convince you to spend on an investment, be assured that he will say, promise and do anything it takes to get your money.

I found I could grow a business twice as fast with a salaried force than with a commissioned sales force. It is much easier to gain and keep a buyer's trust with salaried representatives. While a salaried representative's job still depends upon them signing sales contracts, their monthly income is not directly tied into monthly sales. An annual incentive and salary increase would depend on many months of results. This dials down the desperation level.

 I suspect it would be almost impossible to convince the bank's senior executives that they could get better sales results if financial advisors were salaried. They seem unable to view their financial advisors as anything, but independent businessmen motivated solely by money. Many executives in the investment industry appear to be from the "greed is good" school. How salaried investment advisers could openly and honestly sell investments that are going to benefit the client perhaps more than the bank, would seem impossible to the bank executives.

Like almost all commission sales representative, investment advisers would be measured daily on how much money they have brought into the bank. To keep their jobs, they must meet sales quotas. To be deserving of a promotion, they must generate more sales than their peers.

 When an investment adviser receives the title of Vice President it is seen as a perk. It gives the adviser greater credibility with his clients. It helps increase bank revenue. The title costs the bank nothing. It is a cheap bonus for an outstanding salesperson. Therefore, beware of investment advisers with the title of Vice President on their business card. These may be the real sharks. They have proven they know how to separate investors from their money. A large bank might have hundreds of vice presidents.

The typical investment adviser is believed to handle as many as 150 clients. An employee, on average, works 2,000 hours in a year. If you divide 150 clients into 2,000, this could allow an investment adviser to spend 13 hours with each client. However, clients die. They get lured away by other investment companies. Some clients get discarded when they lose all their money, after following their adviser's advice. There is a natural attrition rate which can result in an investment adviser spending more than half the day hunting for new clients to replace the ones they have lost or will lose. To get one new client may require them contacting more than ten prospective clients.

They seek out lists of high-income individuals to approach. Some banks encourage the tellers in the bank branches to solicit clients. Some use the telephone and social media (Twitter, Facebook, LinkedIn, etc.) to promote their questionable ability to make people rich. Prospective clients are invited to lunch and mailed impressive brochures. Groups looking for cheap entertainment will often ask them to appear and give talks on preparing for retirement or setting up a Registered Retirement Savings Plan. The next time a bank teller suggests you should, "talk to our financial adviser about the $250,000 you have in your savings account", recognize that you are seeing a bank's prospect system at work.

The time spent prospecting, doing clerical work, attending work reviews with their sales managers and other meetings, leaves no time for an investment advisor to research how to increase the value of a client's portfolio. Therefore, the investment adviser must quickly hand an investor's money over to a "professional" portfolio manager. That money is added to a pool of funds, from perhaps thousands of investors. Each investor owns a percentage of that pool.

Hopefully, by delegating the actual investing to another employee the investment adviser may have as much as an hour a year, to communicate with each of his clients. Small accounts may not even get a phone call. Finding new clients is the priority. Existing clients are often taken for granted which can lead to clients taking their money elsewhere.

If you have a portfolio of a million dollars and are paying a 1% annual commission to an advisor, this works out to $10,000. It is doubtful in a year that an investment advisor would spend even 10 hours with a million-dollar client. Is an investment adviser worth more than $1,000 an hour for doing what you can do yourself?

As commission agents of the bank, investment advisers are running their own independent business. If they cut out early to play golf or take long lunches with their associates, no one will chastise them if they can do it and still exceed their quotas.

Investment advisers are not the portfolio managers who invest the money. However, in establishing your portfolio, the investment adviser may suggest that "they" will be spending hours determining where best to place your money. They count on you not asking them to explain in more detail what they might have in mind. You are expected to "trust them" and watch the money roll in.

There is little concern that you would question their investment proposals. The typical client is too timid and ignorant about investing to raise questions. If you did raise a question, those investment advisers, trained in the fine art of "bullshit-baffles-brains", will speak with confidence using investment jargon about incomprehensible investments. Clients nod as if they understand. After all, if they can't trust their investment adviser who can they trust?

The typical client judges their investment adviser by the increase or decrease in their portfolio each month. Investment advisors must pray every night that all their clients' portfolios will never shrink. When the portfolios do not increase, the advisers are trained to "dance around" your questions about the decline.

Some clients when they see a decline in their portfolio's value, move the portfolio to another investment adviser. This is probably a wasted exercise. The results will probably be no better than they were with the previous investment adviser. It is substituting one shark for another shark.

Ms. Innocence had been a typical uninformed investor. She was almost too embarrassed to tell me, that she had regarded banks and churches with the same reverence. Her investment adviser and her priest were put on the same pedestal of respect. She saw investment advisers as saintly individuals whose integrity and selflessness were beyond question. While I am not aware of any investment advisers destined for sainthood, they may exist, I just have not met any. The ones I have met seem to see their purpose in life as being the shifting of as much as possible of the client's wealth into their and the bank's pockets as possible.

When an investment adviser is striving to make you believe they are knowledgeable investment experts, one obvious question to ask to bring the adviser down to earth is, *"Why are you still working?"*

If the purpose of investing is to reach a state of financial independence, why, with such expertise are they still working? Why would an investment adviser endure the corporate politics, the pressure to produce sales, daily commutes, rejection by prospective clients, complaints from unhappy investors and all the other demands that are put upon them? Are they masochistic? Is it, that no matter how much money an investment adviser may acquire that they are still greedy for more?

As a follow up question ask, *"How much money do you have invested in your portfolio?"* Do not be surprised to find out that have far less invested than you do. If they give an evasive answer, or you doubt what they are saying, ask them to send you a copy of their portfolio's last statement so you can gain insight into their investment strategies?" If the investment adviser balks at this invasion of his financial privacy, you might remind him that this is what he expects you to do. Should you be entrusting your life savings to an investment adviser who would not be willing to be open about their own investments?

Do you have any other choice but to employ an investment adviser to manage your portfolio? Yes, you do have a choice. You can manage your own self-directed investment portfolio. The objective of this book is to show you how to invest safely and wisely in shares of public corporations that pay dividends. It does not have to be complicated or beyond your ability to identify a good investment from a bad one.

Just as Ms. Innocence learned how to do it, you too will be able to explain why you chose each stock in your portfolio. You will learn how to find investments that are most likely to grow while paying you a regular dividend income.

 While I will show you how it is done, I will never make a buying decision for you. That is your responsibility. You will understand how to weigh the options and determine, from the thousands of investments available, which stock suits you best. You will learn to have faith in your investment decisions. Never again will you be able to accept without question an investment proposal with which you are being presented. Now, you will be able to ask intelligent questions about investment recommendations.

If you have less than $250,000 to invest, expect to be shunted to a rookie investment adviser. According to the Ontario Securities Commission, most small investors would rarely be in contact with their advisers more than once a year and many would have no contact. Yet, they are paying for investment advice – often through embedded compensation schemes such as trailing commissions in mutual funds. Would you not be better of managing your own investments?

Ms. Innocence made the decision to transfer her large full-service portfolio from her old bank to a self-directed investment account in a new bank. Because she is a nice person, she worried about hurting the feelings of her long-time investment adviser at the old bank. This, despite no longer trusting him and believing that he had been milking her portfolio of tens of thousands of dollars in questionable fees for years.

I warned Ms. Innocence to stay far away from investment advisors at the new bank. They would be no different from the investment adviser she was leaving. Despite my warning, "a nice young man" in the branch immediately arranged for her to meet with the branch's designated investment adviser. She assured me that he must be a "good" advisor because he was a "Vice President" with a long list of important sounding designations on his business card.

Ms. Innocence was made to feel very important at the new branch. Ninety-nine percent of the population would not have the wealth she was bringing to them. She enjoyed the attention. Although she had made it very clear to the new bank that she only wanted a self-directed investment account, she still felt she had to be polite and meet with the financial adviser. She asked me what harm there could be. I warned her again that these were not her friends. She smiled tolerantly at my cynicism.

To transfer a portfolio from one bank to another bank should take no more than two or three days. The bank receiving the portfolio starts the transfer process. They request the new client sign documents that allows them to handle the transfer on their behalf. You leave the transfer in their "capable hands". The client has no need to ever again be involved with the bank they are leaving.

When setting up a self-directed investment account there is no need to be involved with any bank staff. It can be set up online, however, you will first need a chequing account. This may require you to go into the bank branch, but it is also possible to open a chequing account online. The chequing account is necessary as a place to deposit the money that you will transfer in and out of your self-directed trading account.

The new bank can save you money if they handle the transfer of your portfolio from the old bank. The old bank would charge thousands of dollars in cancellation fees to liquidate your investment holding. Enormous capital gain tax charges might also be incurred. If it is a straight transfer of the contents of a portfolio from one bank to another bank, you will avoid any costly surprises. This is something to confirm with the new bank before you make a transfer.

The transfer of Ms. Innocence's portfolio did not go as expected, once the financial adviser got involved. Waving a very large portfolio in front of a financial advisor is like waving raw red meat in front of a shark. Three months after first asking the new financial advisor to make the transfer, thousands of dollars had still not appeared. It resulted in a draft of the following letter (with altered names).

Dear President

Re: Ethics of Full-Service Sales

On December 17th, I went to the bank branch to enquire about transferring my investment account to your bank. I was referred to a Mr. Bird Dog. In a 45-minute meeting, we discussed the transfer of my Full-Service investment account to your bank. I stressed with Mr. Dog that I no longer wanted a full-service account because:

(1) my derived income from the investments was not enough to carry the unnecessary expense of adviser fees.

(2) I wanted total control over my investments.

Mr. Dog said that he knew "just the right person to help me with the transfer". He assured me the transfer would only take 1 to 3 days (It still is not complete as I write this letter almost 3 months later). An appointment was set with a Mr. Big Shark, Vice President.

I was asked to bring a VOID cheque to this meeting and was assured that the cheque would not be retained. Before I left, Mr. Dog opened a Savings Account and a Self Directing Investment account for me. I immediately transferred $4500 into this Investment account.

On December 22, - I met with Mr. Dog and Mr. Shark. Mr. Dog attended the meeting and copied some papers, I had brought detailing my investments at my previous bank.

Mr. Shark launched into a sales spiel about the advantages of having an investment adviser. I wondered if Mr. Dog had not informed him that I did not want a full-service investment account. He asked me if I had a will plus Powers of Attorney for both Financial and Personal. He then pushed me to meet with the person who handled the wills and powers of attorney for his clients so I could decide after that what was best.

The legal papers that my lawyer had recently drawn up for me were perfectly in order. I do not appreciate being pressured by investment advisers who are trying to run up billable fees. Mr. Shark was supposed to be there to assist me in transferring my money to the new self-directed trading account not trying to overwhelm me with financial jargon and canned investment strategies that I neither understood nor was interested in. At this point, I wondered if I had made a mistake in following my friend's advice to do my investing with your bank's self-directed account service.

The day after the first meeting, I asked Mr. Dog to remind Mr. Shark that I was not interested in seeing a third person regarding wills and trusts nor did I wish a full-service account. He assured me that he would make this very clear to Mr. Shark.

A second meeting was held with Mr. Shark. The purpose remained to expedite the transfer of my entire portfolio. I signed one document to authorize the transfer to my self-directed investment account. I confirmed with Mr. Shark that the document's sole purpose was to transfer the portfolio to the self-directed investment account that had already been established. I did not read all the small print on all the pages, but Mr. Shark assured me, in the presence of Mr. Dog, that he would not do anything without first consulting me.

Checking daily, it took ten days, not the two or three I had expected, before I saw money appearing in my investment account. It was only when I was ready to sell one or two funds that I discovered that I did not have the 'SELL' and 'BUY' buttons on my" Holdings" screen. I asked my friend who had been trading in his self-directed account for twenty years, why it appeared I could not sell the funds. He said, "The buttons are always there in a self-directed account." I sent him a photo of my holdings screen to confirm that there were no options to SELL or BUY'. He told me that something was not right and to go back to the branch.

Several times I went to the branch and discussed this problem with Mr. Dog. My money seemed to be there, but I could not transfer or do anything with it. I do not understand why Mr. Dog did not explain to me what was occurring. I assume his loyalties are to Mr. Shark and not to the bank's customer. Getting no where, with Mr. Dog, I phoned the self direct service helpline. This is where I learned that Mr. Shark had converted my self-directed investment account into a full-service investment account, contrary to my directions and wishes.

During one of our meetings, I had asked just out of curiosity, what Mr. Shark's fees would be for handling my account. He had said that while their normal rate was 1.2% of the portfolio, per annum, he was prepared to lower his fee to 1%. I interpret this to mean that on my portfolio he

*expected to receive a significant five figure amount every
year for a service that I did not need.*

*One reason I severed my relationship with the last bank's
full-service investment account was because I had become
aware that for more than ten years, unbeknownst to me, my
investment adviser had been annually taking out of my
investment account thousands of dollars in transactional
fees. This was over and above the flat percentage fee I had
also been paying him each year. This was just one reason I
no longer wanted anyone, but myself, to have access to my
investment account.*

*For many years I owned a successful retail business with
several branches. This brought me in touch with many
unethical, short sighted salesmen who thought this little old
lady was easy pickings. Greed is a terrible thing.*

*I had a third meeting with Mr. Shark and Mr. Dog.
Following it, the account was changed back so I could now
buy and sell in my self-directed investment account. I made
it known to Mr. Shark and Mr. Dog that I was not only
angry but also shocked that your bank would allow an
advisor to change a self-directed trading account into a
full-service account without the customer's
authorization.? What controls does your bank have in
place to stop investment advisors from doing this? I had
understood that Ontario Securities Commission had very
strict guidelines on unauthorized access to a client funds.*

*To further add to the problem, Mr. Shark had taken the
liberty of opening five additional full-service accounts for*

me. Why, I do not know. For weeks I have demanded that these accounts be removed from my profile, yet, they are still there. Dividends and cash from the sale of one of my funds have been in one of them but was inaccessible to me. This has seriously delayed stock purchases I wished to make. When I phoned your helpline, they were not able arrange access to this money. Finally, a regional manager, was assigned to help me. He was under the impression that I was seeking investment webinars, I made sure he understood that what I wanted was order and clarity in my investment holdings.

Since then, I have called this regional manager and other departments repeatedly, trying to determine what happened to my January payments. Not a single cent in income from my investments in January has been received. One of the advisers stated that Mr. Shark had re-invested the January dividends, once again without any authority to do so. When I asked this adviser how that was possible, he told me that it was not his place to comment on what Mr. Shark had done. I would have thought that he would have reported my concerns to authorities high enough in the bank's hierarchy to resolve a customer's concerns about a bank employee's questionable ethics.

Perhaps you would like to explain to me what Mr. Shark has done and whether you condone it. Not only am I concerned, but other investors I am associated with, who have multi-million-dollar portfolios, are also concerned.

I am constantly being told by your staff not to worry and that my money is safe. Is it? Why in March, am I still waiting to have access to my January payments and the two outstanding ones for February? Please explain to me why I, and my friends, should not consider transferring our portfolios to another financial institution.

I wrote the above earlier in the week. Today is March 2nd. The expected money, dividends and payments have finally started to appear in my account. However, I am still waiting for the two February payments and all the January payments to appear.

I look forward to your intervention in clearing up this matter and to your assurances that no one but I, have access to my account.

Sincerely,

Ms. Innocence

I had helped Ms. Innocence with this letter. It was not sent. Why was it not sent? Because, Mister Shark would have been praised by the bank for his aggressiveness. As far as his manager would be concerned Mister Shark was doing his job.

Although Ms. Innocence swore that she never signed a document to become a full-service client, she did admit that she had signed some document that she did not read. Her verbal instructions were ignored. Mister Shark, while dishonest, would have been too experienced and too careful to treat Ms. Innocence as a full-service client without her signature on a document.

You are warned. Stay far away from a bank's investment advisers when you open a self-directed investment account.

The other rather irritating practice Ms. Innocence faced with Mr. Shark was being pushed to complete a "risk tolerance" questionnaire. It is a very intrusive and rather silly questionnaire that all full-service clients must complete. It determined in which investment pool her money was to be managed along with thousands of others who had similarly answered the questions. Ms. Innocence did not know this, otherwise she would have understood that Mr. Shark had disregarded her wishes and was putting her into a full-service account. The bank needs this signed questionnaire to justify to the Ontario Securities Commission the investments the bank has chosen for a full-service client.

This risk assessment evaluation seems to be a pointless bureaucratic effort. The typical uninformed investor does not understand their risk tolerance. They have no experience to measure risk or to provide informed answers to the questions.

The Ontario Securities Commission demands such a questionnaire to stop investment advisers from putting the life savings of naïve investors into highly speculative penny stocks, where they could quickly lose all their money. Since self-directed investors choose their stocks, and are thus safely isolated from investment advisers, no risk tolerance questionnaire is necessary or required.

What investment advisors should explain to a full-service customer is that everything the bank touches will incur a fee. These "small" charges can add up to thousands of dollars in a year. The full-service customers cannot plead ignorance of these fees. They have signed contracts, which few read, agreeing to these charges. The banks deliberately write the terms in legalese, in a crammed format, in tiny print, at the very back of their contracts. This is the reason lawyers often start on the last when analyzing contracts.

The following is an example of the fee legalese that appears in many bank investment contract forms. It has been converted to an easy-to-read format.

THE BIG SHARK'S FEE SCHEDULE

"Fees You Paid. The Operating and transaction fees charged directly to you for the operation, management and transactions related to your account. In some cases, fees may be collected from your account on behalf of a third party. In all cases, fees are reported to you in the account in which they are charged.

If you have directed us to charge fees to a specific account regardless of where the fee was incurred, we have reported the fee where it was charged.

Operating Fees Operating fees represent fees we may have charged you for the operation, transfer or termination of your account, and include applicable federal and provincial sales taxes unless otherwise noted.

Operating fees *include custody fees, interest charges on debit balances, and fees for managed and fee-based programs as outlined in your fee agreement with us.*

Transaction Fees *Transaction fees represent the fees we may have charged you for the purchase and/or sale of securities, including: - Exchange Traded Securities: stocks, preferred shares, exchange traded funds, and options. - Fixed Income Securities: debt instruments. - Investment Funds: mutual funds, money market funds, and hedge funds. - Other: private placements. Fixed Income Security Transactions*

For **debt securities** *purchased or sold for you during the period covered by this report, dealer firm remuneration may have been added to the price you paid (in the case of a purchase) or deducted from the price you received (in the case of a sale). This amount may have been in addition to any commissions you may have been charged.*

Foreign Transaction Tax *A Foreign Transaction Tax may be applied to a transaction when a security is purchased or sold on a foreign exchange.*

Payments Received from Third Parties *We may receive compensation or earn revenue in other forms, in addition to, or in substitution for, direct payments by you. These fees may include: - Issuer Commission: Refers to a commission received from the issuer of a security purchased in your account. These may include new issue securities, GICs, federal and provincial savings bonds, and/or structured notes. –*

Service Fees: Refers to <u>an ongoing trailing commission</u> we may receive in respect to securities or deposit products you owned during the period covered by this report.

Investment funds pay investment fund managers a fee for managing their funds, and we receive an ongoing payment from the manager for the services and advice we provide you.

The amount of the trailing commission depends on the sales charge option you chose when you purchased the fund. You are not directly charged the trailing commission or the management fee; however, these fees affect the performance of the fund. –

Deferred Sales Charge (DSC): Refers to a commission paid directly by the mutual fund manager for mutual fund securities purchased where you pay no up-front commission. –

Referral Fee: Refers to a payment we may receive when you are referred to a dealer, adviser, or fund manager for securities services. –

Other Fees: Refers to commissions earned as a result of corporate actions on the securities held in your account.

Average Market Value of Your Investments The average market value of your account has been calculated based on the ending market value at each month-end (net of debit balances) over the period covered by this report.

Foreign Exchange Rates *Any fees you paid in currencies other than the currency of this report have been converted to the currency of this report using the exchange rate in effect on the date of the transaction."*

With such a buffet of fees is it any wonder that your financial advisor can generate for their employer far more than the 1% you thought you were paying. Self-Directed investing eliminates every fee except the charge for buying the shares. It should be less than $10 no matter how many shares of a stock you buy.

You agree to the full-service fee schedule when you sign the completed form. A bank's lawyers would present this piece of paper as proof of their compliance with the investment guidance you gave them. It would be presented as proof of the bank's due diligence, if you become enraged by the shrinkage in your investment account and initiated a legal action.

Many banks employ platoons of salaried lawyers to protect their interests. To threaten to sue a bank is a bit of a joke, as you are the one who will face having to pay large legal bills, not them.

Opening a self-directed trading account on-line does not require this questionnaire. All Ms. Innocence would have had to provide was a government issued ID, a Canadian Social Insurance number, a permanent Canadian address and an existing account with the bank. I expect all banks, for competitive reasons, have the same easy set up for self-directed investment accounts.

All Ms. Innocent wanted was a "cash stock trading account". This is an account in which you keep enough cash to pay for any stock that you would wish to buy. A bank's fee for processing every trade made would be less than ten dollars, no matter how many shares of a stock you bought.

Ms. Innocence worked hard all her life building a successful business with the belief that the large nest egg she had saved would provide her with a comfortable, stress free retirement. She had mistakenly believed that it required years of experience before you could find and purchase investments that would give you security and a good income.

Within ninety days, after following the steps laid out in this book, Ms. Innocence was buying hundreds of thousands of dollars in good stocks. These were stocks that she found, analyzed and carefully chose for her portfolio. Most bank customers, like her, are unaware of the massive amount of free investment information and services available to protect and grow their wealth.

While business experience teaches entrepreneurs to trust no one with their money, it is surprising when investing, that they will entrust their life savings to an investment adviser just because the adviser works for a large bank. I sent Ms. Innocent an article that appeared in the website "espresso" with the heading, ***"Is Your Financial Adviser Trying to Trick You. Watch Out for These Signs"***. It described twenty areas of concern e.g. pushing to buy or sell a stock, guaranteeing a profit, not being transparent about how advisers earn their money, not finding time to talk to clients, not diversifying your stocks, not supplying references, not being open about the risk, etc. You can view this presentation at https://www.msn.com/en...your-financial-adviser-trying-to-trick-you.../ss-BBU9Ofk

No where in this article, was the safety in self-directed portfolios discussed. There was no warning to stay far away from investment advisers. It was as if this writer assumed that we all must invest through an investment advisor. It made no mention of the hundreds of thousands of dollars that can he saved, over a lifetime, of self-directed investing.

A full-service financial adviser expects you to sign a contract that pays, him every year, from 1% to perhaps 2.5% of the value of your portfolio. The more money you invest the less you should be paying. The investment adviser may try the highest rate possible to see if he can get away with it. Ms. Innocent was paying 1%. She felt this percentage was negligible and was surprised when I told her that one percent was costing her thousands of dollars every year. I calculated that she was paying her investment adviser $5,000 dollars an hour for the time he spent on her behalf.

Since she never looked at her itemized statements, she had missed the additional $7.000 she was paying annually in various fees. The portfolio manager responsible for her portfolio was making more trades in a month than I would make in my portfolio in ten years. While neglecting to point out these fees, the investment adviser told her she could write off whatever he charged, as a legitimate expense on her income tax. Her income was so diminished that there would be no taxable income to write them off against.

The failure to comprehend what is in a stockbroker's fee report is not uncommon. It is believed that these reports are deliberately included with or added to the end of other less important documents. They are disguised as "just another document" to be safely ignored. Few investors understand how indirect fees work and easily underestimate their cost.

Ms. Innocence's gravest error was giving the investment adviser total control over her portfolio. At the time, it seemed to be a wonderful idea and one less task that she would have to be bothered with. For the bank it was like being handed a signed blank cheque. It appears that they did not miss the opportunity to milk her portfolio for all that their conscience and loose laws allowed.

While her portfolio declined each year, she continued to accept his explanation that it was just the nature of investing. The investment adviser had told her he was investing her money conservatively, so she accepted that she should not be expecting any growth.

When Ms. Innocence retired, she began to receive an income from her portfolio each month. That the investment adviser was selling off a bit of her portfolio every month never occurred to her. She never asked how this income was being realized. She assumed it was dividends.

Successful professional athletes who receive multi-million-dollar contracts are more naïve than Ms. Innocence. Few have business experience or investment knowledge. Every athlete's career is short, and they know it can end with one catastrophic injury. They also know, it is wise to invest, enough of their big income, to provide them with a worry free, comfortable lifestyle, after their sports career is over.

Like sugar attracts flies, aggressive investment advisers seek them out. For a tiny annual percentage of their wealth, these advisers offer to manage and grow their wealth. Often athletes suspect that these investment advisers are just salesmen who want to line their pockets. However, they think they must acquire "professional" investment help, like the rest of their teammates. It can become a status thing. All "rich guys" have investment advisers, don't they? No, many "rich guys" are still rich because they stayed away from investment advisers.

According to a study done by Sports Illustrated, 78% of National Football League players within two years of retiring were financially insolvent. The National Basketball Association's players association reported 60% of its members were broke within five years after retiring. The common reason for their lack of savings was the blind trust they put in the investment advisers they had chosen. While most of us worry about funding a retirement for twenty years, an athlete with million-dollar pay cheques needs to worry about funding it for fifty years.

A self-directed portfolio, over a lifetime, can save professional athletes and little old ladies hundreds of thousands of dollars, perhaps even millions of dollars. However, it is stressful for some people to make decisions that involve large sums of money. While it may appear to be less stressful to pay someone to make investment decisions for you, it is not without the stress of constantly debating whether you can trust that person. Some investors also convince themselves that they are too busy to establish and monitor a portfolio. Others may want to deflect decision making responsibility by having an investment adviser to blame, for future investment decisions that may cost them millions.

If you feel you must invest with an adviser, then I hope this book makes you paranoid. Let it make you question your advisor on every recommended investment. As you read further, you will receive measuring sticks that will help you measure the viability of an investment.

Do not give your investment adviser the freedom to have his way with your money. Changes to your portfolio should only be made after you sign off, that you understand the pros and cons of any proposed changes. Keep asking everything about your investments until you understand how you are benefiting from the investment adviser's involvement with your money.

This book will help you communicate with your investment adviser. He will realize that you know enough about investing to catch any effort to try to slide any greedy little thing by you.

You may learn that your portfolio is in the hands of a mysterious portfolio manager and your investment adviser has no control over what goes in or out of it. You may have to blindly accept this reality if you wish the bank's full investment service package. The question then becomes, can you accept full-service when you now know that self-directed investing is a viable, safer option?

Tight control of your expenses is as important as controlling your investment income. If you can not account for how little you have available to invest, I recommend that before continuing, you skip ahead and read Chapter 11 - on frugal living. It may show you where to find thousands of dollars under your control to invest.

Very few people have a six-figure liquidity to invest in the stock market. Those under thirty years of age, have far more debt than assets. Many are trying to pay off large student loans. Just keeping ahead of their bills is a challenge: car payments, the rent and utility bills gobble up most of their income. However, in time, with increased income and fewer debts they too can, if they carefully manage their money, have surplus cash to invest.

A self-directed investment portfolio, no matter how small, is preparation for making important investment risk decisions later in life. There is a payoff for becoming familiar with investment vocabulary; how to sort stock purchases from best to worse; the simple process of acquiring a stock; diversifying stocks; and understanding how businesses are born, survive and die. It could also give a small boost to your income. While investing may appear to be intimidating, with familiarity, it opens the gates to an exciting world.

Fear of making a "mistake" in the investment process often discourages many from opening self-directed investment accounts. It shouldn't. The banks, that offer self-directed investment services, have made it very difficult for a novice investor to make a mistake. For example, some have computer systems that will not allow you to buy more stock than you have the cash to pay for. They always make you reconfirm what you are ordering. If you put in an order higher than the current market price for a stock, they will lower your buying price to the current price. Some banks have expert staff available 24 hours a day, seven days a week who, without charge, will answer any customer questions. They also have free on-line investment courses that can broaden your knowledge and expertise. Take charge of your future happiness by managing your own investment portfolio

CHAPTER 5

STOCKS VS OTHER INVESTMENTS

One of the richest men in the world, Warren Buffet, has a net worth of $82.9 billion. Recognized as being the most successful value investor in the world, he is quoted as saying, *"When we own portions of outstanding businesses with outstanding managements, our favorite holding period is forever…We are just the opposite of those who hurry to sell and book profits when companies perform well."*

Over the years I have invested in stocks, mutual funds, income property, stocks, bonds, savings accounts, paintings, coins, paintings, etc. My insights and conclusions about investing come from my experiences. The objective is to steer you away from mistakes that I initially made and give you insight into aspects of the world of money of which you may not have been aware or even considered.

SAVINGS ACCOUNTS

The best place to start is with the most basic of investments, a bank savings account. If you have never previously had a great deal of money to invest, the first place this money would most likely be invested is a savings account in a major bank. Here you have a secure haven (the Canadian Deposit Insurance Corporation protects up to $100,000 of the Canadian money you have deposited) but this does not make it a "good" investment.

At the time I wrote this, Canadian bank savings accounts were paying between 0.50% and 2.50%. The major Canadian banks were paying the lowest rates. The secondary banks were paying the highest. A quick Google search can provide you with interest rates of thirty or more institution's saving accounts. Only one was paying 2.50%. It was a secondary bank. Most secondary banks were paying closer to 1.50%. To get the higher rates, in some cases, you would need to deposit at least $25,000.

With inflation running close to 2% per annum, money in a savings account is, at best, a neutral investment. If you consider that all the interest you will realize is fully taxable income, you are probably losing money by keeping it in a savings account.

The banks love it that millions of cautious people deposit their money into low interest saving accounts. They then take, what to them is almost free money, and lend it out to businesses and consumers for car loans, mortgages, lines of credit, credit card purchases and more. In return the banks will receive annual loan payments charges from 2% to 20% of the value of their loan from these borrowers. While 2% may not seem like much, when you are lending billions of dollars, it can generate billion-dollar profits.

The shares in Canadian banks pay steady dividends between 3.5% and 5.5% to shareholders. It is far more beneficial to invest your money in bank shares then to deposit your money into a bank's saving account. The side benefit is that as the share price of many Canadian bank stocks rises, the banks steadily increase the money they pay out in dividends. Thus, when you initially bought 1,000 shares in a bank for $50 each paying an annual dividend of 4% you were receiving $2 each per share. When the share price rose to $100, the bank increased what it pays out so that the dividend rate would remain at 4%. You are now receiving $4 a share and putting twice as much money into your pocket as you did when you first bought the shares. Those initial 1,000 shares that you bought for $50,000 and were paying $2,000 a year in dividends are now paying $4,000 a year and are now worth $100,000

Could the shares have dropped below $50. Yes, it is possible, but based on a century of historical patterns it would be for a short period of time. While the share price may drop, you still own the same number of bank shares. The bank is still operating, lending and making a profit. Dividends are paid out of profits. The banks are very unlikely to reduce the amount of dividend money they pay out, just because speculators have driven their share price temporarily down.

Suppose the share price were to drop from $50 to $40 a share, a 20% drop. The amount paid out in dividends would most likely remain at $2 a share. The only thing that changes is the dividend percentage. The $2 payout on a $40 share price would now become 5% instead of 4%. I saw this happen to my bank shares in the market crash of 2008.

While interest you receive on a savings account is fully taxable as income, the dividend income from Canadian companies is lightly taxed if your income is modest. Some investors, whose total income is from dividends, pay no income tax. As well, if you sold none of the bank shares that went from $50 to $100 you would pay nothing on the $50,000 gain in assets. That gain sits there like a reserve and can be almost instantly turned into cash if it were needed.

Canadian banks are conservative institutions very closely regulated by the government. The major ones employ almost a hundred thousand employees in over a thousand branches spread across Canada and the USA. This geographic distribution means that a natural disaster in British Columbia can be offset by boom times in other provinces. Most major Canadian banks have been operating with great success through good times and bad for over 100 years. They are the ultimate safe stock investment and should be represented in all portfolios.

BONDS

Bonds are loans made by companies and governments. They compete with bank loans.

They offer those with cash a better return on their money than they would receive in a typical bank savings account. The money is lent for set periods of times (1 year, 5 years, 10 years, 20 years, 100 years) with a set interest rate being paid at predetermined times (usually twice a year). At the end of the set period you receive back the original money you invested. This gives bonds a level of security that you do not have with shares. However, since it is a loan, and not a share in the company, you do not benefit from any capital gain in the corporation's share price. Unlike a bank savings account the government does not insure them and the interest you receive from a bond is fully taxable. Investors buy them because they are regarded as being "safe".

It is very rare for a corporate bond to default. If it ever did happen, in a corporate bankruptcy, bonds would rank ahead of shareholders and creditors in receiving funds from a disposal of assets.

While stocks are easy and cheap to buy on a public stock exchanges, bonds are not. They must be bought and sold by a broker who takes a percentage of their value as a fee. While I could buy $100,000 worth of shares for $9.95, I have had to pay several thousand dollars to buy $100,000 in corporate bonds. If you wished to sell them before their termination date you may find that in order to sell them, you must accept considerably less than what you paid for them. This can happen if interest rates increased and the interest rate you are receiving is unattractive to investors who can purchase bonds paying a better interest rate.

Corporate bonds pay a better interest rate than government bonds. The financially stronger the corporation, the lower the interest they pay. Government bonds always pay less interest than-corporate bonds because there is supposed to be no risk in lending to governments, however countries have defaulted on bonds. As well, while it is very unusual for a corporate bond to default on paying you back what you have invested, it is not impossible.

Bond rating companies are paid to assess bonds. The best risks are given a AAA rating. Interestingly, the corporations issuing the bond pay the bond rating companies to provide these assessments. The companies getting a AAA rating do not have to pay as high an interest rate to those buying their bonds as those companies whose ratings show they are a higher credit risk. Thus, a AAA rated bond can save the bond issuing company millions of dollars in interest charges. One wonders about the objectivity of the rating companies. A company getting a poor rating might hesitate to engage that bond rating company in the future.

The banks pay bond rating companies to give them access to the ratings of thousands of companies. A company's rating is a determining factor in selecting bonds for their clients' investment portfolios. A bond trader assured me that they find the ratings reliable and sometimes the ratings are negative even though the company issuing the bond paid for the rating. She did agree that the bond rating companies were terribly negligent with their ratings on sub-prime mortgage backed securities in 2008. It caused a serious stock market crash.

Since bond transactions don't occur in a centralized location, you are never certain whether you are buying bonds at a competitive price or not.

The return on stocks is about double the return you can get investing in bonds. Bonds have little to offer investors hoping to double the size of their portfolios over time.

MUTUAL FUNDS & ETFs (Exchange Traded Funds)

. The objective of a mutual fund is to diversify your investments over many stocks and protect you from catastrophic losses However, high expense ratios, front-end and back-end charges, lack of control over investment decisions and diluted returns, do not make mutual funds a good investment. The broker selling them is going to charge you anywhere between 2% and 3% annually for managing the fund. In addition, the mutual funds management company will also charge investors 2% to 4% either at the time they buy or at the time the investor sells the mutual fund. This is expensive when you compare it to an investor with a self-directed trading account, paying a flat one-time $9.95 fee to buy $100,000 worth of shares. By comparison, buying $100,000 worth of mutual fund units could cost you between $2,000 and $7,000, with no guarantee that the mutual fund will make enough money to justify the costs. Be very wary of investment advisers recommending mutual funds from which they will greatly benefit.

Investors in a mutual funds are along for the ride. You have no control over what the mutual fund will invest in. There is nothing prohibiting a mutual fund from dumping the stocks now in their fund and investing the money elsewhere. You have blindly put your trust in someone you don't know, whom you have naively presumed is an expert in selecting stocks that will make you rich. When you don't get rich but lose money, you then have no idea why you lost. You really have no idea what you were invested in and why you were invested in it. The analyst who picked the stocks in the fund may have quit and moved on long ago.

Government regulations now direct mutual fund companies to diversify. They are prohibited from concentrating their portfolios in what a mutual fund manager may consider the best performing area. Like speculators at a casino there is the urge by some mutual fund companies to bet everything on what they think is a certain win. No one can accurately predict the future because economic and social conditions are constantly changing. The odds that a mutual fund can pick the right mix of stocks that can beat stock market averages, year-after-year, have proven to be just about nil.

Stocks pay dividends and bonds pay interest. To derive income from most mutual funds, you often must sell some of your mutual fund's units to get cash. You may have to do this after a mutual fund has shrunken in value. With fewer units, you have diminished your earning power and increased the chances that your portfolio will be worth nothing before you die.

Mutual funds have fallen out of favour with many investors who now prefer to purchase ETFs (Exchange-Traded Funds). The transaction fees are lower than mutual funds because their management charges are lower. Instead of careful stock picks, as is done with a mutual fund, an ETF buys shares of all the stocks listed in an index. For example, if you bought every stock traded on the Toronto Stock Exchange index, historical averages say you would show a capital gain of 6% a year.

 Unfortunately, if an entire index declines in value, the only way to minimize loss is to sell everything in that index. The fund manager then sits on the cash until he thinks the index has recovered. Once the index recovers, he buys back into it. The timing of this selling and buying is speculative and you can lose money if you are unlucky and do not get it right.

Recognizing this problem some ETF's now allow some diversity outside an index. They then end up being more like mutual funds with all the same problems as mutual funds.

REAL ESTATE

You need to live somewhere, so why not live inside what may be your largest single investment. If you live in a large, rapidly growing community, your house or condominium could double its value in five years. The house I live in, is now worth ten times more than what I paid for it 40 years ago. As you approach old age, where living in a stand-alone dwelling becomes impractical, you can sell that asset and, move to a condominium. You can invest any remaining balance, after the sale and purchase, to generating income. For Canadians this is a real benefit because the capital gain you realized on the sale of a primary residence is tax free

Not all communities experience increases in real estate prices. Deciding to purchase a home requires careful analysis. The average home conservatively increases in value about 3% a year. Since you should be able to realize at least 6% from investing in stocks, it may make more sense, in some communities, to rent and invest the money that would have gone to paying a mortgage, insurance, heating, taxes, maintenance, etc. This requires the self discipline of making sure the saved money gets invested.

Another real estate investment option is to buy an income property, where perhaps you may live in one of the apartments. Finding a "well maintained, affordable multi-unit property, in a desirable area" is difficult. The unit you buy, may require significant renovations to bring it up to government standards for rental accommodations. This can be expensive, unless you are prepared to do much of the renovations and maintenance yourself. Costs for fire alarm installations, inspections, lawn mowing, snow clearing, hand railings, intercoms, painting, garbage pickup, laundry equipment, insurance, heating, cooling, security, storage, parking, bathroom and kitchen renovations, etc., can be overwhelming.

When your units are ready to rent, you face advertising expenses and demands on your time to show the apartment to prospective renters. When you do find someone who wants the apartment, it isn't just a matter of signing a lease and getting the first and last month's rent. You must now spend time and money to verify that the tenant will keep on paying their rent and will not destroy the apartment. Why are they leaving their current rental unit? Are you acquiring another landlord's problem tenant? Upon renting the apartment, you need to budget for plumbing and electrical emergencies and setting aside funds to replace appliances and bathroom fixtures

Tenants can encounter problems that prevent them from paying their rent. Now, you face the expense of evicting them or accepting that you have a problem tenant and the easy income you expected has evaporated. Removing a tenant can take months, even years, and can cost thousands of dollars in legal fees.

If you have a separate residence and think you would also like to own a small apartment building, you will find that since this second building is not your primary residence, when you sell the apartment building the capital gain is taxed as regular salary income.

If all your money were invested in a rental property and you needed cash quickly, you can't sell part of a rental building like you can sell part of a stock portfolio. Selling your real estate at the "right price" can take months. The sale involves paying real estate agent commissions, legal fees, transfer taxes, etc. The only other option to get cash out a building is to mortgage it or to increase an existing mortgage, and this can not be done quickly.

To keep ahead of inflation, you will also have to plan on presenting your tenants with a price increase each year. Every time you do this, you risk that they will now seek less expensive accommodation and put you back into the expense of renting a vacant apartment.

While the expectation had been that the rent you charge would cover your expenses, there is a risk that your income property could prove to be an unreliable source of income and a money pit. If you want to own property, buy shares in REITs (Real Estate Investment Trusts) for both a reliable income and a capital gain. Avoid the irate calls in the middle of the night from tenants complaining about the air conditioning or a toilet not working.

HEDGE FUNDS

Hedge funds are like mutual funds but with one big difference. They are marketed to those who think they are rich and want to become even richer. It is said that greed makes even rich people stupid.

To invest in a hedge fund, you would be expected to have an annual income of at least $200,000 and be able to come up with $1,000,000 to invest. I am told the dealer who puts you into the hedge fund immediately gets 2% of what you invest and will take 20% of any future gain. Thus, you are immediately handling over $20,000 to a dealer with no guarantees as to what you will receive in return. Hedge funds are unregulated, and it is understood that few make money.

Those managing the hedge fund speculate on share price gains and share price declines - at the same time. Occasionally there are spectacular wins. These infrequent wins suck in the rich speculators who, like lottery ticket buyers, think the next big win is just around the corner waiting for them.

 If you ever think you would like to invest in a hedge fund, think, of Bernie Madoff. His hedge fund stole billions of dollars from many high profile "rich people". He paid very large dividends to investors by taking money from the deposits of new investors and used it to pay dividends to the old investors. This Ponzi scheme worked until some of the old investors wanted all their money back. Unfortunately, Bernie will die in prison long before he finishes his 150-year sentence. His son committed suicide over the shame of his father's dishonesty and greed.

.

COLLECTIBLES COINS, STAMPS & ART

Paintings, coins, and postage stamps are just a few of the items in which collectors speculate. I have sold collectibles. It is not an easy way to generate income.

In selling paintings, the first thing I learned is that that professional art collectors do not appreciate the aesthetic merits of a painting. These collectors fixate on buying the artist's signature on the painting. Like any investment, supply and demand set the price. Famous dead artist's paintings go up in price because there is now a limited supply of those paintings.

Paintings I considered ugly, and I would not give you $2 for, I have sold to collectors for $15,000 only because the collector had been searching for a painting by this long dead artist for several years. He considered the $15,000 price to be a bargain, and he was right. While the painting was on the way to him in Calgary, I had a call from another collector. He was disappointed to learn the painting was sold. He requested that I ask that buyer to sell him the painting for $20,000. Finding that first buyer had taken me weeks. Interestingly, that buyer was not interested in the $20,000 offer.

Selling your paintings directly to the buyer is unusual. It requires advertising and contacting galleries, museums and others, who may know someone who has an interest in the artist. This takes time. Usually, you want to find a gallery that will take the painting on consignment. They will hopefully find a buyer.

Galleries are very picky as to what they will put on their walls. Their walls are a limited marketing resource. Their commission for selling a painting could be half of the selling price.

Some galleries have terrible reputations for selling your consigned paintings and then "forgetting" to inform you of the sale. Only by visiting the gallery can you confirm your painting is still in the gallery's possession. If the gallery is in another province, where the artist's paintings are in demand, such visits can be impractical. When you do learn about the secret sale, you face trying to collect your money from a gallery, which is often short of funds, and has already shown that they will cheat you.

Sometimes, while the artist's paintings may be in demand, the subject of the painting may not conform to the traditional images for which the artist has become famous. Despite his signature on the bottom, it just doesn't look like one of his paintings. The purpose of buying the painting is often to impress those who recognize the artist. You may spend years trying to find a buyer for such an unusual painting.

Occasionally gallery owners would immediately buy a painting from me. They knew clients that they were certain would want a painting by that artist. Their selling price was going to be far more than what I was asking for the painting. They were taking advantage of me for what they saw as an opportunity for a quick profit. Such is the capitalist way.

While you may find a buyer on your own. The buyer could be thousands of miles away. Getting an expensive painting to them can be difficult. It surprised me to learn a special, climate controlled, truck operated by Ferro Transport, that travels from Montreal to Vancouver, delivering paintings every week to galleries and collectors. I have used this service. One day a huge tractor trailer showed up. It was so large it could not come down my street. I carried the painting to the truck and placed it in special racks. The paintings had to be bubble wrapped for the trip.

There is also an element of speculation in selling paintings. People's tastes change. Something bought twenty or more years ago may be of little interest to current art collectors.

If you enjoy beautiful art, instead of speculating on art, I would suggest going to a website like fineartamerica.com and choosing something you find beautiful from the millions of paintings and prints that are on display. For a few hundred dollars you can enjoy it for the rest of your life. If upon delivery it disappoints, you can send it back. They will refund your money. On-line art galleries have killed off many of the traditional brick & mortar art galleries.

COINS & STAMPS

Many websites, trade shows, and retailers exist which trade rare coins and stamps. These on-line websites and catalogues can give you an almost instant estimation of what your coin or stamp is worth. This prepares you for haggling on a price with a prospective buyer you may have connected with through these websites.

One needs to have a special love of coins or stamps because, buying and selling them requires significant time and effort. Few coins sell for over a thousand dollars. Even a Roman coin, a thousand years old, may only be worth a few hundred dollars.

Being small, coins and stamps are easier and less expensive to ship than paintings. If you can't find a buyer for your old silver coins, some dealers will buy them and melt them down for their silver content. The price of silver rises in tandem with gold prices.

COMMON SHARES

What is a great investment? One that is safe, has the potential to grow, pays out regular amounts of money, protects you from the tax man as it grows and instantly brings millions of buyers and sellers together to establish prices and make immediate sales. It is an investment that you can buy or sell in seconds to potentially millions of people, with minimal effort, while incurring less than ten dollars in transaction expenses, even if that asset is worth hundreds of thousand of dollars. It is an investment with incredible amounts of free statistical data to help you make informed, logical buy and sell decisions. To protect buyers, the government regulates the sale of this investment by passing laws to try to make the process transparent and above board.

This investment is the buying and selling of common shares of public companies on a stock exchange through a self-directed stock trading account with a major financial institution.

So much money is being made and lost in stock markets that it is under constant monitoring. One organization doing this monitoring is the **Investment Industry Regulatory Organization (IIROC).** You can visit their website at **www.iiroc.ca**. In this website you can check for negatives registered against investment advisers or their employers. A free daily email publicizes fines against investment firms and advisers. It is available for the asking.

IIROC is a self- regulating agency that regulates Canadian investment dealers and their 28,000 employees and agents. If approached by dealers or investment advisers not listed with IIROC, you should be extra vigilant.

IIROC seems to fall short of covering the entire industry. One source reported that there are120,000 people registered as financial professionals in Canada. Almost all 120,000 are "dealing representatives" (salespeople registered to sell financial investments). Only about 4,000 of these 120,000 are "financial professionals". Only financial professionals have a fiduciary duty to act in a client's best interest. If you must entrust your portfolio to a third party, it is hoped you would receive a more up-front-honest-service from a registered "financial professional" than you would from a commissioned salesperson.

If you have any doubts that some sharks in the investment industry are fleecing their clients, visit the website for the ***Small Investor Protection Association (SIPA)*** at **https://sipa.ca**. This non- profit organization is a depository of articles from the media. It provides details on "the culture of greed" that pervades the financial industry. It also gives access to legal judgments stored with the Canadian Legal Information Institute. They are available for review if you ever contemplate a legal action involving an investment dispute.

Some deceptions going on in the investment industry verge on the ridiculous. For example, a "financial advisor" – spelled with an "o" is an unregulated title that anyone can use, while "adviser"- spelled with an "e"- can only be used by employees with fiduciary responsibilities. The Ontario Securities Commission confirms that only "adviser" is a legal term under securities law.

Tax avoidance should always be a consideration when investing. Investors only get to keep their net return after tax. Therefore, Canadian investors in stocks should take advantage of all the tax shelters that are available. These include RRSP - Registered Retirement Savings Plans, TFSA - (Tax-Free Savings Accounts) and RESP - (Registered Educational Savings Plans). There are limitations as to how much you can invest in these tax shelters but whatever income you put in an RRSP or RESP gives you an immediate tax reduction. Any dividends and capital gains from sales made, that are kept in these tax shelters, are not subject to tax. This allows you to maximize the growth of your portfolio

You can also create a tax shelter by incorporating a company and leaving some income in the company. The corporate tax rate is lower than your personal rate. To get this tax advantages, the business must have the ability to make a profit. Such a corporation also allows you to write off legitimate business expenses against any taxable revenue the corporation generates. Any operating losses of your corporation can be used to offset capital gains you might realize on your stock investments.

It is important for Canadians who buy stocks inside an RRSP or TFSA to stick to Canadian stocks. Dividends earned from foreign stocks in a TFSA and RRSP may be subject to a withholding tax from a foreign country. Fluctuating foreign exchange rates can also wreak havoc on a portfolio.

All good things, including tax shelters, end. When you turn 71, you must begin to liquidate your RRSP which may have been growing tax free for decades. That first year they require you to withdraw 5%. It will be treated as fully taxable income.

Since you would have earned dividends of at least 5% in your RRSP, and anticipated this withdrawal, you can use this uninvested dividend income to meet your expected tax withdrawal. Doing this avoids having to sell any of the shares in your RRSP. This allows the capital gains in your portfolio to keep on growing and spinning off evermore dividend income.

Each year thereafter, the percentage of government RRSP tax withdrawal increases. If you reach your mid nineties, your RRSP will be reduced to zero with these annual withdraws from it. You will either have spent what you have withdrawn or reinvested it after paying taxes on it in your main trading account.

Capital gain, realized from stock sold from your main trading account, incurs half the tax of employment income. Dividend income is taxed at a reduced rate that fluctuates depending on your total income.

Many REITs (Real Estate Investment Trusts) pay high dividend yields and are an important part of a value investor's portfolio. Tax breaks exist on income realized from them, because a portion of the monthly dividend paid is a tax-free return of invested capital, rather than a straight dividend payment or a capital gain.

Getting all the tax breaks and keeping Revenue Canada happy requires a good accountant. While tax breaks can save you money, they are only of value if you are getting a significant return on your investments. Many investors earn nothing from their investments because they buy a stock at the wrong time (when it has reached its peak price) and sell it at the wrong time (when it has reached its bottom price). Whether you are at the peak or at the bottom, can only be realized after the fact. It is never that obvious when you are making an investment decision, but what is obvious and ignored in pursuit of a "hot" stock are the signs of value: operating margins, price to earnings ratios, dividend payouts, the book value of the stock, etc.

The most you can lose on a stock price is 100% of what you paid for that stock. However, what makes common shares so attractive is that there is no lid on how much you can make on a carefully chosen stock. A big price gain in one stock can easily off-set small losses you might experience in others.

Since no one can accurately predict the future, by investing in several well chosen" good" stocks, you increase the chances of having multiple winners whose price gains will grow your portfolio. Statistically over 50% of your well-chosen stocks will increase in value.

Even in a stock market crash, not all stocks will decline. A 5% "pullback" on the total value of your portfolio will occur a couple of times each year. You will probably not even notice it.

Every three years expect a 10% to 20% "correction" to occur. After such a downturn, you should expect it to take about four months for your portfolio to regain what it lost.

A "bear market" occurs when the average share price decline exceeds 20%. I have been through two. The dotcom implosion saw the Nasdaq Composite index decline by 88% in March 2000 and pull down all other stock indexes in the world. The Nasdaq is where most of these speculative, unprofitable dotcom internet stocks were being traded. While the index's drop was sharp, share prices quickly recovered.

In 2008 there was a 57% drop in the Standard & Poor 500 index. Misinformed speculators invested in mortgage back securities that were anything but secure. At that time, home buyers could buy homes without down payments or background checks, to determine if they could meet the mortgage payments. This caused a supply and demand bubble that drove up house prices at an unprecedented rate. Greedy financiers needed home buyers, any buyer, so they could bundle more and more "sub-prime mortgages" into funds, whose units they could sell to eager investors looking for "safe investments", with high rates of return, "fully secured by real estate".

Unfortunately, a house that originally sold for $500,000 during the frenzy of house buying soon dropped to $100,000 when the bubble of insolvency burst. The mortgage backed securities were as worthless as the mortgages that had secured them. Stock exchanges around the world were staggered by the loss.

There is a credit risk score applied to every adult in the United States. If anyone had wanted to take the time to analyze the mortgage holders who were securing these securities, the pending disaster would have been obvious. However, there are none so blind as those who choose to be. Especially clever financiers, earning huge commissions, caught up in the frenzy of selling a flawed investment, to gullible investors buying something they did not know how to analyze or understand. It took years for house prices to recover and for investors to forget the pain of their losses.

The stock market recovered faster. The lowest point in my portfolio was November 21 of 2008. This was down from its highest point on June 17 of 2008. It finally exceeded that high point by February 10 of 2009.

What do bear markets teach us?

1. Stock markets are cyclical.

2. Speculators buy stocks on emotion. Many seek to get rich with one big win. They bet "the farm".

3. Value investors after careful analysis buy stocks in several profitable companies.

4. Markets recover. Value investors collect their dividends while waiting for the market to recover.

5. Investors fear anticipated losses far more than they like gains.

Much of the fear of investing originates in The Great Depression between 1929 and 1939. It was severe. In 1934 the unemployment rate in Canada was 30%, in the USA, it hit a high of 24%. Compare that to current unemployment rates running at less than 6%.

Stock markets did not recover until the start of World War Two. However, not all publicly traded companies suffered during the depression. Throughout it, the International Nickel Company exported nickel to Hitler's armament manufacturers in Germany.   My father told me stories of the thousands of desperate men, like him, who trekked to Sudbury, Ontario from all over the world to work in the INCO mines. They lined up outside the employment office hoping for employment. INCO hired him and he clung to that job for thirty-eight years. The fear of the return of bad times, kept him there just as it kept many investors out of the stock market for decades.

 The fear mongers herald any bear market now as being the return of "the dirty thirties", instead of a normal economic correction. Bear markets cause many fearful speculators to sell their shares at their lowest historical price and to only re-enter the market when shares are again reaching their peak. This is when greed takes over and many are afraid of losing out in a "hot" stock market. This is often just before inflated prices again decline. In the next chapter we explore how to find the 20 best dividend paying common shares for your portfolio.

PREFERRED SHARES

There is another type of share that company's issue and sell on stock exchanges, called preferred shares. You will recognize them by their stock symbols. Their symbol contains a "PR" or a "PF". As an example, an Enbridge Inc. preferred share is ENB.PR.N and a TransCanada Co preferred share is TRP.PR.F.

Unlike some common shares, preferred shares always pay dividends. Often the dividend is one or two percent more than the dividend of the common share for the same company. However, like a bond, they do not share in the capital gain of the corporation nor do they have any ownership or voting rights in the corporate structure. They are a loan, like a bond.

Preferred shares rank above common shares in realizing money from a company's liquidation but would rank behind the company's bondholders. However, as I have described already, the chances of realizing any kind of payout in a corporate insolvency is just about nil.

You can buy and sell preferred shares on the stock market just like a common share. However, while the dividend payout stays consistent, the share price does not. I did an analysis of all stocks traded on the Toronto Stock Exchange that paid an annual dividend greater than 3.5% of the share price. Six hundred and fifty-four shares met this criterion. Of these, 364 or 56.04% of the shares were preferred shares.

Preferred shares are usually issued at a standard price of $25. Of the 364 shares only 17 companies had a share price exceeding $25 and of these only one was greater than $30. The chance of realizing a capital gain from a preferred share is 1.91%.

183 of the 366 preferred shares (50% of them) had lost at least 20% of their value and were now worth less than $20. Several were trading for less than $10.

Since there is almost no chance of capital gain, speculators seem to have no interest in preferred shares. Only a few hundred shares or at most a few thousand of a company's preferred shares will trade each day. Often no shares are being bought or sold.

The question is why would an investment advisor put preferred shares in a client's portfolio? The dividend rate, which is a perhaps 1% higher than the same company's common share dividend rate, appears to be the only attraction. Unfortunately, what you make on a 1% dividend difference you lose when the preferred share's price drops 20% from its initial placement. Most of the preferred shares seemed to be paying dividends in the 5% to 6% range. There are many good common shares paying more than 7%.

If interest rates decrease and the preferred share's dividend now looks attractive to investors, the corporation who issued the preferred share can call it in and issue new preferred shares paying a lower dividend rate.

Unlike bonds where you get back all the money you invested; with a preferred share you only get back what someone is willing to pay you for your preferred share and 98% of the time that will be less than the $25 you paid for it.

The commission they pay the investment dealers, who sell preferred shares to naïve clients, is believed to be very attractive. Unlike common shares, there is nothing but a mediocre dividend incentive to entice a buyer. None of the usual reference points that encourage you to buy a common stock are available e.g. no operating margin, no book value, no price to earnings ratio, no analyst recommendations, no high volumes of shares being traded, etc. If a company that issued preferred shares ran into financial difficulty, there is nothing stopping a company from suspending all their dividend payments, including those for preferred shares.

Corporations that issue preferred shares must like them. It is a cheaper way to raise money for large capital projects than borrowing from the bank and avoids the monetary commitments that a bond would demand. A company's assets secure their bank loans. The value of these assets limits how much a corporation can borrow. Assets do not secure preferred shares. The number of preferred shares issued is limited by what the corporation thinks it can afford to pay out in dividends.

Corporate executives encourage the use of preferred shares to raise capital because the preferred shares do not dilute the common share price. Thus, the executives who have their annual stock option incentives tied into an ever-rising common share price, need not fear preferred shares removing their chances to make tens or hundreds of thousands of dollars in bonus money.

Ms. Innocence's original portfolio contained a large percentage of preferred shares. Since almost all preferred shares decline greatly in value, it is not surprising that her portfolio lost $300,000 of its value in just a few years.   There really was a good chance that she would have outlived her money had she not substituted common shares for those preferred shares. Dividend income is not enough. You also need capital gain. Preferred shares will not give you capital gain.

CHAPTER 6
Finding 20 Good Stocks?

OPENING A SELF-DIRECTED TRADING ACCOUNT

In the previous chapter we explored where large sums of money could be invested. Opening a self-directed stock trading account with a major bank appeared to be the safest, most cost-efficient destination.

The first step in buying stocks requires that you open a chequing account with the financial institution that will be supplying you self-directed investment service. You deposit money in the chequing account, while you wait for the self-directed trading account to be opened.

How do you choose which major financial institution to invest with? While each of the major banks think they are quite different, I have never seen much difference between them. Their staff appear to be clones of each other. The banks watch each other closely to make sure one bank does not offer any significant service advantage over the other.

I subscribe to an international banker's magazine. It often contains interesting statistical facts like the following list of "The Safest Banks in North America" *(Global Finance/page16/ November 2018/ Global Finance Media,7 E 20th St, 2nd Floor, New York, NY, 10003).*

THE 10 SAFEST BANKS IN NORTH AMERICA

Bank	*Moody's Rating*	*Assets in Dollars*	*Statement Date*
TD Bank	Aa1	1,012,760,000,000	30 Apr 2018
Royal Bank	Aa2	940,707,000,000	31 Oct 2017
Bank of Nova Scotia	Aa2	709,89,000,000	31 Oct 2017
Bank of Montreal	Aa2	550,361,000,000	31 Oct 2017
Canadian Imperial Bank of Com.	Aa2	438,427,000,000	31 Oct 2017
Federation des Caisses. Desjardin.	Aa2	115,943,000,000	31 Dec 2017

AgriBank ,000 31 Dec 2017	Aa3	104,500,000
CoBank ,000 31 Dec 2017	NR	129,211,000
AgFirst 0,000 31 Dec 2017	Aa3	37,811,00

Farm Credit. Bank of Texas	Aa3	22,837,000,000	31 Dec 2017

Since it would confuse readers to present a dozen banks unique, self-directed investment systems, I have chosen to only use the first one on this list, TD Bank. It is just an example. There may be better ones and I know there are worse ones. It is not my intention to endorse TD. Every investor must do their research and make their own decision as to which self-directed investment system suits them best.

To establish a bank account with the TD Bank, you go to the following website **www.td.com/ca/en/personal-banking**.

(American and foreign readers please note that TD has almost as many branches in the USA as it does in Canada. In the US go to www.td.com/us/en/personal banking. For those, outside the USA and Canada, you may be able to gain internet access to their self-directed investment service by phoning the Toronto-Dominion Bank at 1-844-352-1146. TD seems to have now made

*their self-directed investment service available to
investors in more countries).*

Going to this website brings you to a page that reads
"**Browse all accounts**". Click on this box. It takes you
to a page offering "**Chequing**" or "**Saving**" accounts.
Since money will be invested and not saved, choose
Chequing. Several types of chequing accounts are
available. (One that that you should request if you are a
senior is **"All Inclusive With Senior's Rebate"**. It
offers special privileges and discounts).

 Choosing the **TD Unlimited Chequing Account** should
be satisfactory. **TD waives the** $15.95 monthly fee if you
keep $4,000 in the account. You can also make
unlimited transactions without incurring an additional
fee.

This selection now brings you to a page that details the
information needed to open the chequing account. The
most obvious criteria are that you must be the "**age of
majority in your Province**". In small print it states, "**In
some instances you may need to visit a branch to
complete your application**". You are not permitted to
open an account for a 3rd party."

A series of input screens are then presented for
entering: **your name, address, email address, phone,
government issued ID, date of birth, Social Insurance
Number, Work,** etc. The most important of these is your
Social Insurance Number. It allows TD, to verify the
identification data you have entered. Through their online

link to a consumer credit report agency (Equifax or TransUnion) their computer system will order a credit report on you. The Social Insurance Number also links the TD account to the Revenue Canada taxation database.

In your credit report TD will find a history of all your credit card transactions and other risk information. Using their sophisticated risk scoring computer program, they will establish the degree of risk they are accepting in opening your chequing account. It is also a marketing tool that allows them to offer you a credit card with a pre- established limit. It can even offer you a mortgage at a competitive interest rate. This scoring program eliminates the need for you to visit the branch to open an account.

Once your bank chequing account is open, you can open your self-directed stock trading account. You go to the following website "**https://www.td.com/ca/en/investing**" which displays a page headed, "**Investing Solutions Built For You**".

 It provides three choices:

> **(1) I'm a self-directed investor.**
> **(2) I want personalized wealth advice.**
> **(3) I prefer to invest at a branch.**

Choose **"I'm a self-directed investor"**, otherwise you will end up having to contend with personnel from TD's full-service operation. You have read what happened to

Ms. Innocence when she ended up with the investment adviser of a large bank.

At the bottom of this page, you now click on the **"Learn More"** box.

This brings you to a new page headed, **"Introducing TD Direct Investing Goal Assist"**. You skip this option and select the **"Learn More"** box at the bottom or this page.

A page headed, **"Open An Account"** appears and below it they ask, **"How would you like to invest?"**. Skip the first two options, they are additional investment services which they should not be offering to a new, self-directed investor. The first is a **margin trading account** (this is one where TD will lend you money to invest. TD uses the stocks you buy as their security on the loan. They make money by charging you interest). The second service is opening an **options trading account. This** is a complicated investment service in which you only buy an option to buy a stock. They should not be offering this service to a new, self-directed investor.

The third account option **"Cash Account"** is the one you want. You click on the orange box below it, **"Apply Now"**. This takes you to a new page headed, **"Thank you for choosing TD Direct Investing"**. It then states, **"Don't have a TD online login ID?"** Since you do not yet have an account, click on the **"Start Application Here"**.

The application process for opening your self-directed trading account resembles what you went through in opening the chequing account. In the spaces you key in (1) government issued ID (this could be a passport number). (2) social insurance number (3) your Canadian residency address (4) and your newly acquired TD bank account number.

After entering, you acquire (1) A username or Connect ID (2) with a place for your unique, secret password. Never supply this password to another person.

You can now gain access to the following page:

https://www.td.com/ca/en/investing/direct-investing/trading/webbroker

You can just enter **"TD direct investing"** in a Google search and end up on the same page with the following title options:

TD....My Accounts....Ways to Invest....Market Insights....LOGIN

Click on the **LOGIN** box which takes you to a new screen with two options in the top right of the screen: The top option is "**Web Broker On Line Trading**" below this heading is a **login** button. Clicking on it will take you to the next screen.

(The second option was "**EasyWeb On Line Banking**". It also has a **login** button. It takes you to your chequing account screen. Instant access to your chequing account is important as you will be transferring money back and forth between the chequing account and the trading account. To buy a stock you will first transfer money from the chequing account into the trading account.)

Note: The TD phone number provided on this page, **1-800-667-6299**, is a help line that is open 24 hours a day, 365 days a year, if you need help in logging in or have questions about direct investing. TD staff are there. They are patient, knowledgeable and helpful.

The WebBroker Online Trading's login button takes you to a page headed," **WebBroker Login**" where you will enter either your "**Username or Connect ID**" and next your "**Password**". After entering, click the **"login"** button.

At this juncture your search engine may ask you if you wish to save the Connect ID and Password so that you can access the following page in the future without having to enter the ID and Password. I would not recommend it. If your computer were ever left unattended, someone, other than yourself, could gain access to your account. They could then commit all kinds of havoc. With the amount of money that you will have in your trading account this is taking an unnecessary risk.

You have now entered onto your main entry page. From here you will check on all the stocks in your portfolio, do research to find stocks to buy and place your orders to buy and sell stocks. So much information on stocks is available that you could lose yourself for days investigating all the data options. I ignore 95% of the data that is available. Much of it is repeating the same information in a multitude of different ways. I concentrate on the key elements.

In order that this website does not confuse you, I will only cover the information that I think you need to find, buy and monitor good stocks. You will have the rest of your life to explore the fringe information areas.

TD's main landing page for you to go to, is:

https://webbroker.td.com/waw/brk/wb/wbr/static/main/index/html

At the top of the screen, it displays and provides access to the following:

My Account..Contact Us..Products & Services..Life Planning..TD Home..Easyweb..YOUR NAME ..LOGOUT.

Below this line of options, you will click on the following headings to gain access to important applications:

TD..HOME..ACCOUNTS..RESEARCH..TRADING.. GOALS

Below this line are the latest statistics on the TD Composite, the Standard & Poor 500, etc. Not being a speculator, these daily statistics are only of passing interest. Stock markets go up and they go down. As a value investor your intention is to hold the stocks you choose forever.

Below this statistical data, you will find information on where your portfolio stood at the end of the previous day's trading. Since you have not yet transferred cash from your chequing account to your trading account, only zeros will be appearing.

Example:

TOTAL BALANCE (CAD) $1,234,567.05

INVESTMENTS

$1,000,0000

CASH

$234,567.05

YESTERDAY'S CHANGE

$10,567 (-0.53%)

I do record the **TOTAL BALANCE** every day in a diary. It takes three minutes and allows me to spot any unusual change in my portfolio which might cause me to look more closely. From one day to the next these amounts should fluctuate little. Over a month I expect to see a small growth in my portfolio. Growth or loss in an investment portfolio is never in a straight line.

A box, off to the right side of this page, displays a graph entitled **BALANCE TREND DETAILS** for the last month. This is just one of a dozen graphs and charts showing how your stocks are doing compared to different criteria. I pay little attention to it. I am not competing with anyone or with industry standards.

You are now ready to transfer money from your chequing account into your trading account. To do this, you return to your TD chequing account as we described above and sign in on the **Easy Web Login**. You click "**My Accounts**" and up comes your "**Accounts**" page. On the left side are several buttons running vertically down the page. Click on the **"Transfers"** button.

A screen comes up **reading "Between My TD Accounts – Transfer Funds"**. Beneath it, you will see **"Step 1 of 3"** and beneath that you will see that **"From"** and to the right of that it directs you to **"Select From Account"**. There is a **small arrow** to the left of this box which if you click on, it will display all your TD Accounts. Select from this list your chequing account. On the next line is **"To"**. You click on the arrow at the end of this box and then select **"CANADIAN CASH – your account# - $ amount in your trading account"**. Since you have not yet transferred any money into the account, a zero will be appearing.

Now that you have instructed the computer what you want done, you must tell it how much money you want to transfer. Below **"To"** you will see **"Amount"**. Here is where you enter how much money you are transferring from your chequing account. After entering the amount, click on the **"Next"** hi-lighted below.

A new screen appears which is step 2 of the 3 screens involved in a transfer. All this screen does is confirm what you entered in step one. You now click on the hi-lighted **"Finish"** at the bottom of this screen.

The 3rd and final screen confirms that you are transferring money from your chequing account to your trading account. They provide a unique Confirmation code number. You now have cash in your trading account and can buy shares.

You are ready to look for "good" stocks to invest in. What is a good stock? The first rule in investing is never to lose money. Thus, you want to invest in stocks that are least likely to lose money.

Investing is common sense.

Do you want to invest in an unprofitable company? No.

Do you want to invest in a company that pays dividends? Yes.

Why? Because it is the very rare, unprofitable company that can and would pay a dividend. You are buying shares in a company so you can share in its profits. Companies who pay dividends out of profits are sharing their success with shareholders.

The dollar amount of the dividends paid out by companies usually remains steady month-after-month, quarter after quarter, even when their share price drops like a stone in an overall market decline. Your income should remain steady until the stock price recovers. Charts are available for each dividend stock, showing how frequently and how much, they have paid. The charts can go back 10 years.

Stock price fluctuations often reflect the emotional reactions of speculators. These fluctuations often have little to do with the normal income and expense flow in a business. As a commercial risk executive, I studied business failures for over forty years. Business failures are like a slow leak in a tire rather than a sudden tire blow out.

Do you want to invest in companies whose share price is going to increase and in turn increase your wealth? Yes.

Such companies can be identified by how many analysts are saying they are a good buy, by the average number of shares traded daily, by the ratio of their share price to how much they have earned and by comparing their share price to their "book value" (estimated liquidation value divided by the number of shares in the company).

Do you want to invest in a company with high operating margins (profits) or low operating margins? What is the operating margin of a company? It is the company's sales minus the expense to generate those sales. It is that sum of money left over before paying dividends, taxes and investments to improve operations. Some companies have operating margins over 90% while others, with problems, have operating margins that are much less than 1%.

Do you want to buy stocks whose share price are a bargain? Yes. What would be a bargain? A bargain would be a stock that costs you $6 a share to buy, but if liquidated the company shareholders would receive significantly more than $6 per share for their piece of the company. We consider such companies undervalued. More than likely, their share price will increase after you have bought them. The reverse is also a reality. There are some popular stocks that cost over $200 whose liquidation price may only be $5 per share. They are vulnerable to a reduction in their share price. Usually they are speculative stocks, touted as having great potential. You are seduced into buying before they go higher. Speculators not wanting to be left out of the quick riches jump in for fear they will miss an opportunity.

Bre-X Minerals was such a stock. It rose rapidly from pennies a share to $286.50 a share in 1996 after supposedly finding an enormous gold deposit in Indonesia. In 1997 investigators found the company had doctored the ore samples. Some very large Canadian pension funds, who should have known better, lost hundreds of millions of dollars. A few who were not greedy sold before the share price collapsed. They made a fortune.

Do you want to buy companies whose shares trade for pennies or do you want to buy shares that investors are willing to pay at least a few dollars for? You want to invest in stocks that have some established demand in the stock market as reflected in both price and volume of shares traded. A stock that trades only a few thousand shares each day is difficult to both buy and sell. This thin trading causes wide price gaps between what a seller asks and what a buyer will pay for the shares. A share for which you can not easily find a buyer, lacks stability.

Buying a stock is very similar to buying a business. Would you want to buy a poorly run, unprofitable, newly formed business, with nothing solid to recommend it? No, you are looking for well-managed, profitable companies that have operated successfully for years.

Unlike a slot machine in a casino, where all you can do is bet your money, pull the lever and hope for the best, a company traded on the Toronto Stock Exchange offers a wealth of information that you can use to predict whether it is a good company to invest in or not.

To further protect your investment, you do not put all your money into the potential of one company. You spread your risk and increase the chance of buying a stock in a company that may double in value, by investing in several companies that your analysis shows are the best available.

The ideal investment objective is spreading your money evenly among 20 good companies. Why 20? Let us suppose that you have $1,000,000 to invest in the stock market and you want to spread the risk evenly. That puts $50,000 of your wealth (or 5% of your wealth in any one stock). Over ten years the stocks will fluctuate up and down. Expect 80% of your portfolio to be up, and 20% to be below their initial purchase price. Since no one can accurately predict the future, a disaster may occur, and one stock will lose all its value. You may lose the $50,000 you originally invested in that one stock. This is a tolerable loss because the odds are that 80% of your stocks will increase in value. 10% or more of those stocks will double their share price. In addition, to offset any losses, every year you will be receiving dividends from the portfolio that should average 6% or $60,000 from your portfolio of 20 stocks. It is entirely possible with time your $1,000,000 portfolio will more than double in value, despite the possible loss of one stock worth $50,000.

If you reduced the number of stocks in your $1,000,000 portfolio to perhaps 10 stocks, you are reducing your chances of having enough growing stocks to offset losses.

If you increased the number of shares in your portfolio to 40, you reduce the likelihood of significant gains in your portfolio. It is difficult enough to find 20 good shares to buy without having to double the objective. It increases the odds that you will pick losers. It also becomes difficult to research and monitor 40 companies.

Now that we have defined what we want, how do we find these 20 good stocks? The TD computer system makes it easy and fast but accept the reality that the perfect stock does not exist. You will always have to compromise and weigh the pros and cons of each stock before you decide if it is good enough to add to your portfolio. **I created a computer program that will help you compare and score the desirability of prospective stock purchases. It will be useful when you need to choose the best 20 out of 50 potential purchases. I will email this program, free, to all those who have bought this book. Email to <u>idm.score@informus.ca</u> and ask for it. Tell me where and when you bought the book and how much you paid for it.** The matrix I used for the scoring program is in Chapter 12, if you wish to work out scores on a stock manually.

HOW TO SELECT A STOCK

You have established a trading account with the financial institution of your choice. For tax reasons, only stocks traded on the Toronto Stock Exchange are being considered. Why? Because if Canadians invest in US stocks, they encounter both foreign currency fluctuations (as I write this, TD Bank reports that a US dollar equals $1.34 Canadian dollars) and a 30% US withholding tax.

Income tax breaks for Canadians are only available on dividend income from Canadian stocks. There is also the reality that if you live in Canada, you are much more aware of how changes to the laws and the economy affect your stocks.

NOTE: International diversification is realized by buying shares in large Canadian companies, who do billions of dollars in business around the world.

There are 4,468 companies listed on the (TSX) Stock Exchange. Of these, 2,421 are larger companies registered on the Toronto Stock Exchange and 2,047 are smaller companies registered on the more junior (TSXV) the Venture Exchange. The 2,421 larger companies on the TSX must have tangible net assets exceeding $7,500,000 to qualify for listing on the senior TSX.

Out of these 4,468 Canadian stocks we want 20 "good" ones to invest in. Our definition of "good" means paying good dividends, showing the possibility of future share price increase in multiple industries You start this search by going to the search engine (Google) and entering **"TD login"** into the search pane.

It brings you to the main entry page, **"MY ACCOUNTS – TD CANADA TRUST -TD BANK"**.

"MY ACCOUNTS", is highlighted. Over on the right side are two boxes. **"TD Easy Web Online Banking"** will take you to your chequing account. This is not where we now want to go. We want to take the option below it, **"WEBBROKER ONLINE TRADING"**. Click on it.

A screen headed **"WEBBROKER LOGIN"** appears. Beneath it is a pane for you to enter your **"USERNAME OR CONNECT ID"** and below that is a pane to enter your **"PASSWORD"** The "username" is the account number TD gave you when you set up your trading account and created a password. You press the **LOGIN** button to take you to the next screen.

This takes you to the "**HOME**" screen. **HOME** is highlighted in the top left corner. On that same line are four other headings: **"ACCOUNTS...RESEARCH...TRADING...GOALS"**

To find your 20 stocks, click on the **"RESEARCH"** heading.

This takes you to the next screen which is headed up **"MARKETS...INVESTMENTS...TOOLS...EDUCAT ION"**. Underneath the **"TOOLS"** heading is a series of subheadings: **"QUOTES...WATCHLISTS...CHARTS...SCREENE RS...ALERTS**.

Click on **"SCREENERS"** to take you to the next screen.

The new screen is **"SCREENER STOCKS"** below it, the single word **"STOCKS"** appears. Three other headings are on the same line, **"TECHNICAL EVENT...MUTUAL FUNDS...ETFS"**. Below that is a two-line heading that reads **"Pick Your Strategy and follow along easily"**. Just below that, is a little box with the following **"+ ADD NEW"**. Click on that little box.

You are taken to a screen where you will enter the criteria for selecting your stocks.

The heading on this page is "**SELECTION CRITERIA**". Below that it reads, "**SELECT CRITERIA TO BEGIN SCREENING**". A box beneath that says, "**ENTER SEARCH KEY WORD**". Below this box are search criteria to choose from:

"**POPULAR ..COMPANY BASICS..DEBT..DIVIDEND..GROWTH AND EARNINGS...PERFORMANCE...PROFITABILITY ...TECHNICALS TRADING...VALUATION**".

Click on the first one, "**POPULAR**". Here you select the criteria to locate suitable stocks.

A list of criteria appears. Some of these you will load into your search engine. The list presented includes. "**STOCK PRICE...EXCHANGE...MARKET CAPITALIZATION...DIVIDEND YIELD...VOLUME 90 DAY AVERAGE...BULLISH INDICATORS...P/E...EPS GROWTH (5 YEAR HISTORICAL) ...PRICE/BOOK RATIO...DEBT TO EQUITY RATIO.**"

The first one on this list you are going to click on is "**STOCK PRICE**". As soon as you click on it a graph appears at the top of the screen.

On the left, it says "**STOCK PRICE**" as you move the marker to the left you see the words, "**MIN**" (which stands for "minimum") above the start of the dark green bar in the graph. At the other end of the graph is **"MAX"** (which stands for "maximum"). In a box below **"MIN"** the word **"MIN"** is repeated and below '**MAX**" the word "MAX" is repeated.

At each end of the dark green graph are two white boxes. At the right end of the bar under **"MATCHES"** appears the number 12,229. This is the total number of stocks that I could access and buy through my TD self-directed account. Why would this number be so large if the Toronto Stock Exchange only has 4,468 stocks listed? This is because stocks being traded on the US exchanges are also included.

 If you put your cursor on the one close to **"MIN"** and slide it to the right, you will see numbers appearing in the box where the word "MIN" was appearing. This is setting the minimum price that you want to include in your search for a stock. If you go to the other end of the dark green bar and move that white box to the left, you will see a number appear in the box under **"MAX"**. This limits the price of stocks to be considered

To eliminate small value stocks from consideration, arbitrarily set the minimum price as close as you can to **$1.82** and leave the maximum price bar at **MAX.** At the right of the bar, under the heading "MATCHES". The hi and low selectors reduced the number of stocks to **10,246**.

Why is the price of a stock an important selector? Public companies live and die by their share price. Why? Because companies tie executives' incentives to the share price. Executives of large publicly traded companies always want their company share price to go up so they can make money on their stock options (*At the beginning of the year, a senior executive, as an incentive, may receive an option to purchase several thousand shares at a set price at the end of the year. If at the end of that year, the price is higher than the option price set at the beginning of the year, they can sell their optioned shares, without having to buy them, and pocket the difference (the capital gain) between the option price and the new market share price. If given 10,000 optioned shares at $50 and at end of the year, they are now $52 a share, they would have made $20,000 (e.g. $520,000 - $500,000 =$20,000. The tax on capital gains is 50% of the regular income tax rate.)*

 Note: A low share price may show that the company has difficulty in attracting investors. If it can not attract investors, the share price will not realize a capital gain. Lower priced stocks under consideration should get extra scrutiny.

If you are investing 5% of your money in any one stock, a $50 stock limits how many shares you are going to buy. If that 5% represented $50,000, you could only buy 1,000 shares at $50 each. If that same $50,000 was buying $2 shares, you could buy 25,000 shares. If the $50 share goes up $1, you will make $1,000. If the $2 share goes up $1, you will make $25,000 on the same $50,000 investment. If you have chosen a good $2 stock, it is far more likely to double in price than a $50 stock.

Note: I had understood that you could only place orders in blocks of a hundred e.g.100 ...200...500...1,000...100.000. However, it appears there may be some investment dealers who put no restrictions on the number of shares ordered.

Since we are only interested in Canadian stocks. You remove the US stocks by going to the next selector, **"EXCHANGE"** and include it in this search engine.

 EXCHANGE is immediately below "STOCK PRICE". As soon as you click on 'EXCHANGE", the word "EXCHANGE" appears under the "Selection Criteria" and in the middle, on the next line, below the stock price graph the wording **"ANY CANADIAN EXCHANGE"** appears.

On the right, under **"Matches"** a number appears, it now reads that the number of stocks left to select from is "**TOTAL 4468**".

You have successfully removed the US accounts and have 4,468 Canadian companies now meeting the criteria. This is still too many to analyze.

To quickly bring that number down to a manageable size, select the **"DIVIDEND YIELD"** criteria. Using a dividend rate of **"3.5%"**as your minimum dividend criteria and leave the maximum rate at **"MAX"**. It now brings the number of stocks down to **2,317**.

This is still too many. You could increase the dividend percentage to a higher number, like 7%, to bring the number of stocks down to a reasonable number to review. However, it would eliminate many excellent stocks (like major Canadian banks who do not have to offer a high dividend percentage to attract investors).

Banks keep on increasing the dollar amounts they payout in dividends. They do this to maintain their dividend yield percentage at roughly the same number in relation to their share price (e.g. Initially, the share price is $100, and the dividend pay out is $4.50 annually. This equates to a 4.5% dividend yield. When the share price increases to $200, to keep the dividend yield at 4.5%, they would have to increase their payout to $9.00.) If your objective is to realize a dividend yield of 6% from all your stocks, you must take more than just the bank's current dividend yield percentage into consideration.

Most corporations do not pay a dividend. Why are dividends important? If a company is paying a dividend, they know that if the dividend payment to shareholders is eliminated then the stock price will most likely drop drastically. Their executives' bonuses, such as stock options, hinge on increasing the share price. The executives will do everything they can to increase dividends. This not only enriches the executives but the shareholders as well.

You want to own stocks that pay dividends because it is insurance that at least you are going to make something on your investment. The price of a stock will go up and it will go down, but the dollar amount of the dividend paid out will usually remain steady. Dividends allow you to weather those times when the share price may fall.

Beware of stocks paying dividends of 10% or more, especially if the company is operating at a loss. Dividend money must come from somewhere. To stop the share price from declining, some desperate companies may borrow the money to pay the expected dividend or they may even sell assets to pay the dividend. This weakens the company. It is possible for a financially strong company to pay a dividend of 10% or more but it would be unusual. A good company doesn't have to bribe investors with a high dividend to keep its share price high.

A dividend is your share of the annual profits from a successful operation. The company keeps profit money for taxes, research and development and to pay dividends to the shareholders who invested in their company. They may pay as much as 60% of the profit in dividends.

Dividends are taxed at a lower rate than salaried income. A person in the highest income bracket in Canada is paying a 54% income tax. If all your income were from Canadian company dividend, you could, on an income of $75,000, pay as little as $2,000 in income tax. Since the corporation paid income tax on what it earned, having to pay income tax on dividend income is a form of double taxation. The government recognizes this and thus provides a lower tax rate on dividend income

NOTE: As the share price increases the fixed dividend yield percentage will automatically decline and when the share price decreases the fixed dividend percentage will automatically increase.

Dividends instill a discipline on company executives and focuses them on results. Companies that do not pay dividends, argue that they can invest the company's profits better than their shareholders. Studies have shown that companies not paying dividends, do not invest their profits any more wisely than shareholders who receive the dividends.

To bring 2,317 stocks down to a manageable number we next go to **"VOLUME"**. You now set this selector to exclude companies whose stocks trade less than 442,999 shares daily on the Toronto Stock Exchange. This brings the number of stocks for your consideration down to **52**. Out of these 52 stocks you should be able to find 20 good stocks to put in your portfolio.

NOTE: If you can not find enough companies to consider then you could keep reducing the "number of shares being traded daily", to increase the number of stocks being put forward for consideration.

The price of shares has little to do with dividend income. When the market goes down, it only means that the price of most shares has gone down. It does not mean the dividend payments have gone down. One major benefit of owning good dividend stocks is that you can afford to pay minimal attention to their fluctuations in the overall stock market.

For over 100 years, the stock market's value has risen higher after every decline, then it was before each decline. It may take months, even a few years. That is why you do not sell a dividend stock when the market goes down. If you have the cash, you buy good dividend stocks when the market goes down because they will then be at a bargain price and will be the first stock prices to rise.

CHAPTER 7

Scoring Your Stocks

In the previous chapter you identified 52 stocks that met your definition of a good stock. We now want to identify which 20 of the 52 would be best for our portfolio. To keep things simple, I will analyze in depth just one stock of the 52 and four others to a lesser degree.

As you become more familiar with scoring stocks, there may be other data that you will come across that helps you choose the best stocks. However, I have found that the following factors were enough for me to create a good portfolio.

Doing your own stock picking eliminates having to pay investment advisers thousands of dollars. Since you are taking income away from investment advisers, they will scoff and say that it could not be this easy to pick stocks. However, as I am about to show you, it is, and my steady income and the growth in my portfolio are the proof.

When I was working as a vice president for a large international corporation, I was making a salary a little less than my current investment income. However, I was losing 50% of this employment income to income tax. With my current dividend-based income I am now losing about 20%

to income tax. Since I now have far fewer expenses, I am financially far better off. My portfolio and my income grow year after year, with a minimum of effort on my part.

When speaking to novice investors, investment advisers often use unfathomable jargon about incomprehensible investment vehicles. Does the investment industry deliberately make investing money as difficult for investors to understand as they can? Is this their attempt to intimidate clients from even considering that they could trespass into their world? In the aggressive pursuit of commissions, too many of them seem to forget that it is your money that is at risk, not theirs. Ignore their warnings of financial disaster. Peek behind the curtain and find investments that you understand. Paying $10,000 to an investment adviser to invest a million dollars in something you do not understand, makes little sense. Nor does it make sense to keep on paying that investment adviser year-after-year as you watch your portfolio shrink.

In the following, I will use each stock's official stock exchange symbol to save having to write out the full name of the company. For example, "IPL" is the symbol for Inter Pipeline.

Please note that I am neither recommending nor rejecting the stocks being used to illustrate what to look for in a stock. Stock information is never static. It can change in minutes. The following information is historic and not to be used for current decisions.

You will often come across stocks with a "**UN**" after the first letters of their symbol. The "UN" is short for "unit". In some stocks you do not buy shares, you buy units. Real Estate Investment Trusts are where you will see the "UN" appearing. REITs are pools of capital invested in apartment buildings, office buildings, malls, warehouses, etc. In their monthly dividends, you share in the REIT's rental income and its capital gains. REITs usually pay higher than average dividends and have high operating margins. To avoid corporate level taxes, they must distribute almost all their earnings to their unit holders. Less frequently you will come across some "UN" stocks that are not REITS but are a hybrid between a stock and loan. Their payments to investors will be a combination of dividend income and interest. This can provide some tax advantages to investors.

In the previous chapter, 52 stocks met our search criteria. A list appeared at the bottom of the **"Screeners Stocks"** screen, such as the following examples, taken from it:

RANK	SYMBOL	NAME	STOCK PRICE	EXCHANGE	DIVIDEND YIELD	VOLUME 90-DAY	ACTION
(1)	IPL	Inter Pipeline Ltd	22.11	TSX	7.8%	1.71M	Select
(2)	CHE.UN	Chemtrade Logistics Inc	9.14	TSX	13%	446,000	Select
(14)	CM	Canadian Imp. Bank Com	107.39	TSX	5.21%	1,009,163	Select
(26)	TD	Toronto-Dominion Bank	73.91	TSX	4%	5,179,791	Select
(41).	CJR.B	Financial 15 Split Corp	6.02	TSX	3.99%	278,791	Select

The stock price, dividend yield and the average volume of shares traded daily do not give enough information to make a stock buying decision.

To access hundreds of facts on each of these stocks, you click on the **"Select"** button on the extreme right of the line for each stock. A pane with six options then appears:

(1) Buy (2) Sell **(3) Overview** (4) News (5) Charts (6) Option Chain".

Select **"Overview"**. This will bring you to a page containing facts about the IPL and its stock performance.

From this Overview page, we are interested in gathering eight facts. We will record the gathered information on the following form. **It is an input data form for a <u>free</u> <u>computer program available to those who have</u> <u>purchased this book</u> and it may be acquired by sending an email request to:**

<u>idm.score@informus.ca</u>.

On April 1, 2019 there were 654 stocks on the Toronto Stock Exchange paying a dividend of 3.5% or more. These 654 listings were extracted and scored. Their dividend percent, stock price, company name and stock symbol were recorded. **In Chapter 13 you can see a printout of this data sorted by score. Chapters 14, 15 and 16 are additional printouts in alpha, dividend percent and by share price. These sorts can help you to quickly find the 20 stocks for your portfolio.**

In Chapter 12 you will find the matrix which is the origin of the stock scoring program. If you wish, you can manually work out a stock's score by referring to this matrix. It takes a few minutes to calculate the score manually, while the computer program does it in a second.

The higher the score the more reliable the company's dividend and the greater the chance that stock's share price will increase. The highest score I have seen was 78 for one of the major Canadian banks. The lowest score was 8 for a company that appeared to be no longer active.

THE SCORING CHART *(input scoring form)*

    (1) Enter Stock Name or Ticker Symbol

          _____

    (2) Current price of stock _____

    (3) Price 4 years ago _____

    (4) Price/Comparison (current to 4 years ago*)* _____

       (calculated automatically by the computer program)

    (5) Book Value_____

    (6) Book value to Current Price Comparison _____

(calculated automatically by the computer program)

(7) No. of analysts rating a Buy _____

(8) No. of analysts rating a Strong Buy

_____

(9) Yield % _____

(10) Operating Margin % _____

(11) Daily Volume Traded

_____

(12) Price to Earnings _____

(13) Overall Rating _____Score

(total of the scores from #1 to #12)

Using Inter Pipeline Ltd. as an example, the following is a line-by-line review of where to find the information on the **OVERVIEW** page that would go into the above **scoring form.**

(1) **ENTER STOCK NAME OR TICKER –** The first stock on the list, Inter Pipeline Ltd with the stock symbol of **"IPL"**. You would enter IPL into # 1 on the Stock Scoring Chart. You find the symbol "IPL" just below "Inter Pipeline Ltd" in the top left corner. It reads "TSX: IPL" followed by a Canadian flag.

(2) **CURRENT PRICE OF STOCK** – The "LAST PRICE" of the stock (on March 29, 2019 it was **$22.11).** You find the price two lines below "TSX.IPL".

(3) **PRICE 4 YEARS AGO** – To get this figure you go to the horizontal list of option panes below the **LAST PRICE:**

*OVERVIEW… **CHARTS**…NEWS…FUNDAMENTALS… EARNINGS…REPORTS…   CALENDAR…OPTI ONS…TECHNICALS…PORTFOLIO MANAGERS.*

Click on **"CHARTS"**. This brings up a chart with a graph showing the stock's price history for several years. When you put your cursor on the chart a vertical line appears. As you move the cursor, you will see that the vertical line moves with the cursor and the following appears:

"Date…Open…High..Low..Close"

It is just above the green chart. The numbers below change as you move your cursor. The extreme right figure is that historical day's closing price. You stop moving your cursor horizontally as soon as you reach today's date, four years ago. Often you can not get the exact day four years ago. Choose a date as close as you can. The number you want is the closing price of the stock under **"Close"**. *(On April 1, 2015 the price was $31.60.)*

Why is it important to know what the price was 4 years ago? First, it confirms that the company has survived for at least 4 years. It is not a new, risky, unestablished business. The historical chart gives you a feel for the company. Is the current price the lowest price it has been in 4 years? It was as high as $36 four years ago. Taking the current price and this historical price data into consideration, you get both a historical confirmation that this profitable company is a survivor and that the price could move up.

Pipelines are utilities. Their infrastructure is in place. There is little competition. They charge their customers a toll for use of the pipeline. These are all factors that make IPL profitable. They pay dividends out of their profits.

(4) **PRICE COMPARISON** - Automatically the computer program makes a comparison between the current price and the 4-year-old historical price. It calculates and records the score for this line.

(5) **BOOK VALUE** – You find the BOOK VALUE figure for IPL on the Overview screen. *(It is in the column of information on the left side of the page, towards the bottom.)* The BOOK VALUE on this date was $9.82.

I always prefer a BOOK VALUE higher than the current share price, however I suspect if you check several pipeline stocks you will find that a lower BOOK VALUE is typical for pipeline and oil well service industries. A BOOK

VALUE higher than the share price shows that you are getting a real bargain - a stock with a liquidation value of $10 for only $5. Such bargains do not go unnoticed and eventually speculators will recognize that such a stock should have a higher share price. Buying such a bargain increases the chances that you will eventually realize a significant capital gain.

I have seen stocks selling for $200 that have a book value of $35. Will investors suddenly wake up and sell when they recognized that the stock is overpriced. Speculators may also continue to support the $200 price because of anticipated future beneficial changes in the company. Perhaps they would be right, but if you are not a speculator why would you risk having your money in an overvalued stock.?

 BOOK VALUE is an accounting calculation. It divides the tangible assets (e.g. equipment, real estate, etc.) held by the company by the number of shares that are outstanding. It gives you an idea as to what cash they would realize if they liquidated the company. However, something is only worth what someone will pay for it and who knows what would happen in a liquidation. Having analyzed hundreds of bankruptcies, I can only remember one where there was anything left over after the secured creditors, unsecured creditors and trustee had taken their due.

(6) **BOOK VALUE PRICE COMPARISON -**
The computer program automatically works out
the score for this comparison item by
comparing the current share price with the book
value.

(7) **NUMBER OF ANALYSTS RATING A
BUY** – You will find the analyst
ratings prominently displayed toward the top of
the page's right-hand column. 5 analysts rated
IPL as a **"BUY"**. This is more buys than most
stocks receive.

Analysts are playing to speculators who look
for capital gains. I suspect that they looked at
the previous share prices for IPL and the lower
current share price; they are expecting the share
price to increase. The fact that the stock pays a
good dividend, which is a big consideration of
value investors, is of a lesser consideration to
analysts. Since we are value investors, looking
for stocks paying good dividends with a good
capital gains, analysts' recommendations are a
buying signal for us.

I have rarely seen an analyst recommend a
"Sell" until the company seemed to be almost
bankrupt. Be careful how much faith you put in
an analyst's recommendation. Their
recommendations have limited influence on the
share's final score.

Share prices do not necessarily fluctuate on obvious logic. No one can accurately predict where share prices will be. They seem to fluctuate more on emotion than facts. Rumors, totally in contrast to accounting realities, can trigger massive buy and sell movements. The reporting of great increases in profits or losses may not cause share prices to increase or decrease.

(8) **NUMBER OF ANALYSTS RATING A STRONG BUY** – 2 analysts rated IPL a strong buy. **STRONG BUYS** are rarer than **BUYS**. Analysts would lose credibility within their peer group if they were consistently wrong in making such strong predictions. Since no one can accurately predict the future, analysts are cautious. The STRONG BUYs at IPL seem to show a good chance of a capital gain.

(9) **YIELD** -The **DIVIDEND YIELD** of 7.73% is higher than most stocks on the Toronto Stock Exchange, there were only 106 paying a higher dividend then 7.73%. You find the dividend yield in the right hand "FUNDAMENTALS" column towards the top.

The dividend yield figures are obviously critical when your intention is to live off your dividend income. You want to buy a safe stock with the highest dividend possible – but not too high. Look with skepticism at a company paying over 8% of its share price as a dividend.

Why would a dividend be unusually high? A high dividend stops shareholders from selling and causing the share price to drop. If a company must pay such a high dividend, it may be an indicator that there are problems with the company. You may find that the company is borrowing money to pay the dividend. They are digging a hole for themselves as the additional debt load may seriously affect their operating margin.

Successful, popular companies do not see a need to pay extraordinarily high dividends. Most companies traded on the stock exchange do not pay dividends. What you want to look for are companies paying a dividend between 4% and 9% of their share value.

(10)- OPERATING MARGIN - The OPERATING MARGIN of 37.65% is stronger than most companies. The higher this number the better. I own some stocks whose Operating Margin is over 90. You find it at the bottom of the right hand "FUNDAMENTALS" column.

If y our investment objective is never to lose money in a share, then this is one of your most critical figures to consider. The operating margins remain after they subtract the company's

expenses from the company's income. Then, out
of the OPERATING MARGIN dividends, taxes
and future development costs are subtracted. This
37.65% helps to confirm that IPL's dividends
should be safe, and the share price has a good
chance of moving up.

It is a figure that is often ignored by some
speculators, they seem to concentrate on the
potential of an unprofitable company with a "low"
share price that may rise at the first sign of
profitability.

(11) - **DAILY VOLUME TRADED** – It is the
average number of IPL shares traded daily. You
find it at the top of the right column under
"VOLUME". On this day, 1,186,977 shares
traded. This shows it is a vibrant
company. You would have no problem buying
or selling these shares. A company like IPL,
whose shares are at a historic low price, has a
good possibility of increasing. With high
volumes of shares being traded you are likely to
see only small fluctuations in the daily
price. When only a few thousand shares of a
speculative company are available, you often
see great fluctuations in the share price
throughout a day.

(12) PRICE /EARNING -The IPL Price to
Earnings figure of 14.5x is very close to a
traditional average of 15.x for shares. I look at

the P/E as a number that calculates how many years of profits it would take a company to repay the money that I have invested in buying a share in that company (e.g. it would take fourteen and a half years before the profits could repay me for my investment in IPL.)

While a P/E of 15.x is average, you will sometimes see companies whose shares have a P/E as low 5.x. A low P/E is an indicator that you are buying the stock at a bargain price. It is likely to increase. You would get a double value: a good dividend and a nice capital gain from a share price increase.

The lower the P/E number the better. You can often find shares with a P/E between 6.x to 10.x. You can also see the P/E over 200.x or even higher. These overpriced shares would be expected to drop.

Price to Earnings is the stock price divided by its Earnings Per Share. The Earnings Per Share is calculated by subtracting a company's preferred dividends from its net income and then dividing the result by the number of shares outstanding.

(13) OVERALL RATING – After you have entered all 12 figures, you click on the "OVERALL RATING" box and the computer adds up the scores for the 12 lines and gives you the total composite score for the stock.

TEST

Answer the 9 questions about the five test stocks in the boxes below. Refer to the notes below for the explanation of any short forms.

S Symbol	Price	Pr-4y	Bk V	Buys	S.Buys	Dvnd
IPL	22.11	31.6	9.82	6	2	7.73
CHE.UN	9.20	21.4	10.98	4	0	13.04
CM	107.4	96.8	78.91	5	2	5.21
TD	73.91	53.7	43.19	7	3	4
CJR.B	6.02	18.3	7.18	3	2	3.99

S. Symbl	Op. Mgin	Day Volum.	P/E
IPL	37.65	1,100,000	14.5x
CHE.UN	-7.11	239,000	NIL
CM	35.93	1,000,000	9.3x
TD	33.23	5,100,000	12.0x
CJR.B	-41.89	298,000	NIl

NOTES

STOCKS: **IPL** = *Inter Pipeline Ltd*, **CHE.UN** = *Chemtrade Logistics Inc.*, **CM** = *Canadian Imperial Bank of Commerce*, **TD** = *Toronto Dominion Bank*, **CJR.B** = *Corus Entertainment Inc.*

S Symbl = Stock Symbol,

Price = Current Price,

P-4yr = The stock price 4 years ago,

Bk V = Book Value,

Buys = Number of analysts recommending a buy,

S Buys = Number analysts recommending a strong buy,

Dvdn = Percent of the share price paid as a dividend,

Op Mgin = Operating Margin Percent,

Day Volum. = Average number of shares traded daily,

P/E = Price to Earnings ratio.)

NINE QUESTIONS

(1) Which two stocks have book values greater than their current share price?

(2) Which two had the greatest increase in share price over the last four year?

(3) Which stock had the most "BUY" recommendations?

(4) Which stock had the most "STRONG BUYS"?

(5) Which stock is paying the highest dividend?

(6) Which stock had the highest operating margin?

(7) Which stock had the lowest operating margin?

(8) Which stock had the highest volume of shares traded?

(9) Which are the two stocks with the worse price to earnings ratios?

After reviewing the figures in the above table for each stock, enter the Symbol for the 5 stocks below in the order that you think would be the most attractive to least attractive to buy. (*If you have not already requested the stock scoring software you should do so. The scores it calculates, for the five stocks, makes answering this question easy and fast. Another alternative is to calculate the scores manually following the matrix in Chapter 12. The final alternative is to go to Chapter 14, find the stock symbols for each company in the alphabetical sort and read the score for the stock. It is on the extreme left)*

1. _____

2. _____

3. _____

4. _____

5. _____

(1) Why is your number one stock the best?
_____.

(2) Why is your number five stock the worst? _____.

The following were the computer-generated scores for the five stocks:

1. CM = 78

2. TD = 75

3. IPL = 59

4. CJR.B = 41

5. CHE.UN = 35

While it may seem like a great idea to only buy the stocks that have the highest scores, high-scoring stocks are expensive e.g. CM (Canadian Imperial Bank of Commerce) is $107 a share. This limits the number of shares you could buy. You would want to review all Canadian bank stocks to see if there are less expensive bank stocks. Some may have higher scores and pay higher dividends than CM.

It is good to have a few major banks in your portfolio to anchor it. While their dividend percent may only be 4% now, the amount that they pay in dividends is likely to increase as their share price increases. However, if your immediate objective is to achieve an average return of 6% from the dividends of all 20 stocks, you are going to have to find other stocks paying over 6%. They will offset the initial dividend shortfall you will experience with your bank stocks.

To offset a dividend shortfall, you might consider buying a stock like **CHE.UN** (Chemtrade Logistics Inc.) It has a dividend yield of 13%. Unfortunately, the dividend is high because the share price fell when the company's profits shrunk. Its operating margin is now minus 7.1%. The high dividend rate is probably intended to appeal to investor greed and blind them to the risk present in a company with questionable profits.

It has been my experience that dividend rates this high are unlikely to be sustained. The money to pay the dividend must come from somewhere. If the dividend rate gets cut entirely or to a more normal percentage, investors will sell the stock and the share price will drop further.

The beautiful thing about investing in the stock market is that there are hundreds of other stocks to choose from. Just keep looking. Scoring helps you to find a good stock faster.

FULL ANALYSIS OF IPL

IPL (Inter Pipeline Ltd) is probably more typical of the stocks you might buy. The $22.11 price is reasonable. The 59 score is good. The 7.7% dividend is above the 6% you are looking for and would offset the lower dividend that CM is paying. Its 37.7% operating margin is the highest of the five stocks. If its price and book value had been lower four years ago than the current price, it would have been an ideal purchase. However, the perfect stock does not exist. It is always a matter of weighing the positives and negatives before making a stock buying decision.

After scoring all the stocks on a list of potential purchases, you will have a "feel" for the differences between stocks. You will see that having a high score does not mean that you should purchase that share nor should you reject those with lower scores.

You wish to create a diversified portfolio made up of shares from different industries. You might choose to ignore commodity stocks such as oil, mining and lumber companies. They can have rapid price swings depending on world markets. As providers of raw material, there is little to differentiate them from other companies providing the same raw material. A barrel of oil is a barrel of oil no matter who produces it.

Interestingly, speculators like natural resource stocks because they seek volatile stocks whose prices rapidly move up and down. If their timing is right (or they are lucky), speculators can make a huge profit on the volatility. If their timing is not right, they can lose a fortune. It only takes a few pricey losses before you learn that a careful selection of dividend stocks is a better choice if you wish to grow your money.

When someone approaches you with a hot stock tip, you will now be able to say that you want to check it out. If you run that stock's figures against the stock scoring program, you will compare the hot tip to the stocks you already own. Sometimes the tips are good and sometimes they are not, but now you will be able to consider reasons for a stock's attractiveness or lack of appeal.

 You only pay capital gains when you sell a stock. Since you only intend to buy stocks that you intend to hold forever; you will buy more stocks in a year than you will ever sell. If you do not require all your dividend income for your living expenses, you may be constantly adding to the stocks you already own with the excess funds you are receiving from your dividend payments.

On a stock's overview page, you will find two dates. The first is **"Ex-Dividend Date"** and the second is **"Pay Date"**. Check these two dates before either selling or buying a stock.

The directors of a company meet and decide that they are generating enough of a profit to provide a dividend to shareholders. They determine the dividend amount to pay per share. They set a date (*the Ex-Dividend date*) days or weeks later for making this payment.

On the ex-dividend day, you must own shares in their company to qualify for receiving this dividend. Timing becomes important and you need to buy shares a few days prior to the Ex-Dividend Date. This allows enough time for the stock exchange to register your stock purchase. If you waited until the same day, as the Ex-Dividend date, to buy your shares you would not receive the dividend

 The **"Pay Date"** is the day the dividend payment will appear in your trading accounts activity page. Your investment dealer is always very careful to record not just the day you bought your stock, but at what time during the day you made the purchase. Investors would become very upset if an expected dividend payment did not arrive on schedule.

Company Information- appears on the left side of the Overview page for each stock. It is a summary of what the company does and who the officers are. You often cannot tell from a company's name what industry it is in. This information becomes important when you seek greater portfolio diversification. There may be certain industries you wish to avoid.

As an investor, you will find reading the business section of business media becomes much more interesting. You may wonder how the various issues are going to be impact specific stocks in your portfolio. When one of your stocks appears in the media, it will get your full attention.

Similar Industries – Below the Company Information section is a list of a few companies in the same industry as the one being reported on in the Overview report. Sometimes these companies can appear to be a more attractive investment than the one you were considering. This section can also assure you that the company, in whose shares you are considering purchasing, is the best one in that industry. The displaying of the Price to Earnings Ratio and the Earnings Per Share Percentage for these similar companies gives you some insight into the health of each company. The "Market Cap" figure lets you know how the size of the company you are considering compares to its peers. For more information on the similar companies listed here, go to their OVERVIEW page.

What Investment Advisers May Forget to Mention in Pursuit of your Money

An investment adviser working for a large bank is not involved in the selection of the stocks in which your money will be invested. His sole function is to get your money in the bank and to make sure it stays there.

Most clients accept, without question, what an investment adviser recommends because they do not understand what is going on and believe they are dealing with a wise and trusted, expert.

When your money is released to your investment adviser, he immediately forwards it to the bank's portfolio managers, "the backroom boys". It is unlikely you will ever meet them. They add your money to investment pools that thousands of investors may have contributed to. The pools match a full-service investor's stated risk tolerance.

A portfolio manager buys and sells investments for the pools without a client's involvement. Each investor in the pool owns a certain percentage of investments in that pool. All pool transactions show up in your monthly statement as processing fees. It appears that a portfolio manager can make one stock sale in a portfolio and be able to charge a thousand clients in the pool for this one transaction. While you may have thought the bank was motivated to increase the value of your portfolio, thereby increasing their revenue from the annual percentage charge of your portfolio's value, a more reliable source of income for them are the transaction fees. Banks make billions on small fees. For the bank, the portfolio management system is a very cost-efficient way to manage your money

As your stocks are sold by the portfolio manager, there will be capital gains and losses. You have no control over this selling activity even though you are paying for it. There may be unique income tax situations, where you would choose not to sell a stock with a large capital gain. That would not be taken into consideration by the bank.

While portfolio managers may have received specialized training and have impressive credentials, they are caught in a conflict between maximizing portfolio performance for investors and maximizing profits for the bank. As employees of the bank their first loyalty must be to the bank.

If such a conflict bothers you, it is possible to bypass an investment adviser and deal directly with a stockbroker. There are a few still in existence. A stockbroker will charge you for every transaction. It would be a significant percentage of every stock purchase or sale that you would instruct him to make. On-line, self -directed investing, with its minimal fees, has done to stockbrokers what the internet did to travel agents.

CHAPTER 8
VERIFYING YOUR STOCKS

You have sifted through all the stocks on the Toronto Stock Exchange and have identified the first one to add to your investment portfolio. You are sure it is the best of the best. Would it not be embarrassing to learn, after you had bought the stock, that critical information existed that questioned the company's ongoing existence.

The Google search engine is one of your most useful research tools. It takes just a few minutes to make sure that no critical information exists that would stop you from buying a stock.

Using IPL (Inter Pipeline Ltd) as an example, let us search in Google. Put "inter pipeline ltd" in the Google Search pane. You are immediately linked to hundreds of websites. The one at the top of the page is IPL's own website, **www.interpipeline.com**. It contains all the usual information you expect to find in the website of a public company: officers and directors of the company, detailed financial information, news releases, etc. You are unlikely to find any negative information about IPL. This website is designed to sell you on investing in IPL and to sell bankers on lending IPL money.

The **Wickipedia** website reveals information not disclosed in the IPL website. For example, IPL owns storage terminals in the United Kingdom, Germany, Sweden, Denmark and the Netherlands. This could be a positive sign that IPL had diversified beyond being the main pipeline for Alberta's oil sand operations. It might also raise questions as to what might happen if Britain leaves the common market? Will Brexit create a recession and a lessening use of petroleum products? You also learn that IPL's customers include oil industry leaders like Encana, Shell Oil, Chevron and Imperial Oil.

Major financial information websites also report on IPL:

Bloomberg (**www.bloomberg.com**),

Globe & Mail (**www.globeandmail.com/investing/markets/stocks/IPL -t**).

These two, repeat much of the same information you can find in the IPL website.

Yahoo Finance (**https://ca.finance.yahoo.com/q?s=IPL**)

Yahoo does an outstanding job with their graphic displays. Their analysts expect to see IPL rise to $25.50 a share. They also automatically link you to the **"Simply Wall Street"** website, where you learn that insiders own less than 1% of the shares. This is thought to be unusual by the analyst. He appears to like companies where employees and officers hold a significant percentage of their company's shares. Employees who have a vested interest in a company's success would work harder to protect their investment. If the company were to fail or stop paying dividends, the employees would suffer financially. He also noted that institutional investors own 26% of IPL's shares. The institutional investor's analysts, responsible for investing millions of dollars in IPL, would have access to information which may not be available to the public. This gives some reassurance that the stock is a good investment.

The Yahoo site also contained a link to the **"Motley Fool"** website. That site reported positive news that IPL had increased their dividend payout for the 10th straight year and expect a revenue increase of $450,000,000.00 when IPL's $3.5 billion-dollar Heartland Petrochemical Complex opens in a few years.

Not everyone is positive about IPL. You find the naysayers by doing another search, but this time you enter **"Complaints Inter Pipeline"**. This brings up: **"https://stockchase.com**.

NOTE: *Putting "complaints" into any Google company search will often bring up the dark side of most companies, not just those you are considering buying shares in. Before spending hundreds of dollars, you can often benefit from doing "**complaints**" searches. It has saved me from making purchases I would have regretted.*

Stock Chase links you to hundreds of comments about IPL by ordinary investors and professional analysts. One investor commented that if IPL goes into a recession and oil prices fall, it will threaten the dividend. Another comments that IPL is "struggling with storage capacity in its European operation" (whether this is true, and important in making your buying decision is hard to determine). A third wonders, if IPL is earnings only $1.54 per share how can it be paying out $1.71 per share. Another sees a 35% upside on the stock price and recommends buying the stock at $18 per share.

It would be a very rare case where every investor agreed in which direction a share price was heading. For every seller of a stock who thinks the stock price has plateaued there has to be a buyer who thinks the stock price will go higher. If the buyer and seller did not exist, there would be no trading of stocks. It all comes down to you making an informed decision.

An investment decision is a commercial risk decision. No stock purchase is without risk. However, if you do not buy something, then you will never realize a dividend payment nor a capital gain. No one can consistently and accurately predict the future. Accept that occasionally some stocks you buy may never realize the potential you thought they had. More often, because of the care you have taken in choosing your stocks, you will become richer. Having 20 well chosen stocks in your portfolio, instead of two or three, will ensure that you realize your expected dividend income and capital gain.

As a value investor, the losses and gains that a public company experiences today are fleeting when you plan on owning the stock for decades. Every public company has employees dedicated to seeing their company succeed. They are working for you too. Companies are not inanimate blocks of wood. They are "living" entities, constantly trying to adjust to new challenges. A serious set back can inspire employees to work harder to overcome the challenges. Companies can experience a sudden loss in their share price, change direction, and rise from the ashes to greater success.

Put as much thought and research into a stock before selling it as you made in buying it. Do not be impulsive.

CHAPTER 9
Buying Your Stocks

When the overall share prices are down is the best time to buy stocks. That is when you are most likely find good stocks at a bargain price. If the stock scores well, the share price will most likely, in time, exceed its previous high. Dividend stocks are usually the first to rebound because they are the safest place to move your money to during stressful times.

Ms. Innocence asked an interesting question, "Since companies own all their shares would it hurt the company if the stock price declines?"

Companies do not own all the shares. Individual shareholders own the shares. There can be millions of shareholders owning a public company.

The shares exist because the founding directors of the company sold pieces of the company (shares) to investors. Their motivation is often to raise money for corporate growth and expansion or to reward the founders for establishing the company. The investors buy the shares because they expect the shares will increase in value and reward them with a capital gain. While it is possible for one company to sell its shares directly to a few investors, it is much more efficient to create a marketplace (e.g. Toronto Stock Exchange) where thousands of companies with shares to sell can interact with millions of investors interested in buying shares.

There are a limited number of shares in any one company available to buyers. What sets the price of a share is the law of supply and demand, as illustrated in the following:

A farmer has advertised that he is bringing the most delicious, juicy, sweet oranges to the market tomorrow. Lovers of oranges, and others, eagerly await their arrival. The farmer arrives at the market and before ten o'clock and quickly sells every orange he has at $1.00 an orange. His price was deemed reasonable to the buyers. He returns to his farm a happy man and invests the money in buying more acreage to grow even more oranges.

Many who wanted to buy his oranges could not buy them because they were all sold by the time they arrived at the market. That afternoon a rumour circulates that a frost has wiped out the orange crop. It will be months before local oranges are again available.

The next day, those who would really like one of those delicious oranges to eat, go to the market and post a notice on the community bulletin board that they will pay $1.50 for one of those oranges. They hope that this will entice someone, who bought the oranges at $1.00, to sell them an orange and earn a fifty-cent profit.

Some orange lovers got there ahead of them. They posted notices that they will pay $1.75 for an orange. If orange lovers do not beat the $1.75 price, they will not be getting an orange. Those who were willing to pay $1.50 now cross out the $1.50 and write in $2.00. They check all the other notices. No one is higher. They have set a new market price at $2.00.

Some of those who bought oranges yesterday were not lovers of juicy, sweet oranges. They were just interested in making money. These speculators knew this farmer had a reputation for growing delicious oranges. They purchased oranges with the anticipation that people the next day would pay far more than $1.00 for the oranges. They gambled that they could make a profit reselling their oranges. The next day, those speculators were checking the market's bulletin board to see if anyone had posted a notice saying they wanted to buy oranges and what price they would pay for them.

It pleased the speculators when they saw the notices on the bulletin board confirming a demand for the oranges greater than the $1.00, they paid. Some speculators think the price would go even higher than $2.00, so they hold on to their oranges. Other speculators are happy to sell their oranges at $2.00. They know that while oranges are perishable, importers could fly oranges in from other countries to meet the demand for less than $2.00.

People are finicky. Tomorrow, they may prefer to buy bananas instead of oranges especially if they think the sellers priced their oranges too high.

This analogy is my attempt to describe what goes on in a stock market. A Stock Exchange is a convenient communication vehicle that allows buyers and sellers of shares to trade with each other. No one wants to sell shares for less than what they paid for them. However, sometimes they sell, not to make a profit but to avoid a loss. They may see signs that there may be a future decline in the share price. Every buyer thinks the sellers are wrong about the future price declining. Only time and fate will determine who is right about tomorrow's price.

To complete a share sale the buyer's bid price must meet the seller's asking price. A stock exchange brings together millions of buyers bidding for the shares of a few thousand companies. Buyers and sellers can instantly see stock price increases and decreases on the stock exchange's electronic bulletin board. A stock with little potential will receive few bids from buyers. To encourage buyers, the sellers will keep dropping the price until a buyer sees the price as a bargain.

Stock exchange prices are beyond the control of the companies listed on the stock exchange. They are also beyond the control of those selling and buying shares. It is the invisible hand of the marketplace that is setting prices. Millions of individuals are making independent decisions to buy and sell. Keeping a stock exchange independent and beyond manipulation is difficult. Laws exist to prevent interference in the marketplace, as much as it is possible.

The major shareholders, who sit on a public company's board of directors, control the future of that company. These directors approve the hiring of the Chief Executive, who in turn hires other executives to operate the company. They are tasked by the directors with doing everything they can to increase the company's share price. An increase in the company's share price increases the wealth of all shareholders.

The Chief Executive officer of a public company wants to suppress all adverse information about the company because it may cause a drop in the company's share price. Employees are restricted from speaking to the media. They are also isolated from the board of directors. The fear is that they might inadvertently, or intentionally, reveal information that could threaten the CEO's job.

To the best of his ability the CEO controls any information that could negatively impact his relationship with the directors. Those directors have the power to fire a CEO if the share price drops to what they see as an intolerable level. Being an executive in a large public corporation is like being forced to cross a minefield, fearing that the next step will trigger an explosion.

To make sure the executives of the company are working in the best interest of the major shareholders, the board of directors grant the senior employees "stock options". This is an annual bonus system which can put tens or hundreds of thousands of dollars into the pockets of those who are running the corporation, but ONLY if the stock price increases.

Stock options motivate the company's executives to keep share prices up. They can do this by manipulating the company's expenses and revenues e.g. not paying "living wages" to employees; taking money from profits to buy shares in the company to inflate the share price; asking suppliers to hold large invoices until the next fiscal year to make the current year's profits look better; booking sales into the current year to inflate sales and profits but not delivering or incurring the expense of these sales until the next fiscal year; selling off property to increase the company's revenue and then leasing it back at an exorbitant rate, etc.

The Chief Financial Officer in a major public corporation is paid a large salary to make the corporation look wonderful. The corporation's annual financial statements that they prepare are expected to be impressive documents meant to bedazzle investment analysts, bankers, their directors, their existing and potential stockholders.

The law requires the company to send shareholders these annual financial statements and to invite you, as a shareholder, to "your company's" annual meeting. The directors would prefer that no one attended these annual meetings and often only a handful of people out of thousands of shareholders attend the meetings.

While you may own a few thousand shares, the CEO and others at the annual meeting, may control hundreds of thousands, even millions of shares. Those who control the most shares control the company. The chief executive may ask you to give him your proxies (each share has one vote) and trust him to vote them for you, on any resolutions put forth at the annual meeting. Does he really vote these proxies in your best interest or his own?

You and thousands of others minority shareholders are just along for the ride. Public companies are not democratic organizations, even though they try to give the appearance that the minority shareholders have a voice. Go to a few annual meetings just to watch the performance by wealthy individuals, who often reluctantly appear in public. It is a stressful annual event for them. They can't totally control the meeting. There is always the potential, that a shareholder may ask an embarrassing question that they really do not want to answer.

While a public company's manipulation of financial data may not be illegal, it wanders into the area of the sin of omission. You will rarely see a major company's warts until the warts are so big that the company can no longer hide them. Then you could see the shares of a large public company, that was once selling at $100 per share, dropping to a few cents per share. This is a buying signal for some speculators, who will buy millions of these penny shares, in the hope that after the settlement of all obligations there may something left for them to feast on.

Fortunately, public companies do not become insolvent overnight. It can take years. There are signs, such as unprofitability and speculations by the financial press. Therefore, you must periodically score your shares and try to keep abreast of what is being reported on "your" companies by doing some Google searches.

Companies are in constant flux. In the next ten years there may be one or two stocks of the 20 stocks that you have so carefully chosen, that you would be wise to sell. They may shrink to a shadow of what they once were and finally disappear.

Investing isn't totally the Wild West. You are not totally on your own. There is a sheriff that supposedly keeps the public companies and the investment dealers in line. For the Toronto Stock Exchange, it is the Ontario Securities Commission (a provincial government department). They will step in when someone brings to their attention a blatant violation of one of their rules or when they notice a company has missed filing an important document with them. Their objective is to make the stock market a fair and even playing field. For example, every investor, at the same time, supposedly receives important information that could affect the price of a stock.

The OSC carries a big stick. They can issue a "cease trading order" which halts all trading on a stock. You can then neither buy nor sell shares in that company. This certainly gets the media and the public's attention. Often when it happens, it is just to announce the sale or purchase of a company or some other housekeeping issue. Trading of the stock often resumes the next day.

They also try to control those in the industry who get carried away with their greed and illegally help themselves to their client's funds. Unfortunately, their rules contain grey areas, and are open to interpretation. This is one reason you want to invest in simple, easy to judge stocks, that you can buy and sell without a third party's involvement. Stay as far away from the sharks as you can.

Since you are buying and selling stocks on your PC, through your internet connection, you have eliminated the possibility that someone, other than yourself, can touch your portfolio. Your investment dealer's computer system makes it easy for you to order the 20 stocks you have chosen. Their system has several double checks built into it, so it is almost impossible to order the wrong stock, in the wrong quantity, at the wrong price.

When you enter the bank's computer system to buy a stock, it presents you with dozens of options that you can ignore. The objective is to keep stock ordering and selling as simple as possible. All you need to know is how to buy a specific stock at the price you want to pay for it.

Once again, using the TD investment system, the first step is to sign into your TD self-directed account.

Up comes the screen title **"WEB BROKER-HOME PAGE"**.

Below the heading are four subheadings:

*HOME....ACCOUNTS....RESEARCH....***TRADING***....TR ADING PLATFORM*

Since you are buying stocks, you click on **TRADING** this brings up another screen with the following headings:

BUY/SELL*.... TRADE....MANAGEMENT....TRADING PLATFORMS*

Since we are buying a stock, we click on **BUY/SELL**. This brings up five choices:

STOCKS & ETFS..*OPTIONS..STRATEGIES..MUTUAL FUNDS..FIXED INCOME..NEW ISSUES*

As we are buying stocks we click on **"STOCKS & ETFS"**. This takes us to the main order screen headed as follows:

TD DIRECT INVESTING....(with your unique TD account number) ...**CAD CASH**

The first line, below the heading, displays **"SYMBOL OR NAME",** in the pane to the right, enter the **symbol of the stock** you are interested in buying. As you to enter your symbol (in capital letters) the computer system will anticipate and start displaying the symbol that they think you are entering. When you see the symbol you want, click on it and the stock symbol will immediately appear in the pane.

The next line is "**ACTION**" to the right of it, **"BUY...SELL"** appear.

Since you are buying, click on **"BUY".** If you were selling, click on SELL.

To the right of the BUY option, the label **"QUANTITY"** appears and beside it is a pane for entering the number of shares that you wish to buy. The minimum number of shares the computer system allows you to buy is 100. You must round off the shares you are buying to hundreds (it may be less in some systems).

To buy stocks you must first have **transferred money** from your chequing account to your self-directed trading account. This amount will appear in the top right corner as being available. Therefore, you cannot make an error of ordering more stocks than you have the cash to pay for. Their computer system will not allow it.

Below the ACTION line is the **PRICE** heading. The default option of "**MARKET**" appears beside it. If you click on "MARKET" the following options appear:

MARKET…**LIMIT**…*STOP MARKET*…*STOP*
LIMIT…*TRAILING STOP MARKET*…*TRAILING STOP*
LIMIT.

I never buy using the MARKET price. There is always a
chance that you will get the stock at a price lower than the
then current market price. I always choose **LIMIT** so that I
can set the price. Usually I initially bid below the
MARKET price just to see what will happen. If I get the
stock at a lower price, I save a little money. If I do not get
it, then I gradually increase my bids until a seller accepts
the bid and I acquire the stock. There is nothing preventing
you from adjusting your bids as often as you wish. They
have made it easy to make such adjustments.

Since you are buying stocks that you intend to hold
"forever" the matter of a few cents saved can become
irrelevant. If you were a speculator, those few cents could
really matter because you might be risking every penny you
own or could borrow on that one stock. A speculator's
intention is to sell the stock as soon as they see their
expected capital gain. The important thing is to not get
caught up in the unreasonable fear, that if you do not buy
this stock now, the price will escalate, and you will never
again be able to buy it at this "low" price. Share prices
never move in a straight line. They go up and
down. Sometimes, it is a waiting game.

The next heading is **"GOOD'TIL"** and the default option
displayed is **"DAY"**. If you click on "DAY" it presents you
with the option of **"SPECIFY"**. If you click on SPECIFY a
calendar pops up. You can go to this calendar and click a

future date. Your bid will stay open until that date. You can leave your bid out there for weeks if you want to, as you wait for the share price to drop down to what you have bid.

NOTE: According to conventional wisdom, you have the best chance of buying a stock at its lowest price in the first and last hour of trading each day. Supposedly Monday mornings and Friday afternoons display the greatest fluctuations in price. Perhaps this is true, but it would only be a significant consideration for speculators.

The next line provides a space to enter your **PASSWORD** into a pane. As you enter your **PASSWORD** a new display appears on the right side of the screen, **"FUNDS AVAILABLE TO TRADE CASH $____**. It is showing the cash that was transferred from your chequing account to your trading account so you could buy shares. You now click on **PREVIEW ORDER**. A screen with a summary of what you have ordered appears.

This summary first displays the **SYMBOL** of the stock you are ordering, then the current price of the stock. Next it shows whether the stock price has gone up or down since its opening price that morning. If it is up, it shows the amount it has increased, with a green arrow pointing upwards. If it decreased, they will display it in red with an arrow pointing downwards.

Following this display, you will see **"BID/ASK"** and two amounts. The first is the amount a buyer is bidding for the stock and next to it is the amount a seller is asking for the stock. To immediately buy the stock, you enter the asking price. If the asking price has not changed in the last few seconds, you should get it.

The next display is **"LOTS"**. This is telling you how many shares are being offered to buyers in blocks of 100. If you saw 47 under the BID, this would mean that buyer or buyers want 4,700 shares at the price being bid.

The line below this, the heading **"OPEN"** informs you of the price that stock opened at that morning.

The heading **"VOLUME"** lets you know how actively traded the stock is that day. If you worked out a score for this stock, you know what the average number of shares being traded in a day are. An unusually large number might cause you to look for news on this stock, especially if the price for the stock has increased or decreased significantly.

This brings you to the final confirmation screen which has the heading of **"CONFIRM ORDER"**.

The stock symbol appears with a small Canadian flag to show the transaction is in Canadian funds on the Toronto Stock Exchange.

The next line will appear as:

ACTION ....QUANTITY....PRICE ......GOOD'TIL

BUY   YOUR #   YOUR$ YOUR EXPIRY DATE

This is followed by what this trade is costing you

EST. TOTAL $\_\_\_\_\_CAD ($ *your total* **PRINCIPAL +
$9.99 COMMISSION)**

At the bottom of the page you are presented with two
options

CHANGE ORDER ………..SEND ORDER

If you made a mistake entering the order, click on
CHANGE ORDER. If the order meets with your approval,
click on **SEND ORDER.** This then takes you to a new
screen confirming for a second time that this is the order
you want to place.

This screen displays **"THANK YOU"** followed by:

**TD DIRECT INVESTING (YOUR ACCOUNT #) CAD
CASH (A UNIQUE REFERENCE#)**

YOUR ORDER WAS RECEIVED

**STOCK SYMBOL …(CANADIAN FLAG) GOOD'TIL
(DATE)**

ACTION ……QUANTITY……PRICE

LIMIT

LIMIT PRICE

NEW ORDER

Click on the **"GO TO ORDER STATUS"** button at the bottom to go to the final screen.

The final screen in this ordering process is **"ORDER STATUS"**. Followed by the date and time.

A linear display once again summarizes the order under the following headings:

ACCOUNT..ACTION..SYMBOL..QUOTE..PRICE..GOOD'TIL..ORDER DATE..STATUS

If the **STATUS** says **OPEN,** a seller has not yet accepted your bid. If it shows **FILLED,** congratulations, you are now a true capitalist. Your purchase of the shares is complete.

Periodically during the day, you can check on the status of an unfilled order by signing into your portfolio. Click on **ACCOUNTS,** choose the trading account the shares are going to, then click on **BALANCE,** this shows how much cash is in this account and the total value of all shares held in it, then click on **TRADING,** this brings up a menu and in that menu you click on **ORDER STATUS**, which shows the number shares purchased. Sometimes your order for shares may take hours or a few days to get all the shares at the price you want. You can always adjust the price in your order or extend the date to keep your order open.
Shares bought in dribs and drabs should not change the small flat fee the financial institution is charging for fulfilling your order.

A few days after completing your purchase of a stock, you will receive via postal mail a printed confirmation of the transaction. If you go to the **ACTIVITY** screen in your trading account, you will also see that money has been taken to pay for the shares. In the **ACCOUNTS** screen you will now see the shares have been added to your portfolio. It takes two days to complete all the paperwork involved in making a trade.

Note: If you place an order during the weekend, it will obviously not go through because the stock market is closed. They will categorize the order as **OPEN**. If you have second thoughts about the order you can always cancel it before the stock market opens on Monday morning and revise it.

If you want to Invest no more than 5% of your wealth in one stock, you can divide the proposed share price into that 5% of your wealth, to arrive at the number of shares you require (e.g. you are investing a total of $1,000,000 into 20 stocks which each represent 5% of your wealth. You wish to invest approximately $50,000 in each of these 20 stocks. A stock is available for $10. You divide $10 into $50,000 which allows you to buy 5,000 shares). You must round the number off to the nearest 100 shares.

If you put in a bid higher than the current price, the stock is trading at, the stock exchange will tell you before processing your order. If during the day the share price should drop below the share price you bid, you will automatically get the remaining shares at the lower price.

Having bought the shares just sit back and watch the share price increase and collect your dividends. Don't look for sudden, dramatic increases because stable, profitable stocks do not have large daily fluctuations. Check individual stocks monthly, not daily or weekly. The following chapter is about monitoring your portfolio.

CHAPTER 10

Monitoring Your Stocks

Your self-directed investment service provider offers a wealth of free tools for tracking the historical value of your portfolio and individual stocks. So much information is available that you can get lost in it. Investment advisers are certainly not stressing themselves daily, over the individual stocks in a client's portfolio. Nor do investment advisers have checklists tracking every dividend payment made to each of their clients.

Before Ms. Innocence took back control of her portfolio, she was not aware of dividend payments being made to her account. After Ms. Innocence had learned enough to pick 20 good dividend-paying stocks for her portfolio, she contacted me in an agitated state. It upset her that the bank's computer program was not projecting as much of an annual dividend income as she expected.

She had found an income projection program in her bank's website which projected her total dividend income for the year. While I had never noticed that such a program existed, I thought it could be an interesting reference tool. Ms. Innocence's concern was she was not going to realize the generous 6% dividend income that I had predicted she would receive.

I responded that for me to determine why she was not getting the 6% income; I needed to see the actual dollar amounts of the dividends being deposited into her account for each stock and the deposit dates. With that information I could see which stock was or was not paying the expected dividends. I also needed to know the purchase dates of her shares.

I finished my note by telling her that the stock's dividend percentage that she was using to calculate her expected income could be misleading. The dividend percentage of a stock changes daily because it is the expected total of dividends paid out in a year calculated as a percentage of a stock's daily fluctuating price. I suggested in calculating a more accurate estimate of her projected income she should add up all the expected dividend payouts for the year and calculate what percentage it was of the total value of all stocks in her portfolio. It should work out to 6%. When Ms. Innocence took 6% of her portfolio's total value, she found the bank's income project program was low because her portfolio did not yet include 15% of the money that she had yet to invest in dividend-paying stocks.

With millions of customers depending on the accuracy of their computer systems, banks are unlikely to make mistakes. Carefully check your calculations before assuming an error has been made.

Monitoring a portfolio's results can cause undo stress. One of my speculator friends is always very concerned that his portfolio growth is "doing better" than the stock market averages. When he "beats the market" averages, he sees it as a sign of his superior investing skill.

Speculative investors, worrying about being able to pick stocks that will show unusual increases in share price do not fit into the objectives of value investors. If you buy 20 stocks to hold for decades, through fluctuating markets, the daily movement of various stock market indices are mostly irrelevant. I hope that Ms. Innocence's insecurity whenever the Toronto Stock Exchange's daily index declines, will fade with time. All she needs to be concerned about is how her total portfolio is doing.

After investing for years, and not being concerned about fluctuating stock market indices, I see that my portfolio is 90.23% ahead of where it was December 31, 2010. Has this increase in wealth changed my life? It hasn't. If I were to convert all my shares to cash, it would mean that the ever-increasing dividend income I receive each year would disappear. Liquidating my portfolio would be killing the goose that lays a golden egg every month. Therefore, when you look at your portfolio's statistics, keep the long-term picture in mind and become deaf to the media's constant warnings of an imminent financial apocalypse.

Each morning, I go to my stock portfolio in my investment dealer's website and record two numbers in a book that I have kept for 15 years. In it I keep track of the previous day's total portfolio value and the total amount of cash in the account. Before I retired 15 years ago, I used to invest the dividend income, now the monthly dividend income that shows up in this account gets transferred to my chequing account to pay my living expenses.

 I can estimate how much cash will appear each morning, depending on which day of the month it is. Dividends are mostly paid at the middle and at the end of the month. If I see unexpected cash appearing at other times of the month, I will check the **"ACTIVITY"** screen to see why cash has arrived.

Since the total amount in the portfolio changes very little in a day, it rarely causes me to look more closely. By listening to the business news on the radio and watching the stock ticker on television for a few minutes each day, I am rarely surprised by changes in my portfolio., However, sometimes there can be a significant anomaly that bears investigation. When that happens, you need a permanent historical snapshot of what your portfolio looked like to refer to.

Every three to six months, I could review an Excel spreadsheet that I created. It lists each stock in my portfolio. For each stock I should update the following information horizontally in the following sequence. However, my concern is primarily those stocks who are not performing up to my expectations. Usually I only update their information.

It seems unnecessary to update those that I have had large increases in their share price and whose dividends are being paid consistently year-after-year. Such stocks represent most of my portfolio. Until you gain such experience with your stocks, you may feel more comfortable updating them all.

(1) The Date I entered the Data

(2) What the stock's score was that day

(3) The price of the stock that day

(4) The book value of the stock that day

(5) The dividend yield % for the stock that day

(6) The stock's operating margin %

(7) The stock's trading symbol

(8) The full name of the stock

(9) The Price of the stock 4 years ago

(10) The Price to Earnings ratio

(11) The number of analysts recommending stock a buy

(12) The number of analysts recommending strong buy

(13) The volume of shares trading that day

(14) Notes

I constructed this spread sheet using Microsoft's Excel software. It allows me to use colours, different font sizes and bold text to make negatives and positives stand out. When adding new information, I can insert a new line below the earlier line. It is then easy to spot trends and significant changes in a stock. The Excel format also allows for the entering of unlimited notes on the same line to explain any unusual observations.

This spread sheet is the extent of the in-depth portfolio monitoring I do. I might also check the various information screens provided by the bank if I spot a problem with one of my stocks. To do this, using the TD investment system as our system model, I would sign in to:

td.com/ca/en/investing/direct investing

This takes me to the screen where I LOGIN to WEBBROKER. Up comes the WEBBROKER LOGIN screen where I enter my "USERNAME OR CONNECT ID" and my "PASSWORD

The next screen brings up the following options:

TD
*HOME...**ACCOUNTS**...RESEARCH...TRADING...GOAL S*

This time I click on **ACCOUNTS.** I am immediately presented with 7 sub-headings:

(1) **BALANCES** *(2)* **HOLDINGS** *(3) ACTIVITY (4) PERFORMANCE (5) GAIN + LOSS (6) PROJECTED INCOME (7) DOCUMENT E-SERVICES*

Clicking on the first option, **BALANCES,** they present you with the **"TOTAL BALANCE $_____"** of your portfolio and beside it the **"RATE OF RETURN ___%"**

Beneath this it states **"TD DIRECT INVESTIN – ACCOUNT #_____"**

The next heading is **SUMMARY,** followed by the following headings and beneath are the headings:

 ACCOUNT...*CASH...INVESTMENTS...TOTAL ...MARG IN.*

Your account number would appear under **ACCOUNT** along with the amount of cash available in the account. Under investments would appear the current value of all your stocks. The two figures are added together, and this amount appears under **TOTAL.**

 Since you are not borrowing money from TD to buy stocks, you ignore the **MARGIN** heading.

The next area to explore is **"HOLDINGS.** When you click on that heading, it opens a screen headed "**ACCOUNT DETAILS"**. It displays your account number, cash available, the current value of all your stocks plus the book cost of all your investments. By **"book"** they mean the price you originally paid when you bought the stocks. What makes this page so important is that it lists all the stocks you own and how the share price fluctuated since you bought them.

This display begins with the **stock's symbol**, followed by the **company name**. Beside this are two boxes. One says "**BUY"** and the other says **"SELL"**. If you wanted to buy more shares of this stock, you would click **BUY** and the stock ordering screen appears and if you clicked **SELL,** the screen to make the sale appears.

 If BUY and SELL do not appear on your screen, then you do not have a self-directed account. An investment adviser has taken control of your account and has blocked you from either buying or selling.

For each stock in the list you can see the following in a horizontal display:

How many shares you own (under **QUANTITY**),

The current **price** of the stock (under **PRICE**),

The average price you paid for the stock (under **AVG COST**).

The total dollar value of this company's shares you own are under **"MKT VALUE"**.

The **"BOOK COST"** is the official calculation of what you paid for these shares. You may have bought the shares in this company at different times and paid different prices.

The **"GAIN LOSS"** heading showing how much money you have gained or lost owning these shares. It also shows the percentage of gain or loss. If it is a gain, it displays the information in green. If it is a loss, the display is red.

Finally, the **percentage of your total portfolio** this stock represents is displayed. If the objective was to own 20 stocks of approximately the same dollar value, then **"% OF**

PORTFOLIO" should be near 5%. Since some share prices increase more rapidly than others, after a few months, you will see that some stocks now represent over 5% of your portfolio while other stocks who have not grown will now be less than 5% of your total portfolio.

When the occasional stock in your portfolio shrinks down below the price you paid for it, you need to determine if this is a temporary fluctuation. Does the stock still have a good score, good operating margin, paying a good dividend or is it something more serious which might require you to consider selling the stock.

 Sometimes when a good stock drops below the price you paid for it, you are being presented with an opportunity to buy more at a bargain price. A declining stock price is not necessarily a negative. Put faith in your calculations that showed this was a good stock.

The next subheading under **"ACCOUNTS"** is ACTIVITY. Click on **"ACTIVITY".** This takes you to the accounting screen. **Every dollar, going in and out of your portfolio, is being recorded on this screen.** When I spend those two or three minutes each day checking on total value of my portfolio and its cash, the **ACTIVITY** page is the first page I go to, if I see an unexpected amount showing up in the **CASH** for the portfolio,

The heading for the page is **"ACCOUNT DETAILS AS OF** (DATE AND TIME). As on the other screens, it identifies your account number, how much cash is in your portfolio and the total value of your stocks in Canadian dollars. Then, line-by-line, you will see in chronological order a record of all transactions that have taken place in your portfolio under the following headings:

**"TRADE DATE..SETTLE DATE
.DESCRIPTION..ACTION..QUANTITY..PRICE..COM
MISSION..NET AMOUNT**

The **TRADE DATE** would be the date the purchase or sale took place.

The **SETTLE DATE** would usually be the same day as the **TRADE DATE,** but sometimes certain investments may take several days to appear in your portfolio.

The **DESCRIPTION** might describe a transfer of funds to another account, a purchase or sale of stock, a dividend payment, an interest payment, etc.

Under **ACTION,** each transaction has a code, such as **WBW** for a cash transfer between a bank account and a trading account; **DIV** would be a dividend payment, **TXPDV is** a tax paid dividend in a REIT, **INT** is interest being paid. This information is important to your accountant because they tax these items at different rates.

PERFORMANCE

Clicking on the **PERFORMANCE** subheading brings up a screen that shows you how your investment strategy is working.

You can see whether the total value of your portfolio was ahead of the totals for last month, last quarter, last year, 3 years ago, 5 years ago and even since the day you first opened your self-directed trading account.

AFTER ACHIEVING YOUR INCOME OBJECTIVE

Your objective was to invest enough money in your trading account so that its passive income would give you the option to never need to work again. After achieving that objective, you may now wish to invest the surplus cash in a RRSP – Registered Retirement Saving Plan. There, it would be in reserve.

The government deducts the surplus money you put in the RRSP from your income for that year. This will lower your annual income tax and generate even more surplus income for you. While Revenue Canada gives you a bit of a break, there are restrictions on how much they allow you to put in your RRSP each year. If you live into your late nineties, you will end up having paid income tax on the all the money you put in your RRSP.

After you turn 71, you can no longer put money into an RRSP. Now they require you to withdraw money from the RRSP. The withdrawal starts at 5% and each subsequent year, the percentage you are required to withdraw increases slightly.

You may have more disposable cash at 71 then you have had in your life. All your major life expenses will most likely be behind you e.g. mortgage, education expenses, raising children, etc.

By the time I turned 71, I had enough cash being generated in the RRSP that I could easily take out the required 5% from the dividend cash that my RRSP portfolio was generating. This meant I did not have to liquidate any of the dividend producing stocks inside the RRSP portfolio. The RRSP continues to grow and generate even more dividend income to pay for the next annual withdrawal.

After paying the income tax on the 5% extraction I now had surplus cash to reinvest. I could not contribute to the RRSP portfolio and if I put it into my trading account, it would generate taxable income. The solution was to open a TFSA -Tax Free Saving Account. Like an RRSP there are limits as to how much you can put in a TFSA. It was around $6,000 a year with the ability to do a catch up for any years that you had missed making contributions.

While, the TFSA contribution restrictions were greater than on an RRSP every tax saving helps. The bank you invest with will be more than happy to open a TFSA account for you. They will also tell you how much you can to put into it.

You can invest the TFSA money the same way as you now invest in your trading account. Even with rigid restrictions on how much money you could put into a TFSA, apparently, a few investors (speculators, no doubt) have grown their TFSA to more than a million dollars.

The joy of a TFSA is that the money you make in it or take out of it is tax free. The only thing you must remember is that if you take out money this year, be sure to check with your bank to determine when you can put money back into it and how much you can put in. It can be tricky, and you do not want to incur a penalty.

Ms. Innocence chastised me for not having given her any guideline as to when to sell a stock? When do you sell a stock? The simple answer is you sell a stock when it no longer produces a high enough dividend income to meet your expectations.

Ms. Innocence was asking this question because she had purchased a stock that had cut its dividend from 9.19% to 6%. This caused some investors to sell the stock which lowered the share price. The value of her shares in that stock were now down a few thousand dollars from the original purchase price. She was ready to join some of the others and sell this stock.

The stock was an investment company that financed "start-ups". It takes as security, a percentage of the ownership in these companies. I pointed out to Ms. innocence that the company had not cut the dividend to zero. The 6% they were now paying was still a good dividend percentage compared to most stocks. She still owned the same number of shares. Stocks fall in and out of favour. I told her to do a Google search and see if she could determine why it fell out of favour and to also analyze the stock in the same way she did when she first chose it.

She did this analysis and found: The share price and the book value of the share were now about the same. This indicated the share price was attractive and likely to increase. The current price to earnings ratio of 10.9x indicated the share price would likely increase as it appeared undervalued. The operating margin of 62.29% was very strong, almost double what a large bank's operating margin would be. This was also a sign the share price would increase. Four analysts were still recommending it as a BUY which would encourage investors to buy it and cause the share price to increase. The 20,939 shares traded that day, indicated it was active and trading at an acceptable level.

 No stock is perfect. Stocks go up and stocks go down. Just because, the share price drops this month does not mean that within months the shares could not be worth much more than what you originally paid for them. Patience and analysis win out in the long run if you own a good stock. Further investigation reported that the stock had had a temporary problem with a company in which they invested. The problem was now being corrected.

If you are looking for black and white rules in investing, there are no black and white rules. There is only common sense and logic. You need to analyze each situation before acting.

When you first invest, you have not gone through periods where you see your stocks plunge down and then roar ahead and perhaps plunge again. The reason you invest in 20 stocks is that while some are going down others are going up. You will most likely never see all 20 going in the same direction at the same time. That is why the total health of your portfolio is better judged by the gain or loss of the total portfolio, rather than by individual stocks in it.

On average share prices gain about 6% a year. A year from now I would expect Ms. Innocence to be showing a significant gain in her total portfolio. This share price cushion means that she will no longer obsess over the fluctuations of a few thousand dollars in one stock in her portfolio. (She has already seen a significant gain in her portfolio). Until she reaches that level of experience, at the first negative sign, she will be convinced that all her money will disappear, and it will leave her in poverty unless she does "something". The only "something" she feels is open to her is to sell the stock and cut her losses. This would be a mistake.

First, losing all her money will not happen. She carefully chose 20 good dividend stocks. It takes time to gain faith in your analytical ability.

Constantly re-investing in new stocks creates the problem of it becoming harder and harder for you to find good stocks. There is not an infinite supply of good stocks. You do not want to dilute your portfolio that you so carefully chose, nor do you want to increase you monitoring workload by exceeding 20 stocks.

CHAPTER 11

On Being Frugal

One definition of "frugal" is *"simple, plain and costing little"*. The hard part with being frugal is that you must first accept that you can't "have your cake and eat it too." If you are going broke trying to "look rich", then you need to accept the reality that your whole attitude towards money must change.

Your objective is to obtain financial independence. You want a passive income from your investments that allows you to live well with no need for employment. This requires you to sacrifice now for future rewards. You need to accumulate enough cash to invest in dividend-paying stocks which have the potential for capital gains.

For many, it first requires paying off all debts with intolerably high interest rates. If married, this includes your spouse's debts and your own. For a shared goal of financial independence, you both need to buy into frugality **now**, not next week, next month or next year. Since married couples are usually responsible for one another's debts, financial compatibility is important. You are going to be making large financial decisions together and most likely be sharing a bank account.

A survey, conducted by SlickDeals.net of 2,000 people, found that 90 percent of the respondents viewed frugality as an appealing trait to have in a prospective spouse. That same survey also found that 53 percent of the respondents would avoid a relationship with someone who was debt burdened. 60 percent had been in relationships with partners who were reckless with money. They now avoided relationships with the financially irresponsible.

Although it does not sound very romantic, a dating service called CreditScoreDating.com exists. They provide credit scores on those using their service. Another website, Marriage.com, states that while infidelity is the number one reason for divorce, the number two reason is money.

It has been my experience, from designing credit risk scoring systems based on millions of records, that 80% of any population behaves responsibly in managing their affairs. It is that remaining 20% that cause varying degrees of grief. A quarter of this 20% are very toxic.

 Someone who regularly reaches the limit on their credit card is broadcasting their financial irresponsibility. Often, when they cannot charge more on their credit card, they attempt to seek an additional card from another financial institution. I say "attempt", because each month financial institutions transmit their customers' credit card experiences to credit reporting agencies. This creates a risk pool that warns them of potential problem accounts.

These institutions also frequently match credit scores against all their customers. While they like "good" customers, who carry high credit card balances (the interest these card holders are paying is very profitable), they don't like are bad debt losses.

Maxed out on your credit card? Eliminating that debt takes priority over any investing objectives. The stock market is not a casino or a lottery. Do not expect the stock market to reward you with a lump sum to pay off your credit card debt. There is no point in investing money to earn a 6% dividend, when you are paying 20% interest per year on a credit card debt that is compounding monthly.

The convenience of credit cards blinds many borrowers to considering the use of less expensive borrowing options, like a line of credit or a bank loan. These two options charge a quarter of the interest you would be paying in credit card interest.

A credit card is a convenient buying tool. A frugal investor pays off the credit card balance every month, before the card's due date, to avoid paying interest charges. This requires organization and discipline. It also requires accepting the difference between "needs" and "wants". You want your money invested and earning income, not paying outrageous bank interest.

Until you are free of high interest obligations, you must question every dollar spent. The people, I know, who have worked hard to accumulate millions of dollars in assets, don't drive overly expensive show cars, wear expensive designer clothes, live in 10,000 square foot mansions nor live an overly extravagant lifestyle. Before they spend a dollar, they think about the realizable cost benefit of that dollar. These are not impulsive people. They have a goal and they have a plan.

In the legendary1996 book, **"The Millionaire Next Door"** *(Authors: Professors Thomas J. Stanley, Ph.D. and William D. Dank, Ph.D./ Publisher: Longstreet Press Inc., Marietta, Georgia, USA,)* the authors best describe how 50 years ago they began studying the wealthy. They started their research in what they thought was the most logical place, the well-to-do areas across the USA. They soon discovered that people in the impressive upscale homes who drove expensive cars rarely had wealth. Many of those with true wealth did not live in upscale areas. The book is well worth reading. It gives interesting insights into the behaviour and problems of the wealthy.

About 20% of the population work hard at making you believe they are wealthy. They flaunt their expensive clothes, their status cars and their impressive addresses. When I was president of a small collection agency it opened my eyes to the illusion of wealth. We collected the long past due accounts for the most expensive clothing store in the city. Their customers were professional people, well educated, doctors, dentists, lawyers, engineers and executives. While they had high incomes, they were spending more than they earned and were drowning in debt.

 The cost of creating this illusion of wealth removes any chance of them ever achieving real wealth. They will never achieve the financial independence that would allow them to stop working and still maintain their lifestyle. Perhaps you can not blame them. Our society gears us to keeping us working for the rest of our lives. No one directs students towards achieving financial independence as quickly as possible.

Not all debt is bad. People can use credit wisely to increase their wealth. Taking a 2.9% mortgage on an investment property, versus liquidating stocks that are paying a 7% dividend to buy the property, makes sense. This is especially true when property prices are growing annually at 4% or more. It is amazing how easy it is to obtain a mortgage at the best rate from a bank, when your stock portfolio is many times greater than the amount you wish to borrow.

What expenses would I cut if I were one of those high-income, low wealth individuals maxed out on my credit cards.

1. **Automobile expense** - Each vehicle you own could be costing you $8,000 or more a year (insurance, fuel, parking, repairs, car payments, licensing and maintenance). The interest on car loans is now averaging about 5% per annum.

   Can you cut back to one car? Using Uber, walking and public transportation could save you thousands of dollars. If you do need a second car, look for a low mileage, small, well maintained, second-hand, fuel-efficient vehicle. Pay a mechanic to check this used car to make sure you are not purchasing one that will soon require expensive repairs.

A new car loses between 20% and 30% of its purchase price as soon as you drive it it off the dealer's lot. Let someone else take the depreciation loss. With the money you have saved in buying a used car, you will be able to keep the car in good repair.

To get the ultimate return on your investment in a car, plan on keeping it until it accumulates 200,000 kilometres.

Pamper your car. Avoid unnecessary use of it. Plan your trips, do all your errands at once.

2. **Accommodation expense** - If you are spending over 40% of your income on accommodation, then you might be classified as "house poor". If you are in such a situation, consider selling your existing home and buying a more affordable residence. Apply the equity you might gain in the sale of your unaffordable house to paying off debts and building your investment portfolio. The sooner you become debt free, and have a portfolio that is generating investment income, the quicker you will achieve the goal of financial independence. With a smaller house, your monthly expenses will shrink e.g. lower taxes, heating, cooling, maintenance, services and insurance costs. To minimize commuting cost, live close to

your work or close to a major public transportation corridor.

If you are no longer working or have a job that allows you to work remotely, consider relocating. Living in a large city is expensive. The average price of a small home can easily exceed $600,000. To rent a modest apartment can exceed $2,000 per month. Moving to a small town may be a viable option.

There are many towns where you can buy a nice home for less than $100,000. An extreme example would be Elliot Lake, a town of 11,000 people, in Northern Ontario, where you can buy a well-maintained condominium apartment for less than $50,000. While, moving to a distant town, away from family and friends, can be unappealing, living with a mountain of debt is both stressful and unhealthy. The cost of maintaining social contact with distant family and friends through electronic media has become very affordable.

3. **Electronic communication expense** - Cable television, satellite television, telephone and internet access can cost thousands of dollars annually. If you must have cable or satellite television, negotiate with your suppliers. Play one supplier against the other. Never accept the first price they offer for their services. Tell them their competitors are offering almost the identical service for a third less. This is often enough for them to find a way around your price objection.

Electronic communications are one of the few expenses that seem to get better and costs less each year. Check with your current supplier every six months to see if a better deal is available. Technology is transforming and reducing costs. Do not assume the price you are now paying is one with which you should be satisfied.

Every year many suppliers will sneak in a small price increase. They know that a certain percentage of customers will neither notice nor challenge the increase. Do not expect to be notified of any price decreases that are available. You must ask for them.

If you have internet service, it is debatable whether you still require a cable television service. Online streaming services, like Netflix and Amazon Prime, are good entertainment alternatives. Hundreds of internet news services can keep you fully informed and will even customize the news to your specific interests.

Online telephone services can reduce telephone costs. Consider buying a phone service like MagicJack. I purchased this service for my business line, and they gave me 5 years of service for a flat fee of $165. Not only can I phone anyone in North America without an additional charge, but I can communicate with anyone in the world who also has the MagicJack service, without a charge. When I travel abroad, the phone service travels with me. It is immediately activated as soon as I plug it into any internet modem or my laptop. This gives me free North American phone service.

4. **Books -** Buying printed books, newspapers and magazines can be expensive. Buy electronic publications that can be read on tablets, e-readers and computers. A mountain of e-books is available for free or for less than five dollars (e.g. *"100 Great Novels You Should Read Before You Die"* - for 99 cents). Many public libraries now provide free access to e-books (however their restrictions on accessing their e-books may make them a less attractive reading source than KOBO or Kindle. For a few dollars, you can often buy the book you want from these e-book distributors).

There are not enough hours available in a day to access all the free news services. Not only can you eliminate cable television service but printed newspapers and magazines as well.

5. **Tobacco, Coffee and Alcohol -** Tobacco, coffee and alcohol consumption can be a pleasurable social, habit. However, they are not a necessity. If you can eliminate or reduce their consumption, you may not only be saving thousands of dollars annually but banishing habits that are not contributing to good health. Dropping a lifetime habit is never easily done.

6. **Vacations -** If you must go deeply into debt to go on a vacation, then you should question whether you can

afford such a vacation. Everyone needs a break from their normal routine. Can you plan a vacation that will minimize your debt, not increase it? Trading houses with someone in another country for a few weeks is a possibility. Travelling by car to explore a city you have never previously explored, can save the thousands of dollars in flight expenses and be an interesting escape from your routine.

On achieving financial independence, your whole life can become one extended vacation. You will then have the freedom to travel to a foreign country for several months instead of for only a week or two. I found the travel costs for several months of vacation can be equivalent to what I used to spend on a two-week vacation. Thanks to the internet, you can manage your money from almost anywhere in the world. Many friends, with whom you now primarily communicate by telephone or e-mail, will not realize that you are away.

7. **Non-Residency** - If you live abroad for over six months, as a non-Canadian resident you can avoid paying income tax. However, it creates some complications such as losing your free provincial medical coverage. You would have to prove to Revenue Canada that you really have severed your Canadian residency. This would require closing bank accounts and all other registered connections.

For several hundred thousand dollars, citizenship in several countries without income tax law can be purchased.

Abandoning your citizenship is probably one of the most difficult life decisions anyone would ever have to make.

8. **Food -** Eating fabulous meals, paired with exquisite wines, in renowned restaurants is an expensive form of entertainment. The bragging rights may make you feel good for a few days. In a week it will be difficult to remember exactly what had been so good. Frequent gourmet dining will delay you reaching your objective of financial independence. Once financial independence is achieved, wine and dine to the extent of your dividend income.

9. **Gifts -** Until you get out of debt, try to avoid social situations where expensive gifts are expected. You can no longer afford to accept every invitation to weddings, showers or birthday parties. This may be the hardest sacrifice you will have to make to achieve your goal of financial independence. Celebrations in your social network are not only important but fun.

Charitable donations fall under gifts. Moderate your charitable donations now, so you can be financially secure in the future? Be generous when you can finally afford to be generous.

10. **Accounting** - Pay your bills electronically. This not only saves postage but creates a historical record of expenses that can be instantly referred to at tax time.

Companies do make billing mistakes. If you think that a monthly invoice is larger than normal, review the previous bills you have paid over the last 18 months. Are there any unexplained increases? If there are, ask the vendor for an explanation. Use this call as an opportunity to also ask how you could lower your monthly billing. They will often offer discounts if they feel a customer relationship is in jeopardy.

Thousands of companies distribute discount coupons. Some are instantly available online from services such as canadiancoupons.net.

11. Credit Cards - Never pay for the use of a credit card. Never incur a past due charge. The banks count on half of card holders not paying their card debt by the due date. They want to charge an interest of almost 2% per month on unpaid balances. In addition, the banks are also receiving up to 2.5% from the stores who accept your credit card. Despite this charge, retailers still love credit cards because they know that customers with credit cards do not pay as much attention to price as those who pay cash. They especially love those who see shopping as a form of entertainment.

Some retailers complain how unfair it is for banks to take a percentage of every sale charged to a credit card. They ignore the reality that if they established their own in-house credit card service, they would not only incur administrative costs, but on average, they would lose 5% of their sales to bad debt. This is what retailers traditionally lost before credit cards were introduced. Therefore, the 2.5% the retailer might pay a bank is a bargain.

Credit consultants will often recommend that those addicted to credit card spending should destroy their credit cards and revert to either cash or debit cards. While credit cards are a convenience and have almost become a necessity, it is important that you recognize that you are being manipulated to spend more money than you need. Good times or bad, the banks always make billions of profitable dollars from their "small" charges. This may sound like a hypocrisy, but bank stocks give any investment portfolio a good solid dividend base.

11. While managing your own investments you will continue to be solicited by investment advisers. The following statistics are what some investment advisers accept as gospel. I have added my *rebuttals, where applicable in brackets*. You can find these statistics and others interesting data at ***https://planwell.com/how-it-works***.

Expect investment advisers to do their best to dissuade you from self-directed investing.

"Conservative investors should expect a to receive an annual return of 3.91% on their investments". (*obtaining a 6% dividend return is easy*)

"A conservative growth return would be 4.34%". (*In addition to a 6% dividend return expect your portfolio to show a significant capital gain*)

"A moderate growth return would be 4.67%". (*In addition to a 6% dividend return expect a capital gain*)

"A maximum growth return would be 5.63%". (*In addition to a 6% dividend return expect your portfolio to have a capital gain*)

The annual (25-year historical average) inflation rate is 1.83%. In calculating how much money you need for retirement, the assumed life expectancy used is 90 years. If you retired at 60 and did live until 90 almost 60% of your savings would be eaten up by inflation (e.g. 90 minus 60 = 30 years X 1.83). This leaves you with much less to survive on than you may have counted on.

Some economists calculate that the average life expectancy for someone who retires at 65 is only 9.7 years. Who at 65 wants to bet their savings on being dead at 75? I sure don't. By investing in dividend stocks with good scores there is no reason that your portfolio should ever decline.

Investment advisers often throw out "the 4% rule". It states, to outlive your money, you should only withdraw from your savings 4% a year. If you retired at 60 and took out 4% a year for 30 years, that would represent 120% of your savings. You would have depleted your portfolio long before you reached 90, unless the income from the portfolio was sufficiently high to cover not only the 4% you were withdrawing every year, but also 2% for inflation and probably 2% for the fees the investment adviser was charging you. This adds up to 8%. If investment advisers thought you are doing well to get a 5.63% return from your portfolio, make sure you die long before you reach 90. Is there any wonder, retirees who use investment advisers, fear outliving their savings?

Not wanting to deplete your portfolio is something investment advisers do not seem to understand. Your purpose in life is not to provide an investment adviser with a steady income for decades as they nibble away at your portfolio. I am quite sure they do not want you to take out more than 4% a year from a portfolio it could jeopardize their future income.

"Your emergency cash fund should be equivalent to 3 months of your income". (If you invest your money in common stocks that you can convert to cash in a day for a $9.99 service charge, 3 months of cash not earning dividends seems excessive. Getting cash out of bonds and mutual funds can cost you thousands and take days.)

 "They assume the target retirement income from passive investments to be 70% to 80% of your current income (without government subsidies)". (You can probably live as well on half the income you once enjoyed. Much of your income was being lost to income tax. With age and a dividend income, comes lower income taxes. Your income keeps growing as your portfolio grows even after you retire.

Your objective is to reach a point in your life where your passive income exceeds your needs and you no longer face the problem of wondering how to pay your bills. Your biggest concern becomes trying to decide whether to invest your surplus cash or to spend it on now affordable, but questionable, luxuries. These may be luxuries that your frugal lifestyle had eliminated. I warn you that frugality is a hard habit to break. Once you accept that you are being seduced by retailers to spend, spend, spend; it takes much of the joy out of shopping.

After reading this chapter one of editors told me she thought a frugal lifestyle would take all the joy out of living. However, unless you are focused on your financial objective, an occasional exception can quickly become the norm and you will never establish a large enough financial cushion to protect yourself from unforeseen setbacks. Frugal living and investing do require discipline.

This raises the question of how much money is too much money to save? There are cynics who suggest that the financial service industry scares investors into saving-too-much, so that the adviser can receive an ongoing high commission income from your portfolio.

While this cynicism may be justified, I have not met any retirees who complain about having too much money invested. All the retirees I know have health issues of a minor or major nature. They are spending more and more on health and pain reduction products. A large, growing stock portfolio is "living-a-comfortable-life" insurance for them.

CHAPTER 12

Scoring Stocks

This chapter explains how the stock score is calculated. It is no deep, dark, incomprehensible secret. You can easily work out the score manually on any stock by just matching the characteristics of a stock to the items in each of the eleven categories. Record the score for each category. Add all 11 scores to determine the total desirability score for the stock.

The higher the total score the greater the chances that a dividend will be secured and the greater the chance the share price will increase. The lowest score I have encountered was 8 for an unprofitable penny stock and the highest was 78 for a major bank. Few of my stock purchases fall below 50 or above 70.

Instead of calculating a stock's score manually, those who have purchased this book can send an email to idm.score@informus.ca and ask for the free IDM SCORING PC computer program. It will be emailed back to you. It is simple to use. You enter the data from your investment service's "OVERVIEW" page and the program instantly does the score calculations.

(1) The Current Price of the Stock

1. $0 to 99 cents scores =1
2. $1 to $1.99 scores ...=2
3. $2 to $4.99 scores... =3
4. $5 to $9.99 scores... =4
5. $10 to $14.99 scores =5
6. $15 to $19.99 scores =6
7. $20 to $29.99 scores =7
8. $30 to $49.99 scores =8
9. $50 to $99.99 scores =9
10. over $100 scores......=10

(2) The Price of the Stock 4 Years Ago

1. $0 to 99 cents scores = 1
2. $1 to $1.99 scores... = 2
3. $2 to $4.99 scores... = 3

4. $5 to $9.99 scores …= 4
5. $10 to $14.99 scores = 5
6. $15 to $19.99 scores = 6
7. $20 to $29.99 scores = 7
8. $30 to $49.99 scores = 8
9. $50 to $99.99 *scores = 9*
10.   over $100 *scores ....= 10*

(3) % Difference Between Current Price of Stock and Four Years Ago
(The program automatically calculates this score)

1.   The Stock has been sold for less than 4 years
= 0
2.   The Current Price is less than the price 4 years ago, by more than 50.50% = 1
3.   The Current Price is less than the price 4 years ago, by 11.50% to 50.49% = 2
4.   The Current Price is less than the price 4 years
by .50% to 10.49%   = 5
5.   Current Price is within .51% to 1.49% of the price it was at 4 years ago   = 6
6.   Current Price is 1.50% to 10.49% more than the price 4 years ago   ... = 7
7.   Current Price is 10.50% to 99.4% more than the price 4 years ago   = 9
8..   Current Price is more than 99.50% greater than the price of 4 years ago   = 10

(4) The Book Value of Stock

1. $0 to 99 cents scores = 1

2.	$1 to $1.99 scores	= 2
3.	$1 to $4.99 scores	= 3
4.	$5 to $9.99 scores	= 4
5.	$10 to $14.99 scores	= 5
6.	$15 to $19.99 scores	= 6
7.	$20 to $29.99 scores	= 7
8.	$30 to $49.99 scores	= 8
9.	$50 to $99.99 scores	= 9
10.	over $100 scores	= 10

(5) % Difference Between Current Stock Price & Book Value of the Stock. *(The program automatically calculates this score)*

1.   Current Price is less than the Book Value by more than 49.49% = 10

2.   Current Price is less than the Book Value by 10.50% to 49.50% = 8

3.   Current Price is less than the Book Value by 0.50% to 10.49% = 6

4.   Current Price is between 0.51% and 1.49% of the Book Value   = 4 5.   Current Price is 1.50% to 9.49% greater than the Book Value   = 2

6.   Current Price is 9.50% to 49.49% greater than the Book Value   = 1

7.   Current Price is 49.50% greater than the Book Value = 0

(6) Number of Analysts Rating the Stock a "Buy".

1.   0 analyst   = 0

2. 1 analyst   = 2
3. 2 to 3 analysts   =3
4. 4 to 5 analysts   = 4
5. 5 or more analysts   =5

(7) Number of Analysts Rating the Stock a "Strong Buy."

1. 0 analysts   = 0
2. 1 analyst   = 3
3. 2 to 4 analysts   = 4
4. 5 or more analysts   =5

(8) The % of the Share Price that the Dividend Represents

1. No Dividend Paid   = 0
2. 0.001% to 1.49% Dividend = 1
3. 1.50% to 2.49% Dividend   = 4
4. 2.50% to 4.49% Dividend   = 6
5. 4.50% to 7.49% Dividend   = 8
6. 7.50% to 10.49% Dividend = 10
7. Over 10.50% Dividend   =2

(9) The Company's Operating Margin %.

1. A margin less than 1.49% = 0
2. 1.50% to 4.49%   = 1
3. 4.50% to 9.49%   = 2

4.	9.50% to 14.49%	= 3
5.	14.50% to 19.49%	= 4
6.	19.50% to 29.49%	= 5
7.	29.50% to 49.49%	=6
8.	49.50% to 69.49%	= 8
9.	69.50% to 79.49%	= 9
10.	Over 79.50%	*= 10*

(10) The Average Daily Volume of Shares Traded by this Stock

1.	Fewer than 10,000 shares	= 0
2.	10, 001 to 30,000 shares	= 1
3.	30,001 shares to 50,000 shares	= 2
4.	50,001 to 100,000 shares	= 3
5.	100,001 to 250,000 shares	= 4
6.	250,001 to 500,000 shares	= 5
7.	500,001 to 750,000 shares	= 6
8.	750,001 to 1,000,000 shares	=8
9.	1,000,001 shares to 2,000,000	= 9
10.	Over 2,000,001 shares	= 10

(11)   The Stock's Price to Earnings Ratio

1.	0 or a minus figure = 0
2.	01 to 5.49	= 10
3.	5.50 to 15.49	= 9
4.	15.50 to 20.49	= 8
5.	20.50 to 25.49	= 7

6.   25.50 to 30.49   = 6
7.   30.50 to 35.49   = 5
8.   35.50 to 40.49   = 4
9.   40.50 to 99.99   = 2
10.   100 or more   =1

CHAPTER 13

The 654 By Score

(Data Extracted May 6, 2019)

Following are all 654 stocks that paid a dividend of 3.5% or more on the Toronto Stock Exchange. (My intent is to reissue this book annually with updates of this data.)

 In this chapter, the 654 stocks are sorted in descending order by their **score**. (*In* **Chapters 7** *and* **12** *you will find details on how scores are calculated*.) The higher the score the more likely you will find a stock that pays a safe dividend and show an ever-increasing share price in the months and years to come.

In the three following chapters, you will find the same information as in Chapter 13 but it is sorted in three additional ways: (**Chapter 14**) **alphabetical** *by company name,* (**Chapter 15**) *in descending order by the annual* **dividend** *percentage paid and* (**Chapter 16**) *in descending order by the company's share* **price**. *The item being sorted is highlighted in each of these chapters.*

These four chapters can help you to quickly find the 20 stocks that you would want to add to your portfolio e.g. *you may want to find stocks for your portfolio that will cost you between $6 and $10, pay a dividend over 7% and have a score greater than 50.*

Before buying a stock based on the sorting of this data, recalculate the score. The scores can change daily with fluctuations in stock prices and volume of shares being traded. One, that scored 53, was down to 32 only a month later.

Of the 654 shares, 366 or 56.04% of the stocks were preferred shares. Almost all the preferred shares had low desirability scores (between 17 and 28). Unlike common shares, operating margins, book values or price to earnings are not available when scoring preferred shares which accounts for their low scores. Since most preferred shares show capital losses and their trading volumes rarely trade above a few hundred shares a day, analysts rarely if ever seem to recommend them. It is assumed the analysts see them as having no interest to speculators.

Of the 366 preferred shares, the scores for the five highest were SNI.PR.A with a score of 63, IGM.PR.B with a score of 57, TXT.PR.A with a score of 49, EML.PR.A with a score of 40 and EFN.PR.L with a score of 36.

The highest score of all 654 stocks was 76. Only 10 stocks achieved a score exceeding 70 and half of these were Canada's largest banks. Only one of these 10, the Canadian Imperial Bank of Commerce was paying a dividend exceeding 4.99%.

While many of the stocks scoring over 60 cost more than $30 per share, there were a few that cost under $10 including one at $2.01. It paid a dividend of 8%.

The lowest score was 7, for what appeared to be an inactive company that was selling for 20 cents a share. It was on this list because it paid an astounding dividend of 400%. There is obviously a story here. No shares appeared to be trading for this company.

The following list of stocks has been divided into those who score over 50 and those who score under 50. There are 99 stocks scoring over 50. These are the ones who are most likely to show capital gain (*have their share price increase*) and to provide reliable dividend payments year after year. Unfortunately, many of these high scoring stocks pay out dividends less than 6% of their share value. Therefore, if the objective is to average a dividend payout of 6% for your entire portfolio, then you may have to purchase some stocks that score below 50 who are paying dividends in excess of 7%. to offset those good solid stocks paying less than 6%.

Your aim is not only to average this 6% dividend return on your portfolio but to also diversify the industries that you are invested in. This includes avoiding volatile commodity shares and infrequently traded preferred shares. Out of the 654 shares, 366 were preferred shares and of these only 2 *(Sonor Investments and IGM Financial)*. were included in the 99 stocks scoring over 50.

Chapters 14, 15 and 16 will also help you in your research to find the best 20 stocks for your portfolio. They contain the same data, on the 654 shares, as this chapter, but the data is provided in different useful sorts.

THE TOP 99 STOCKS ON TORONTO STOCK EXCHANGE PAYING DIVIDENDS OVER 3.5%, IN DESCENDING ORDER BY SCORE

Columns

#1 = Score

#2 = Stock Symbol

#3 = Company Name

#4 = Stock Price

#5 = Dividend % paid

#1	#2	#3	#4	#5

#1	#2	#3	#4	#5
76	RY	ROYAL BANK OF CAN	107.00	3.80%
75	TRP	TRANSCANADA COPR	63.07	4.80%
74	BMO	BANK OF MONTREAL	106.00	3.80%
74	BNS	BANK OF NOVA SCOTIA	73.46	4.70%
74	TD	TORONTO-DOM. BANK	76.38	3.90%
73	CM	CANADIAN IMP. BANK	113.00	5.00%
72	MIC	GENWORTH MI	41.90	4.90%
71	SU	SUNCORP ENERGY	43.11	3.90%

70	CNQ	CAN. NATURAL RESOURC.	37.68	3.70%
70	FTS	FORTIS INC	49.63	3.60%
69	BCE	BCE INC	56.69	5.30%
69	GRT	GRANITE REIT	60.93	4.60%

68	DRG	DREAM GLOBAL REIT	13.84	5.80%
68	SLF	SUNLIFE FINANCIAL	55.41	3.60%
68	T	TELUS CORP	49.45	4,40%
67	MFC	MANULIFE FIN. CORP	24.64	4.00%
67	PPL	PEMBINA PIPELINE	47.53	5.10%
66	VET	VERMILLION ENERGY	32.03	9%
65	ARX	ARC RESOURCES	8.06	7.40%
65	EMA	EMERA INC	50.31	4.70%

65	FCR	FIRST CAPITAL REALTY	21.48	4.00%
65	INQ.UN	INOVALIS REIT	10.33	8%
64	MRG.UN	MORGUARD NA REIT	17.80.	3.80%
64	NA	NATIONAL BANK	63.70	4.10%
64	NXR.UN	NEXUS REIT	2.01	8%
64	NPI	NORTHLAND POWER	23.80	5%
64	REI.UN	RIOCAN REIT	25.90	5.60%
64	D.UN	DREAM OFFICE REIT	23.51	4.30%

63	LB	LAURENTIAN BANK	42.78	6.10%
63	SNI.PR.A	SONOR INVESTMENTS	8	9%
62	ACO.X	ATCO LTD	45.14	3.50%
62	CPX	CAPITAL POWER CORP	30.23	5.90%
62	IPL	INTER PIPELINE	21.29	8.10%
62	NVU.UN	NORTHVIEW APRT, REIT	28.26	5.80%
62	PIF	POLARIS INFASTRUCTURE	11.79	6.90%
62	POW	POWER CORP	30.40	5.00%

62	PRV.UN	PRO REAL ESTATE INV	2.30	9%
61	UFS	DOMTAR CORP	63.31	3.70%
61	EIF	EXCHANGE INCOME CO	35.30	6.20%
61	HR.UN	H&R REIT	22.95	6.10%
60	ENB	ENBRIDGE	49.40	6.00%
60	RUF.U	PURE MULTI-FAMILY REIT	8.96	5.70%
59	AQN	ALGONQUIN POWER	15.20	4.50%
59	APR.UN	AUTOMOTIVE PROPERTIES	10.58	7.60%
59	BPY.UN	BROOKFIELD PROPERTY	28.06	6.30%
59	CRR.UN.	CROMBIE REIT	14.42	6.20%

59	FCD	FIRM CAPITAL	6.31	7.50%
59	PEY	PEYTO EXPLORATION	5.82	4.20%
59	PWF	POWER FINANCIAL	31.27	5.60%
59	SRU.UN	SMARTCENTRES	33.76	5.30%
58	AD	ALARIS ROYALTY	18.07	9%
58	ALA	ALTAGAS LTD	18.79	5.10%
58	MRT.UN	MORGUARD REIT	12.30	7.80%
58	NFI	NFI GROUP INC	32.94	4.60%

57	AFN	AG GTOWTH	57.74	4.20%
57	BEP.UN	BROOKFIELD RENEWABLE	42.06	6.60%
57	CU	CANADIAN UTILITIES	36.88	4.60%
57	CRT.UN	CT REIT	13.89	5.40%
57	DIR.UN	DREAM INDUS. REIT	11.58	6.10%
57	ESI	ENSIGN ENERGY	5.33	9%
57	IGM.PR.B	IGM FINANCIAL	24.99	5.90%
57	PZA	PIZZA PIZZA	10.35	8.70%

57	SOT.UN	SLATE OFFICE REIT	5.96	6.90%
57	WIR.U	WPT INDUSTRIAL	18.59	5.40%
56	BIP.UN	BROOKFIELD INFASTRUCT,	55.96	4.80%
56	KMP.UN	KILLAM APT. REIT	18.81	3.50%
56	SJR.B	SHAW COMMUNICATIONS.	27.12	4.40%
56	TNT.UN	TRUE NORTH REIT	6.63	9%
55	AX.UN	ARTIS REIT	10.56	5.10%
55	ACO.Y	ATCO LTD	45.50	3.60%
55	AI	ATRIUM MORTGAGE	13.36	6.70%

55	CHR	CHORUS AVIATION	7.58	6.30%
55	MBN	MBN CORP	6.65	4.80%
54	BTB.UN	BTB REIT	4.85	9%
54	CJ	CARDINAL ENERGY	3.03	4.20%
54	KEY	KEYERA CO	30.60	5.90%
54	SMU.UN	SUMMIT INDUS REIT	12.05	4.30%
54	VNR	VALENER	26.12	4.60%
53	AW.UN	A&W REVENUE	43.68	4.30%

53	CAI	CALEDONIA MINING CO	7.70	4.80%
53	CIX	CI FINANCIAL	19.35	3.70%
53	IVQ	INVESQUE	9.40	11%
52	BEK	BECKER MILK	14.10	5.70%
52	CGX	CINEPLEX	25.58	6.80%
52	FN	FIRST NATIONAL	29.55	6.20%
52	GWP	GREAT WEST LIFECO	32.14	5.20%
52	MKP	MCCAN MORTGAGE	15.76	8.10

52	RNW	TRANSALTA RENEW	13.89	6.80%
51	AND	ACADIAN TIMBER CO	16.70	6.90%
51	FC	FIRM CAPITAL	13.48	7.00%
51	MRD	MELCOR DEV. LTD	13.50	3.80%
51	TGL	TRANSGLOBE ENERGY	2.50	7.40%
50	CU.X	CANADIAN UTILITIES	36.90	4.60%
50	DIV	DOVERSIFIED REALTY	3.36	5.80%
50	FCA	FIRM CAPITAL	9.40	4.40%

50	IGM	IGM FINANCIAL	35.81	6.10%
50	SRT.UN	SLATE RETAIL REIT	12.44	9.00%
50	NWC	THE NORTH WEST CO	29.15	4.50%
50	WCP	WHITECAP RESOURCES	5.11	6.70%

STOCKS SCORING 3.5% WITH A SCORE BELOW 50

Following are the remaining 565 companies on the Toronto Stock Exchange who paid a dividend greater than 3.5% and whose scores were lower than 50. They are sorted in descending order by their score. Of these, 364 of them are preferred shares whose chances of showing a capital gain appear to be about 1 in 100. You can identify them by the "PR" or the "PF" in their stock symbols.

To fit the available space, many of the company names have been abbreviated. A stock symbol search will provide you with the full name, if required.

You are reminded that these scores were calculated in the Spring of 2019. Before buying a stock, check the most recent information, rescore them and do a verification search. You want to confirm that they are still have potential for a share price increase and are still paying close to your dividend expectation.

Note: Display of Stocks with a Score Under 50 has changed to the following

1st Row = Stock Symbol

2nd Row = Stock Score

3rd Row = Company Name

4th Row = Stock Price

5th Row = Dividend % Paid

PLZ.UN	**49**	PLAZA RETAIL REIT	4.13	6.70%
ET	**49**	EVERTZ TECHNOLOGIES L	17.00	4.20%
RUS	**49**	RUSSEL METALS INC	23.29	6.60%
SPB	**49**	SUPERIOR PLUS CORP	11.42	6.30%
KEG.UN	**49**	THE KEG ROYALT INC FUN	17.49	6.50%
TXT.PR.A	**49**	TOP 10 SPLIT TRUST	12.43	6.30%
BPF.UN	**48**	BOSTON PIZZA ROYALTY	17.56	7.80%
CCS.PR.C	**48**	CO-OPERATORS GEN. INS	23.74	5.30%
INE	**48**	INNERGEX RENEW ENERG	14.20	5.00%
OLY	**48**	OLYMPIA FINANCIAL CORP	55.50	5.00%
RME	**48**	ROCKY MOUNTAIN DEAL	8.73	5.60%
AGF.B	**47**	AGF MANAGEMENT LTD	5.24	6.00%
CUF.UN	**47**	COMINAR REIT	11.48	6.30%
GEI	**47**	GIBSON ENERGY INC	21.7	6.10%
MR.UN	**47**	MELCOR REIT	7.6	9%
NWH.UN	**47**	NORTHWEST HEALTH REIT	11.45	7%
PSK	**47**	PRAIRIESKY ROYALTY LT	18.75	4.20%
SIA	**47**	SIENNA SENIOR LIVI CORP	18.52	5.00%
SGY	**47**	SURGE ENERGY INC	1.39	7.10%
TOG	**47**	TORC OIL & GAS LTD	4.66	5.70%
TCL.B	**47**	TRANSCONTINENTAL INC	15.77	5.60%
BLX	**46**	BORALEX INC	18.31	3.60%
BRE	**46**	BROOKFIELD REAL EST SE	16.9	8.10%
HPS.A	**46**	HAMMOND POWER SOLUT	7.70	3.60%

ITP	46	INTERTAPE POLYMER GRP	18.13	4.10%
LNF	46	LEON'S FUNITURE LTD	14.22	3.90%
TCL.A	46	TRANSCONTINENTAL INC	15.71	5.60%
WJX	46	WAJAX CORP	15.82	6.40%
FCA	45	FIRM CAPITAL AMERICAN	7.07	4.40%
OSB	45	NORBORD INC	33.52	4.70%
PSI	45	PASON SYSTEMS INC	20.48	3.50%
CUP.U	44	CARIBBEAN UTILITIES CO	20.80	4.50%
HLF	44	HIGH LINER FOODS INC	7.8	7.40%
ISV	44	INFORMATION SERVICES C	16.26	4.90%
DR	44	MEDICAL FACILITIES CORP	15.69	7%
PEGI	44	PATTERN ENERGY GROUP	30.93	7.30%
TF	44	TIMBERCREEK FINANCIAL	9.48	7.40%
WFC	44	WALL FINANCIAL CORP	24.50	4.10%
ACD	43	ACCORD FINANCIAL CORP	10.25	3.50%
BNP	43	BONAVISTA ENERGY CORP	0.85	4.50%
CSH.U N	43	CHARTWELL REITIREMEN	14.55	4.10%
CHW	43	CHESSWOOD GROUP LTD	10.2	8.56%
FRU	43	FREEHOLD ROYALTIES LT	8.73	7.20%
GS	43	GLUSKIN SHEFF & ASSOC	14.46	6.90%
RCO. UN	43	MIDDLEFIELD CAN. REIT	12.25	5.30%
SRV.U N	43	SIR ROYALTY INCOME FUN	16.36	7.70%
ACQ	42	AUTOCANADA INC	10.67	3.70%
CMG	42	COMPUTER MODELING GR	5.97	6.60%

XTC	42	EXCO TECHNOLOGIES LTD	8.93	4.00%
M	42	MOSAIC CAPITAL CORP	5.72	7.20%
DII.B	41	DOREL INDUSTRIES INC	11.77	12%
GXO	41	GRANITE OIL CORP	0.92	13%
HWO	41	HIGH ARTIC ENERGY SERV	3.85	5.10%
NEXA	41	NEXA RESOURCES SA	13.83	4.90%
PIC.A	41	PREMIUM INCOME CORP	6.77	12%
ACI	40	ALTAGAS CANADA INC	19.35	3.60%
BCF	40	BUILDERS CAPITAL MORT.	9.85	8%
CSW.A	40	CORBY SPIRIT AND WINE	17.99	4.90%
FDI	40	FINDEV INC	0.46	6.50%
KML	40	KINDER MORGAN CA LTD	14.97	4.30%
MDF	40	MEDIAGRIF INTER TECH.	10.09	4.00%
RSI	40	ROGERS SUGAR INC	5.93	6.10%
EML.PR.A	40	THE EMPIRE LIFE INS CO	25.89	5.60%
AWI	39	ADVENT-AWI HOLDINGS I	1.10	4.50%
CSW.B	39	CORBY SPIRIT AND WINE	17.44	5.00%
DII.A	39	DOREL INDUSTRIES INC	12.51	11%
GH	39	GAMEHOST INC	9.92	6.90%
SPS.A	39	SPORTSCENE GROUP INC	6.80	4.60%
HOT.UN	38	AMERICAN HOTEL REIT	6.89	12%
AFCC	38	AUTOMOTIVE FINCO CORP	1.34	16%
IAM	38	INTEGRATED ASSET MAN	2.62	4.60%
LUC	38	LUCARA DIAMOND COPR	1.61	6.30%
SJR.A	38	SHAW COMMUNICATIONS	28.80	4.20%

WEF	38	WESTERN FOREST PROD IN	1.80	5.00%
SES	37	SECURE ENERGY SERVICE	7.56	3.60%
SIL	37	SPROTT INC	3.00	4.00%
ALA.P R.B	36	ALTAGAS LTD	14.61	7.40%
SBC	36	BROMPTON SPLIT BANC	12.37	9%
CWX	36	CANWEL BUILDING MAT.	4.81	11%
CHE. UN	36	CHEMTRADE LOGISTICS IN	8.54	14%
CRW N	36	CROWN CAPITAL PARTNER	9.64	6.30%
FSZ	36	FIERA CAPITAL CORP	12.33	6.80%
MTL	36	MULLEN GROUP LTD	9.75	6.10%
RET	36	REITMANS (CANADA) LTD	3.21	6.10%
KPT	35	KP TISSUE INC	7.9	9%
MPVD	35	MOUNTAIN PROV DIAMON	1.42	11%
RET.A	35	REITMANS (CANADA) LTD	3.27	6.10%
ZZZ	35	SLEEP COUNTRY CA HLDG	17.56	4.20%
FAP	34	ABERDEEN ASIA-PACIFIC	3.83	10%
H	34	HYDRO ONE LTD	21.75	4.20%
SOX	34	STUART OLSON INC	4.50	5.30%
HRR. UN	33	AUSTRALIAN REIT INCOM	11.01	5.90%
KWH. UN	33	CIRUS ENERGY TRUST	8.69	9.60%
EFN.P R.A	33	ELEMENT FLEET MANAG	21.57	8%
GWO. PR.L	33	GREAT-WEST LIFECO INC	25.35	5.60%
MFC.P R.G	33	MANULIFE FINANCIAL CO	20.74	4.70%
SXP	33	SUPREMEX INC	3.07	9%

SWP	33	SWISS WATER DECAF. COF	5.54	4.40%
BIR.PR.A	32	BIRCHCLIFF ENERGY LTD	25.42	8.20%
BBD.PR.C	32	BOMBARDIER INC	20.75	7.50%
CHP.UN	32	CHOICE PROPERTIES REIT	13.4	5.50%
EXE	32	EXTENDICARE INC	7.94	5.90%
FRO.UN	32	FRONSAC REAL ESTATE IN	0.62	3.60%
INE.PR.C	32	INNERGEX RENEWABLE E	22.82	6.30%
STUS.A	32	STARLIGHT US MULTI-FAM	9.3	7%
TD.PF.G	32	THE TORONTO-DOM BANK	26.04	5.30%
AX.PR.E	31	ARTIS REIT	20.36	6.80%
AX.PR.G	31	ARTIS REIT	21.75	5.70%
AZP.PR.A	31	ATLANTIC POWER PREFER	15.48	8%
AZP.PR.B	31	ATLANTIC POWER PREFER	18.48	7.50%
AZP.PR.C	31	ATLANTIC POWER PREFER	18.52	7.40%
ERE.UN	31	EUROPEAN RESIDEN REIT	4.43	8%
MKZ.UN	31	MACKENZIE MASTER LP	0.95	14%
SLF.PR.A	31	SUN LIFE FINANCIAL INC	22.2	5.30%
ABT	30	ABSOLUTE SOFTWARE CO	8.98	3.60%
BPS.PR.U	30	BROOKFIELD OFFICE PROP	34.50	5.10%
BPS.PR.A	30	BROOKFIELD PROPERTY S	25.35	5.70%
BPS.PR.C	30	BROOKFIELD PROPERTY SP	25.25	5.10%
BRF.PR.A	30	BROOKFIELD REN POWER	15.58	5.40%

CWL	30	CALDWELL PART INTERN.	1.2	7.40%
CEE	30	CENTAMIN PLC	1.59	4.40%
DE	30	DECISIVE DIVIDEND CORP	4	9%
DRA. UN	30	DREAM HARD ASSET ALT	7.56	5.20%
EFN.PR.C	30	ELEMENT FLEET MAN CO	20.4	7.90%
ENB.PR.V	30	ENBRIDGE INC	29.02	6.90%
FTN	30	FINANCIAL 15 SPLIT CORP	7.69	19%
FEC	30	FONTERA ENERGY CORP	11.93	4.10%
FFN	30	NORTH AMERICAN FIN SPL	6.56	18%
VNR.PR.A	30	VALENER INC	25.00	4.60%
BIR.PR.C	29	BIRCHCLIFF ENERGY LTD	25.08	7%
BBD.PR.D	29	BOMBARDIER INC	11.57	9%
BPS.PR.B	29	BROOKFIELD PROPERTY SP	25.30	5.00%
WN.PR.A	29	GEORGE WESTON LTD	25.6	5.70%
WN.PR.E	29	GEORGE WESTON LTD	22.68	5.20%
GWO.PR.F	29	GREAT-WEST LIFECO INC	25.56	5.80%
POW.PR.C	29	POWER CORPORATION	25.55	5.70%
POW.PR.G	29	POWER CORPORATION	25.5	5.50%
PWF.PR.I	29	POWER FINANCIAL CORP	25.8	5.80%
PWF.PR.G	29	POWER FINANCIAL CORP	25.50	5.80%
PWF.PR.H	29	POWER FINANCIAL CORP	25.47	5.60%
AKT.A	28	AKITA DRILLING LTD	2.98	11%

HOT. U	**28**	AMERICAN HOTEL REIT LP	6.91	12%
BAM. PF.C	**28**	BROOKFIELD ASSET MAN	21.07	5.80%
CF.PR. C	**28**	CANACCORD GENUITY GP	17.08	7.20%
CU.PR .E	**28**	CANADIAN UTILITIES LTD	22.77	5.40%
CU.PR .D	**28**	CANADIAN UTILITIES LTD	22.9	5.40%
CU.PR .F	**28**	CANADIAN UTILITIES LTD	21.2	5.30%
CU.PR .G	**28**	CANADIAN UTILITIES LTD	21.15	5.30%
CIU.P R.A	**28**	CU INC	21.35	5.40%
ELF.P R.H	**28**	E-L FINANCIAL COPR LTD	24.99	5.50%
ELF.P R.F	**28**	E-L FINANCIAL COPR LTD	24.08	5.50%
ELF.P R.G	**28**	E-L FINANCIAL COPR LTD	22.07	5.40%
EFN.P R.G	**28**	ELEMENT FLEET MAN	21.66	7.50%
ELC	**28**	ELYSEE DEV CORP	0.38	11%
EMA. PR.E	**28**	EMERA INC	20.48	5.50%
ENB.P F.C	**28**	ENBRIDGE INC	17	6.40%
ENB.P R.T	**28**	ENBRIDGE INC	16.26	6.10%
ENB.P R.A	**28**	ENBRIDGE INC	24.69	5.60%
EQB.P R.C	**28**	EQUTABLE GROUP INC	24.74	6.40%
FTS.P R.F	**28**	FORTIS INC	22.65	5.40%
WN.P R.D	**28**	GEORGE WESTON LTD	24.27	5.40%
WN.P R.C	**28**	GEORGE WESTON LTD	24.13	5.40%
GWO. PR.H	**28**	GREAT-WEST LIFECO INC	22.41	5.40%

GWO.PR.T	28	GREAT-WEST LIFECO INC	23.98	5.40%
GWO.PR.Q	28	GREAT-WEST LIFECO INC	23.97	5.40%
GWO.PR.G	28	GREAT-WEST LIFECO INC	24.16	5.40%
GWO.PR.P	28	GREAT-WEST LIFECO INC	24.97	5.40%
GWO.PR.R	28	GREAT-WEST LIFECO INC	22.50	5.30%
GWO.PR.S	28	GREAT-WEST LIFECO INC	24.73	5.30%
IAF.PR.B	28	IA FINANCIAL CORP	22.10	5.20%
L.PR.B	28	LOBLAWS CO LTD	24.94	5.30%
MFC.PR.C	28	MANULIFE FINANCIAL	21.01	5.30%
MFC.PR.B	28	MANULIFE FINANCIAL	21.9	5.30%
MID.UN	28	MINT INCOME FUND	6.66	7.20%
NEW.PR.D	28	NEWGROWTH CORP	32.17	4.10%
PVS.PR.D	28	PARTNERS VALUE SPLIT	25.58	4.40%
POW.PR.A	28	POWER CORP OF CANADA	25.09	5.60%
POW.PR.D	28	POWER CORP OF CANADA	22.65	5.50%
POW.PR.B	28	POWER CORP OF CANADA	24.35	5.50%
PWF.PR.O	28	POWER FINANCIAL CORP	25.53	5.70%
PWF.PR.T	28	POWER FINANCIAL CORP	18.86	5.50%
PWF.PR.F	28	POWER FINANCIAL CORP	24.03	5.50%
PWF.PR.E	28	POWER FINANCIAL CORP	25.34	5.50%
PWF.PR.L	28	POWER FINANCIAL CORP	23.48	5.40%
PWF.PR.S	28	POWER FINANCIAL CORP	22.11	5.40%

PWF.PR.R	28	POWER FINANCIAL CORP	25.65	5.40%
RZE	28	RAZOR ENERGY CORP	2.71	5.40%
RY.PR.UN	28	ROYAL BANK OF CAN	24.00	5.10%
RY.PR.W	28	ROYAL BANK OF CAN	25.05	4.90%
RY.PR.C	28	ROYAL BANK OF CAN	25.18	4.60%
SLF.PR.E	28	SUN LIFE FINANCIAL INC	21.10	5.30%
SLF.PR.B	28	SUN LIFE FINANCIAL INC	22.65	5.30%
SLF.PR.C	28	SUN LIFE FINANCIAL INC	21.00	5.30%
SLF.PR.D	28	SUN LIFE FINANCIAL INC	21.00	5.30%
XTD	28	TDB SPLIT CORP	6.29	9.60%
AQN.PR.A	27	ALGONQUIN POWER UT	19.75	6.50%
BCE.PR.C	27	BCE INC	16.65	6.70%
BDT	27	BIRD CONSTRUCTION INC	7.55	5.10%
SBC.PR.A	27	BROMPTON SPLIT BANC	10.28	4.90%
BRF.PR.E	27	BROOKFIELD RENEWAB	19.69	6.30%
BRF.PR.F	27	BROOKFIELD RENEWAB	19.8	6.30%
CPX.PR.X	27	CAPITAL POWER CORP	20.08	6.80%
CPX.PR.E	27	CAPITAL POWER CORP	19.73	6.60%
EFN.PR.E	27	ELEMENT FLEET MAN	19.88	7.90%
ENB.PF.V	27	ENBRIDGE INC	26.94	6.70%
ENB.PR.F	27	ENBRIDGE INC	17.61	6.70%
ENB.PF.U	27	ENBRIDGE INC	26.08	6.30%

ENB.PR.U	27	ENBRIDGE INC	26.23	6.30%
GMP	27	GMP CAPITAL INC	2.03	5.00%
INP	27	INPUT CAPITAL CORP	0.69	5.70%
PL	27	PINNACLE REN ENERGY	12.12	5.20%
PWF.PR.K	27	POWER FINANCIAL CORP	22.7	5.50%
RY.PR.E	27	ROYAL BANK OF CAN	25.23	4.50%
RAY.A	27	STINGRAY GROUP INC	6.47	4.10%
BCE.PR.A	26	BCE INC	15.9	5.70%
BCE.PR.K	26	BCE INC	14.03	5.20%
BGI.UN	26	BROOKFIELD GLOBAL	6.72	9%
CSE.PR.A	26	CAPSTONE INFAST	13.17	6.20%
DFN.PR.A	26	DIVIDEND 15 SPLIT CORP	10.09	5.20%
ENB.PF.N	26	ENBRIDGE INC	19.01	6.70%
ENI.UN	26	ENERGY INCOME FUND	1.82	6.60%
IAF.PR.G	26	IA FINANCIAL CORP	21.64	4.40%
LBS.PR.A	26	LIFE & BANC SPLIT CORP	10.09	5.40%
MBK.UN	26	MANULIFE US REG BANK	11.57	4.30%
NPF.UN	26	NORTH AMERICAN PREFX	18.8	7.30%
NPI.PR.A	26	NORTHLAND POWER INC	15.85	5.50%
PAR.UN	26	PARTNERS REIT	1.7	11%
PPL.PR.S	26	PEMBINA PIPELINE CORP	23.55	5.30%
RY.PR.Z	26	ROYAL BANK OF CANADA	18.48	5.50%

RY.PR.G	**26**	ROYAL BANK OF CANADA	25.20	4.50%
RY.PR.F	**26**	ROYAL BANK OF CANADA	25.16	4.40%
TA.PR.H	**26**	TRANSALTA CORP	18.5	7.10%
TA.PR.J	**26**	TRANSALTA CORP	19.11	6.90%
AKT.B	**25**	AKITA DRILLING LTD	4	9%
AQN.PR.D	**25**	ALGONQUIN POWER UT	21.32	5.90%
BMO.PR.W	**25**	BANK OF MONTREAL	18.10	5.20%
BCE.PR.O	**25**	BCE INC	20.49	5.20%
RBN.UN	**25**	BLUE RIBBON INCOME F	8.27	7.20%
BAM.PR.N	**25**	BROOKFIELD ASSET MAN	20.5	5.80%
BAM.PR.M	**25**	BROOKFIELD ASSET MAN	20.67	5.80%
BAM.PF.D	**25**	BROOKFIELD ASSET MAN	21.5	5.70%
BK.PR.A	**25**	CANADIAN BANC CORP	10.40	5.20%
CM.PR.O	**25**	CANADIAN IMPERIAL BNK	18.35	5.30%
CM.PR.P	**25**	CANADIAN IMPERIAL BNK	17.77	5.30%
CF.PR.A	**25**	CANNACORD GENUITY GR	14.1	6.90%
EIT.UN	**25**	CANOE EIT INCOME FUND	11.38	11%
YCM.PR.B	**25**	COMMERCE SPLIT CORP	5	7.50%
DF.PR.A	**25**	DIVIDEND 15 SPLIT CORP II	10.04	5.20%
FFH.PR.F	**25**	FAIRFAX FINANCIAL HOLD	14.69	6.30%
FFH.PR.M	**25**	FAIRFAX FINANCIAL HOLD	22.50	5.20%
FTS.PR.J	**25**	FORTIS INC	21.93	5.50%

GWO.PR.I	25	GREAT-WEST LIFECO INC	21.13	5.30%
NA.PR.S	25	NATIONAL BANK OF CAN	18.51	5.50%
FFN.PR.A	25	NORTH AMERICAN FIN. 15	10.04	5.50%
PPL.PR.A	25	PEMBINA PIPELINE CORP	17.59	7%
PPL.PR.E	25	PEMBINA PIPELINE CORP	18.77	6.70%
PPL.PR.I	25	PEMBINA PIPELINE CORP	21.32	5.60%
PIC.PR.A	25	PREMIUM INCOME CORP	14.64	5.90%
PDV.PR.A	25	PRIME DIVIDEND CORP	10.2	6.10%
SBN.PR.A	25	S SPLIT CORP	10.35	5.10%
SRT.U	25	SLATE RETAIL REIT	12.43	9%
TD.PF.B	25	THE TORONTO-DOM BNK	18.40	5.20%
TA.PR.F	25	TRANSALTA CORP	15.83	6.40%
VB.PR.A	25	VERSABANK	10.1	6.90%
ALA.PR.G	24	ALTAGAS LTD	16.58	7.20%
ALA.PR.E	24	ALTAGAS LTD	19.09	7.10%
ALA.PR.U	24	ALTAGAS LTD	26.1	6.80%
BMO.PR.T	24	BANK OF MONTREAL	18.15	5.40%
BMO.PR.S	24	BANK OF MONTREAL	18.75	5.30%
BCE.PR.Y	24	BCE INC	15.53	6.40%
BCE.PR.Q	24	BCE INC	19.85	6.10%
LCS.PR.A	24	BROMPTON LIFECO S	10.04	6.20%
BAM.PF.E	24	BROOKFIELD ASSET	17.9	6.20%

BAM. PF.A	**24**	BROOKFIELD ASSET	20.74	6.10%
BAM. PF.G	**24**	BROOKFIELD ASSET	19.14	5.90%
BAM. PF.B	**24**	BROOKFIELD ASSET	18.50	5.60%
BAM. PF.H	**24**	BROOKFIELD ASSET	25.60	4.90%
BIP.P R.A	**24**	BROOKFIELD INFAS	20.59	5.50%
BPO.P R.T	**24**	BROOKFIELD OFFICE	18.9	7.10%
BPO.P R.A	**24**	BROOKFIELD OFFICE	16.9	7%
BPO.P R.P	**24**	BROOKFIELD OFFICE	15.71	6.70%
BPO.P R.N	**24**	BROOKFIELD OFFICE	15.74	6.10%
BPO.P R.R	**24**	BROOKFIELD OFFICE	17.3	6.00%
BRF.P R.C	**24**	BROOKFIELD RENEW	17.19	6.40%
HOM. U	**24**	BSR REIT	13.01	5.10%
CM.P R.Q	**24**	CANADIAN IMP BANK.	20.30	4.50%
LFE.P R.B	**24**	CANADIAN LIFE SPLIT	10.04	6.50%
CU.PR .C	**24**	CANADIAN UTILITIES	18.20	4.70%
CWB. PR.B	**24**	CANADIAN WEST BANK	18.57	5.80%
DGS.P R.A	**24**	DIVIDEND GROWTH SPL	10.12	5.20%
DRM. PR.A	**24**	DREAM UNLIMITED CO	7.49	6.80%
EMA. PR.C	**24**	EMERA INC	20.2	5.80%
EMA. PR.F	**24**	EMERA INC	18.84	5.60%
ENB.P R.H	**24**	ENBRIDGE INC	16.15	6.80%
ENB.P R.D	**24**	ENBRIDGE INC	16.72	6.60%

ENB.PR.P	24	ENBRIDGE INC	16.95	6.50%
ENB.PR.J	24	ENBRIDGE INC	17.18	6.40%
ENB.PF.G	24	ENBRIDGE INC	17.15	6.40%
ENB.PF.A	24	ENBRIDGE INC	17.07	6.40%
ENB.PF.E	24	ENBRIDGE INC	17.15	6.40%
FFH.PR.D	24	FAIRFAX FINANCIAL	18.1	6.50%
FFH.PR.C	24	FAIRFAX FINANCIAL	18.37	6.30%
FFH.PR.K	24	FAIRFAX FINANCIAL	19.33	5.90%
FN.PR.A	24	FIRST NATIONAL	13.25	5.30%
FTS.PR.G	24	FORTIS INC	19.10	5.80%
FTS.PR.K	24	FORTIS INC	17.67	5.50%
FTS.PR.M	24	FORTIS INC	19.18	5.30%
HSE.PR.C	24	HUSKY ENERGY INC	18.96	6.00%
HSE.PR.E	24	HUSKY ENERGY INC	20.7	5.50%
IFC.PR.C	24	INTACT FINANCIAL	18.40	4.50%
LB.PR.H	24	LAURENTIAN BANK	16.76	6.40%
MFC.PR.K	24	MANULIFE FINANCIAL	19.16	5.80%
MFC.PR.J	24	MANULIFE FINANCIAL	20.69	5.60%
MFC.PR.L	24	MANULIFE FINANCIAL	17.62	5.60%
MFC.PR.M	24	MANULIFE FINANCIAL	18.47	5.30%
MFC.PR.N	24	MANULIFE FINANCIAL	18.21	5.20%
MFC.PR.I	24	MANULIFE FINANCIAL	21.21	5.10%

MFC.PR.H	**24**	MANULIFE FINANCIAL	22.43	4.80%
NA.PR.W	**24**	NATIONAL BANK	17.61	5.50%
NPI.PR.C	**24**	NORTHLAND POWER	19.85	6.40%
PPL.PR.C	**24**	PEMBINA PIPELINE	17.42	6.40%
PPL.PR.G	**24**	PEMBINA PIPELINE	17.76	6.30%
PPL.PR.O	**24**	PEMBINA PIPELINE	17.75	6.30%
PPL.PR.Q	**24**	PEMBINA PIPELINE	19.38	6.20%
RY.PR.H	**24**	ROYAL BANK	18.80	5.20%
BMO.PR.Y	**24**	ROYAL BANK	21.11	4.50%
RY.PR.A	**24**	ROYAL BANK	25.16	4.40%
RY.PR.M	**24**	ROYAL BANK	20.30	4.40%
SLF.PR.I	**24**	SUN LIFE FINANCIAL	20.63	4.60%
SLF.PR.H	**24**	SUN LIFE FINANCIAL	17.80	4.00%
XTD.PR.A	**24**	TDB SPLIT CORP	10.06	5.20%
TD.PF.A	**24**	TORONTO-DOM BANK	18.40	5.30%
TD.PF.C	**24**	TORONTO-DOM BANK	18.41	5.10%
TD.PF.E	**24**	TORONTO-DOM BANK	21.60	4.30%
TS.B	**24**	TORSTAR CORP	0.73	14%
TA.PR.D	**24**	TRANSALTA CORP	12.28	5.60%
TRP.PR.E.	**24**	TRANSCANADA CORP	16.75	6.30%
TRP.PR.G	**24**	TRANSCANADA CORP	19.21	5.00%
VB.PR.B	**24**	VERSABANK	10.22	6.50%

BCE.PR.J	23	BCE INC	15.58	6.40%
BCE.PR.B	23	BCE INC	15.65	6.40%
BCE.PR.S	23	BCE INC	15.65	6.40%
BCE.PR.E	23	BCE INC	15.6	6.30%
BCE.PR.H	23	BCE INC	15.59	6.30%
BCE.PR.D	23	BCE INC	15.59	6.30%
BCE.PR.Z	23	BCE INC	15.65	6.20%
OSP.PR.A	23	BROMPTON OIL SPL	9.71	5.10%
BAM.PR.E	23	BROOKFIELD ASSET	16.9	5.80%
BAM.PR.T	23	BROOKFIELD ASSET	15.6	5.40%
BAM.PR.X	23	BROOKFIELD ASSET	14.05	4.80%
BAM.PR.R	23	BROOKFIELD ASSET	16.01	4.70%
CLR	23	CLEARWATER SEAFD	4.95	4.00%
DS	23	DIVIDEND SELECT 15	7.44	9.80%
ECF.UN	23	EAST COAST INVEST	9.20	5.20%
EMA.PR.A	23	EMERA INC	15.45	4.10%
ENB.PR.B	23	ENBRIDGE INC	15.35	5.50%
FFH.PR.I	23	FAIRFAX FINANCIAL	16.55	5.60%
FFH.PR.G	23	FAIRFAX FINANCIAL	15.49	5.40%
FTN.PR.A	23	FINANCIAL 15 SPLIT	9.9	5.60%
GMP.PR.B	23	GMP CAPITAL INC	11	8.56%
IFC.PR.A	23	INTACT FINANCIAL	15.8	5.40%
MCS	23	MCCHIP RESOURCES	0.66	9%

PWF.PR.P	23	POWER FINANCIAL	14.17	4.10%
SJR.PR.A	23	SHAW COMMUNIC	14.40	4.90%
TRP.PR.D	23	TRANSCANADA COR	17.03	5.70%
WFS.PR.A	23	WORLD FINANCIAL	9.95	5.30%
ALA.PR.A	22	ALTAGAS LTD	14.42	5.90%
BCE.PR.F	22	BCE INC	15.30	5.10%
BCE.PR.T	22	BCE INC	15.12	5.00%
BCE.PR.M	22	BCE INC	14.48	4.80%
BCE.PR.G	22	BCE INC	15.10	4.60%
BCE.PR.I	22	BCE INC	15.14	4.50%
BAM.PR.B	22	BROOKFIELD ASSET	11.68	5.70%
BAM.PR.G	22	BROOKFIELD ASSET	16.54	4.20%
BRF.PR.B	22	BROOKFIELD RENEW.	15.75	6.70%
CPX.PR.A	22	CAPITAL POWER CORP	13.81	5.50%
YCM.PR.A	22	COMMERCE SPLIT COR	5.1	5.90%
ENB.PR.Y	22	ENBRIDGE INC	15.71	6.40%
FFH.PR.E	22	FAIRFAX FINANCIAL	14.20	5.10%
FTS.PR.I	22	FORTIS INC	14.3	5.30%
FTS.PR.H	22	FORTIS INC	14.51	4.30%
GMN	22	GOBIMI INC	0.35	4.20%
HSE.PR.A	22	HUSKY ENERGY INC	12.55	4.80%
INE.PR.A	22	INNERGEX RENEW	14.45	6.20%

IFB.UN	22	INVESTMENT GRADE	8.11	6.20%
JE	22	JUST ENERGY GROUP	4.94	10%
XMF.PR.C	22	M SPLIT CORP	5.23	7.30%
MFR.UN	22	MANULIFE FLOAT	7.63	9%
PWF.PR.A	22	POWER FINANCIAL	13.60	5.00%
BSD.PR.A	22	SOUNDVEST SPLIT	9.52	6.30%
TRP.PR.F	22	TRANSCANADA CORP	14.86	6.10%
TRP.PR.H	22	TRANSCANADA CORP	12.32	6.00%
TRP.PR.A	22	TRANSCANADA CORP	15.10	5.40%
TRP.PR.C	22	TRANSCANADA CORP	13.13	4.30%
CLIQ	21	ALCANNA INC	26.1	6.80%
BBD.PR.B	21	BOMBARDIER INC	11.3	9%
BAM.PF.Z	21	BROOKFIELD ASSET	20.00	5.80%
BAM.PR.K	21	BROOKFIELD ASSET	11.64	5.80%
BAM.PR.C	21	BROOKFIELD ASSET	11.67	5.70%
BPO.PR.W	21	BROOKFIELD OFFICE	10.68	6.40%
BPO.PR.Y	21	BROOKFIELD OFFICE	10.76	6.30%
BPO.PR.X	21	BROOKFIELD OFFICE	10.75	6.10%
CIQ.UN	21	CANADIAN HIGH-INC	7.57	8%
DFN	21	DIVIDEND 15 SPLIT	8.66	14%
ERM	21	ECLIPSE RESIDENTIAL	9.34	8%
PCD.UN	21	PATHFINDER INCOME	7.96	7.50%
TRI.PR.B	21	THOMSON REUTERS	13.08	5.10%

TRP.PR.B	21	TRANSCANADA CORP	12.35	4.30%
TSL	21	TREE ISLAND STEEL	2.06	3.90%
BPO.PR.C	20	BROOKFIELD OFFICE	25.78	5.80%
EIT.PR.A	20	CANOE EIT INCOME	25.19	4.80%
CIU.PR.C	20	CU INC	13.62	4.10%
GWO.PR.M	20	GREAT-WEST LIFECO	25.44	5.70%
GWO.PR.N	20	GREAT-WEST LIFECO	14.79	3.70%
ICL	20	ITASCA CAPITAL CORP	0.32	245%
MFC.PR.F	20	MANULIFE FINANCIAL	14.32	3.70%
SLF.PR.G	20	SUN LIFE FINANCIAL	15.00	3.80%
TXT.UN	20	TOP 10 SPLIT TRUST	3.29	9%
FTU.PR.B	20	US FINANCIAL 15 SP	7.89	10%
WBE	20	WESTBOND ENTER	0.18	5.70%
CDD.UN	19	CORE CANADIAN DI	5.74	6.50%
JE.PR.U	19	JUST ENERGY GRP	29.23	9.80%
MMP.UN	19	PRECIOUS METALS	1.33	9.20%
RAY.B	19	STINGRAY GROUP	6.50	4.00%
USF.UN	19	US FINANCIALS INC	7.23	6.90%
SAT	18	ASIAN TELEVISION	0.11	18%
BMO.PR.Z	18	BANK OF MONTREAL	24.79	5.00%
BMO.PR.D	18	BANK OF MONTREAL	22.50	4.90%
BMO.PR.C	18	BANK OF MONTREAL	23.79	4.70%
BNS.PR.I	18	BANK OF NOVA SCO	22.60	5.40%

BAM. PF.J	18	BROOKFIELD ASSET	23.03	5.10%
CM.P R.T	18	CANADIAN IM BANK	25.4	5.50%
CM.P R.R	18	CANADIAN IM BANK	22.81	4.80%
ENS	18	E SPLIT CORP	14.75	10%
NA.PR .A	18	NATIONAL BANK	25.85	5.20%
PPL.P F.A	18	PEMBINA PIPELINE	22.89	5.40%
PDV	18	PRIME DIVIDEND	7.15	9.50%
RY.PR .S	18	ROYAL BANK	21.6	5.60%
RY.PR .Q	18	ROYAL BANK	25.92	5.30%
TD.PF. D	18	TORONTO-DOM BANK	21.02	4.30%
TRP.P R.K	18	TRANSCANADA CORP	25.51	4.80%
W.PR. N	18	WESTCOAST ENERGY	25.73	5.00%
ALB.P R.C	17	ALLBANC SPLIT	26.50	4.60%
ALA.P R.K	17	ALTAGAS LTD	20.54	6%
ALA.P R.I	17	ALTAGAS LTD	22.96	5.70%
AX.PR .I	17	ARTIS REIT	24.69	6.10%
BMO. PR.E	17	BANK OF MONTREAL	22.33	5.40%
BMO. PR.B	17	BANK OF MONTREAL	25.75	4.70%
BNS.P R.E	17	BANK OF NOVA SCO	29.52	5.30%
BNS.P R.G	17	BANK OF NOVA SCO	26.15	5.30%
BNS.P R.H	17	BANK OF NOVA SCO	25.80	4.70%
PRM	17	BIG PHARMA SPLIT	12.2	10%
BAM. PF.I	17	BROOKFIELD ASSET	24.55	4.90%

BIP.PR.E	17	BROOKFIELD INFA	21.99	5.60%
BIP.PR.B	17	BROOKFIELD INFA	25.13	5.50%
BIR.PR.D	17	BROOKFIELD INFA	22.65	5.40%
BIP.PR.C	17	BROOKFIELD INFA	25.00	5.30%
BEP.PR.K	17	BROOKFIELD RENEW	22.01	5.60%
BEP.PR.E	17	BROOKFIELD RENEW	21.6	6.50%
BEP.PR.M	17	BROOKFIELD RENEW	20.4	6.10%
BEP.PR.I	17	BROOKFIELD RENEW	25.34	5.70%
BEP.PR.G	17	BROOKFIELD RENEW	24.72	5.60%
CM.PR.S	17	CANADIAN IMP BANK	20.59	5.50%
CU.PR.H	17	CANADIAN UTILITIES	24.6	5.30%
CWB.PR.C	17	CANADIAN WEST BANK	25.81	6.10%
CWB.PR.D	17	CANADIAN WEST BANK	25.75	5.90%
EIT.PR.B	17	CANOE EIT INCOME	25.10	4.80%
CPX.PR.G	17	CAPITAL POWER CORP	26.00	5.80%
CPX.PR.I	17	CAPITAL POWER CORP	25.25	5.70%
DC.PR.E	17	DUNDEE CORP	13.99	14%
DC.PR.D	17	DUNDEE CORP	12.57	11%
DC.PR.B	17	DUNDEE CORP	12.6	11%
ECN.PR.A	17	ECN CAPITAL CORP	21.95	7.40%
ECN.PR.A	17	ECN CAPITAL CORP	21.19	7.30%
EFN.PR.I	17	ELEMENT FLEET MAN	20.1	7.10%

EMA.PR.H	17	EMERA INC	23.70	5.20%
ENB.PF.K	17	ENBRIDGE INC	22.89	5.30%
ENB.PR.I	17	ENBRIDGE INC	25.12	5.10%
GRP.PR.A	17	GLOBAL RESOURCE	25.49	6.10%
GMP.PR.C	17	GMP CAPITAL INC	11.15	10%
IAF.PR.I	17	IA FINANCIAL CORP	22.7	5.30%
IFC.PR.G	17	INTACT FINANCIAL	20.56	6.00%
IFC.PR.F	17	INTACT FINANCIAL	24.49	5.40%
IFC.PR.E	17	INTACT FINANCIAL	24	5.40%
KML.PR.C	17	KINDER MORGAN	23.67	5.50%
KML.PR.A	17	KINDER MORGAN	23.83	5.50%
LB.PR.J	17	LAURENTIAN BANK	25.79	5.70%
MFC.PR.O	17	MANULIFE FINANCIAL	26.15	5.40%
MFC.PR.R	17	MANULIFE FINANCIAL	25.12	4.80%
NA.PR.G	17	NATIONAL BANK	21.85	5.70%
NA.PR.X	17	NATIONAL BANK	26.04	5.40%
NA.PR.C	17	NATIONAL BANK	22.65	4.90%
PVS.PR.E	17	PARTNERS VALUE	25.75	5.30%
PPL.PR.K	17	PEMBINA PIPELINE	25.92	5.60%
PPL.PR.M	17	PEMBINA PIPELINE	25.88	5.50%
PWF.PR.Z	17	POWER FINANCIAL	23.62	5.40%
RY.PR.R	17	ROYAL BANK	26.05	5.30%

RY.PR.P	17	ROYAL BANK	25.25	5.20%
TD.PF.J	17	TORONTO-DOM BANK	21.75	5.40%
TD.PF.F	17	TORONTO-DOM BANK	24.06	5.10%
TD.PF.I	17	TORONTO-DOM BANK	23.17	4.80%
TD.PF.H	17	TORONTO-DOM BANK	25.74	4.70%
TRP.PR.J	17	TRANSCANADA CORP	26.07	5.30%
W.PR.K	17	WESTCOAST ENERGY	25.60	5.10%
AX.PR.A	16	ARTIS REIT	21.89	6.50%
BCE.PR.R	16	BCE INC	15.7	6.60%
BAM.PR.S	16	BROOKFIELD ASSET	16.15	6.10%
BAM.PF.F	16	BROOKFIELD ASSET	19.4	5.80%
BSO.UN	16	BROOKFIELD SELECT	3.87	15%
BK	16	CANADIAN BANC COR	11.32	9.50%
DGS	16	DIVIDEND GROWTH	5.38	22%
ENB.PR.C	16	ENBRIDGE INC	15.85	6.50%
FFH.PR.H	16	FAIRFAX FINANCIAL	15.8	6.50%
FFH.PR.J	16	FAIRFAX FINANCIAL	17.2	6.50%
IFC.PR.D	16	INTACT FINANCIAL	18.43	5.80%
MFC.PR.Q	16	MANULIFE FINANCIAL	20.70	5.70%
NA.PR.E	16	NATIONAL BANK	20.35	5.70%
NPI.PR.B	16	NORTHLAND POWER	16	6.80%
PVF.PR.U	16	PARTNERS VALUE	26.19	5.80%

RY.PR.J	16	ROYAL BANK	20.76	4.30%
SLF.PR.K	16	SUN LIFE FINANCIAL	17.56	5.40%
BCE.PR.N	15	BCE INC	14.71	6.40%
BCE.PR.L	15	BCE INC	14.17	6.30%
PRM.PR.A	15	BIG PHARMA SPLIT	10.28	4.90%
CU.PR.I	15	CANADIAN UTILITIES	26.01	4.30%
DF	15	DIVIDEND 15 SPLIT	5.14	23%
ENS.PR.A	15	E SPLIT CORP	10.19	5.10%
EMA.PR.B	15	EMERA INC	15.5	5.30%
FN.PR.B	15	FIRST NATIONAL FIN	13.68	6.80%
GDV.PR.A	15	GLOBAL DIVIDEND	10.23	4.90%
GWO.PR.O	15	GREAT-WEST LIFECO	14.78	5.00%
HSE.PR.B	15	HUSKY ENERGY INC	13.15	6.40%
MFC.PR.B	15	MANULIFE FINANCIAL	14.28	5.00%
PTG	15	PIVOT TECHNOLOGY	1.28	13%
PWF.PR.Q	15	POWER FINANCIAL	14.58	5.10%
RY.PR.O	15	ROYAL BANK	24.10	5.10%
SJR.PR.B	15	SHAW COMMUN	14.75	6.00%
SLF.PR.J	15	SUN LIFE FINANCIAL	15.00	5.10%
TA.PR.E	15	TRANSALTA CORP	13.02	7%
TRP.PR.I	15	TRANSCANADA CORP	13.83	5.70%
BSC.PR.C	14	BNS SPLIT CORP II	20.18	3.90%

PFT.UN	14	CANADIAN PREFER	8.04	5.00%
LBS	14	LIFE & BANC SPLIT	8.13	15%
STUS.U	14	STARLIGHT US MUL	12.17	7.20%
LCS	12	BROMPTON LIFECO	4.8	18%
CCI.UN	12	CANADIAN CONVER	4.97	13%
0SP	10	BROMPTON OIL SPI	2.85	42%
GDV	9	GLOBAL DIVIDEND	10.8	11%
HSE.PR.G	9	HUSKY ENERGY INC	20.00	5.60%
RE	9	RE ROYALTIES LTD	0.9	5.90%
CBL	8	CALLIDUS CAPITAL	0.67	185%
HFC.PR.A	8	HAMPTON FINANCIAL	5.5	15%
PT	8	PINE TRAIL REIT	0.13	6%
HFC	7	HAMPTON FINANC	0.2	400%

CHAPTER 14

The 654 Alphabetically

(Data Extracted May 6, 2019)

Following are the 654 stocks that paid a dividend of 3.5%
or more on the Toronto Stock Exchange. In this chapter
they are sorted **alphabetically** by company name.

In the two Chapters that follow, you will find the same
information sorted two additional ways: (*Chapter 15*) *in
descending order by the annual **dividend** percentage paid
(Chapter 16) in descending order by the company's share
price*. The four sorts of the 654 stocks will help you find
the 20 stocks that you would want to add to your portfolio.

**Before you make a decision on buying a stock based on
the sorting of this data recalculate the score. Dividend
percentages and the scores can change daily with
fluctuations in stock prices and volume of shares being
traded.**

The following alphabetical sort may help you to find the
scores, prices and dividends paid by companies who have
been recommended to you. It also gives you insight into
how some major corporations rely upon preferred shares to
raise development money. You can quickly see that the
dividends of their preferred shares are only a percent or two

higher than the dividend paid on their common shares. It is surprising how most preferred shares are now worth much less than the $25 that it is believed they were at when first issued.

Company Name, in Alphabetically order, display is

#1 = Score

#2 = Stock Symbol

#3 = Company Name

#4 = Stock Price

#5 = Stock's Dividend

#1	#2	#3	#4	#5
53	AW.UN	**A&W REVENUE ROYALT**	43.68	4.30%
34	FAP	**ABERDEEN ASIA-PACIFIC**	3.83	10%
30	ABT	**ABSOLUTE SOFTWARE**	8.98	3.60%
51	ADN	**ACADIAN TIMBER CORP**	16.7	6.90%
43	ACD	**ACCORD FINANCIAL CO**	10.25	3.50%
39	AWI	**ADVENT-AWI HOLDINGS**	1.10	4.50%
57	AFN	**AG GROWTH INTERNAT.**	57.74	4.20%
47	AGF.B	**AGF MANAGEMENT LTD**	5.24	6.00%
28	AKT.A	**AKITA DRILLING LTD**	2.98	11%
25	AKT.B	**AKITA DRILLING LTD**	4	9%
58	AD	**ALARIS ROYALTY CORP**	18.07	9%
21	CLIQ	**ALCANNA INC**	26.1	6.80%
27	AQN.PR.A	**ALGONQUIN POWER UT**	19.75	6.50%
25	AQN.PR.D	**ALGONQUIN POWER UT**	21.32	5.90%
59	AQN	**ALGONQUIN POWER UT**	15.20	4.50%
17	ALB.PR.C	**ALLBANC SPLIT CORP II**	26.50	4.60%
40	ACI	**ALTAGAS CANADA INC**	19.35	3.60%
36	ALA.PR.B	**ALTAGAS LTD**	14.61	7.40%
24	ALA.PR.G	**ALTAGAS LTD**	16.58	7.20%
24	ALA.PR.E	**ALTAGAS LTD**	19.09	7.10%
24	ALA.PR.U	**ALTAGAS LTD**	26.1	6.80%
17	ALA.PR.K	**ALTAGAS LTD**	20.54	6%
22	ALA.PR.A	**ALTAGAS LTD**	14.42	5.90%
17	ALA.PR.I	**ALTAGAS LTD**	22.96	5.70%
58	ALA	**ALTAGAS LTD**	18.79	5.10%
28	HOT.U	**AMERICAN HOTEL INCO**	6.91	12%

38	HOT.UN	**AMERICAN HOTEL INC**	6.89	12%
65	ARX	**ARC RESOURGES LTD**	8.06	7.40%
31	AX.PR.E	**ARTIS REIT**	20.36	6.80%
16	AX.PR.A	**ARTIS REIT**	21.89	6.50%
17	AX.PR.I	**ARTIS REIT**	24.69	6.10%
31	AX.PR.G	**ARTIS REIT**	21.75	5.70%
55	AX.UN	**ARTIS REIT**	10.56	5.10%
18	SAT	**ASIAN TELEVISION**	0.11	18%
55	ACO.Y	**ATCO LTD**	45.50	3.60%
62	ACO.X	**ATCO LTD**	45.14	3.50%
31	AZP.PR.A	**ATLANTIC POWER PREF**	15.48	8%
31	AZP.PR.B	**ATLANTIC POWER PREF**	18.48	7.50%
31	AZP.PR.C	**ATLANTIC POWER PREF**	18.52	7.40%
55	AI	**ATRIUM MORTGAGE INV**	13.36	6.70%
33	HRR.UN	**AUSTRALIAN REIT I**	11.01	5.90%
42	ACQ	**AUTOCANADA INC**	10.67	3.70%
38	AFCC	**AUTOMOTIVE FINCO**	1.34	16%
59	APR.UN	**AUTOMOTIVE PROPERTI**	10.58	7.60%
17	BMO.PR.E	**BANK OF MONTREAL**	22.33	5.40%
24	BMO.PR.T	**BANK OF MONTREAL**	18.15	5.40%
24	BMO.PR.S	**BANK OF MONTREAL**	18.75	5.30%
25	BMO.PR.W	**BANK OF MONTREAL**	18.10	5.20%
18	BMO.PR.Z	**BANK OF MONTREAL**	24.79	5.00%
18	BMO.PR.D	**BANK OF MONTREAL**	22.50	4.90%
18	BMO.PR.C	**BANK OF MONTREAL**	23.79	4.70%
17	BMO.PR.B	**BANK OF MONTREAL**	25.75	4.70%
74	BMO	**BANK OF MONTREAL**	106.00	3.80%
18	BNS.PR.I	**BANK OF NOVA SCOTIA**	22.60	5.40%
17	BNS.PR.E	**BANK OF NOVA SCOTIA**	29.52	5.30%
17	BNS.PR.G	**BANK OF NOVA SCOTIA**	26.15	5.30%
74	BNS	**BANK OF NOVA SCOTIA**	73.46	4.70%

17	BNS.PR.H	BANK OF NOVA SCOTIA	25.80	4.70%
27	BCE.PR.C	BCE INC	16.65	6.70%
16	BCE.PR.R	BCE INC	15.7	6.60%
23	BCE.PR.J	BCE INC	15.58	6.40%
15	BCE.PR.N	BCE INC	14.71	6.40%
23	BCE.PR.B	BCE INC	15.65	6.40%
24	BCE.PR.Y	BCE INC	15.53	6.40%
23	BCE.PR.S	BCE INC	15.65	6.40%
23	BCE.PR.E	BCE INC	15.6	6.30%
23	BCE.PR.H	BCE INC	15.59	6.30%
23	BCE.PR.D	BCE INC	15.59	6.30%
15	BCE.PR.L	BCE INC	14.17	6.30%
23	BCE.PR.Z	BCE INC	15.65	6.20%
24	BCE.PR.Q	BCE INC	19.85	6.10%
26	BCE.PR.A	BCE INC	15.9	5.70%
69	BCE	BCE INC	59.69	5.30%
26	BCE.PR.K	BCE INC	14.03	5.20%
25	BCE.PR.O	BCE INC	20.49	5.20%
22	BCE.PR.F	BCE INC	15.30	5.10%
22	BCE.PR.T	BCE INC	15.12	5.00%
22	BCE.PR.M	BCE INC	14.48	4.80%
22	BCE.PR.G	BCE INC	15.10	4.60%
22	BCE.PR.I	BCE INC	15.14	4.50%
52	BEK.A	BECKER MILK CO LTD	14.10	5.70%
17	PRM	BIG PHARMA SPLIT COR	12.2	10%
15	PRM.PR.A	BIG PHARMA SPLIT COR	10.28	4.90%
32	BIR.PR.A	BIRCHCLIFF ENERGY LT	25.42	8.20%
29	BIR.PR.C	BIRCHCLIFF ENERGY LT	25.08	7%
27	BDT	BIRD CONSTRUCTION IN	7.55	5.10%
25	RBN.UN	BLUE RIBBON INCOME F.	8.27	7.20%
14	BSC.PR.C	BNS SPLIT CORP II	20.18	3.90%

21	BBD.PR.B	**BOMBARDIER INC**	11.3	9%
29	BBD.PR.D	**BOMBARDIER INC**	11.57	9%
32	BBD.PR.C	**BOMBARDIER INC**	20.75	7.50%
43	BNP	**BONAVISTA ENERGY CO**	0.85	4.50%
46	BLX	**BORALEX INC**	18.31	3.60%
48	BPF.UN	**BOSTON PIZZA ROYALTIES**	17.56	7.80%
12	LCS	**BROMPTON LIFECO SPLI**	4.8	18%
24	LCS.PR.A	**BROMPTON LIFECO SPLI**	10.04	6.20%
10	0SP	**BROMPTON OIL SPLIT C**	2.85	42%
23	OSP.PR.A	**BROMPTON OIL SPLIT C**	9.71	5.10%
36	SBC	**BROMPTON SPLIT BANC**	12.37	9%
27	SBC.PR.A	**BROMPTON SPLIT BANC**	10.28	4.90%
24	BAM.PF.E	**BROOKFIELD ASSET MA**	17.9	6.20%
16	BAM.PR.S	**BROOKFIELD ASSET MA**	16.15	6.10%
24	BAM.PF.A	**BROOKFIELD ASSET MA**	20.74	6.10%
24	BAM.PF.G	**BROOKFIELD ASSET MA**	19.14	5.90%
23	BAM.PR.E	**BROOKFIELD ASSET MA**	16.9	5.80%
16	BAM.PF.F	**BROOKFIELD ASSET MA**	19.4	5.80%
21	BAM.PF.Z	**BROOKFIELD ASSET MA**	20.00	5.80%
25	BAM.PR.N	**BROOKFIELD ASSET MA**	20.5	5.80%
28	BAM.PF.C	**BROOKFIELD ASSET MA**	21.07	5.80%
21	BAM.PR.K	**BROOKFIELD ASSET MA**	11.64	5.80%
25	BAM.PR.M	**BROOKFIELD ASSET MA**	20.67	5.80%

21	BAM.PR.C	**BROOKFIELD ASSET MA**	11.67	5.70%
22	BAM.PR.B	**BROOKFIELD ASSET MA**	11.68	5.70%
25	BAM.PF.D	**BROOKFIELD ASSET MA**	21.5	5.70%
24	BAM.PF.B	**BROOKFIELD ASSET MA**	18.50	5.60%
23	BAM.PR.T	**BROOKFIELD ASSET MA**	15.6	5.40%
18	BAM.PF.J	**BROOKFIELD ASSET MA**	23.03	5.10%
17	BAM.PF.I	**BROOKFIELD ASSET MA**	24.55	4.90%
24	BAM.PF.H	**BROOKFIELD ASSET MA**	25.60	4.90%
23	BAM.PR.X	**BROOKFIELD ASSET MA**	14.05	4.80%
23	BAM.PR.R	**BROOKFIELD ASSET MA**	16.01	4.70%
22	BAM.PR.G	**BROOKFIELD ASSET MA**	16.54	4.20%
26	BGI.UN	**BROOKFIELD GLOBAL IN**	6.72	9%
17	BIP.PR.E	**BROOKFIELD INFASTRU**	21.99	5.60%
17	BIP.PR.B	**BROOKFIELD INFASTRU**	25.13	5.50%
24	BIP.PR.A	**BROOKFIELD INFASTRU**	20.59	5.50%
17	BIR.PR.D	**BROOKFIELD INFASTRU**	22.65	5.40%
17	BIP.PR.C	**BROOKFIELD INFASTRU**	25.00	5.30%
56	BIP.UN	**BROOKFIELD INFASTR**	55.96	4.80%
24	BPO.PR.T	**BROOKFIELD OFFICE PR**	18.9	7.10%
24	BPO.PR.A	**BROOKFIELD OFFICE PR**	16.9	7%
24	BPO.PR.P	**BROOKFIELD OFFICE PR**	15.71	6.70%
21	BPO.PR.W	**BROOKFIELD OFFICE PR**	10.68	6.40%

21	BPO.PR.Y	**BROOKFIELD OFFICE PR**	10.76	6.30%
21	BPO.PR.X	**BROOKFIELD OFFICE PR**	10.75	6.10%
24	BPO.PR.N	**BROOKFIELD OFFICE PR**	15.74	6.10%
24	BPO.PR.R	**BROOKFIELD OFFICE PR**	17.3	6.00%
20	BPO.PR.C	**BROOKFIELD OFFICE PR**	25.78	5.80%
30	BPS.PR.U	**BROOKFIELD OFFICE PR**	34.50	5.10%
59	BPY.UN	**BROOKFIELD PROPERTY**	28.06	6.30%
30	BPS.PR.A	**BROOKFIELD PROPERTY**	25.35	5.70%
30	BPS.PR.C	**BROOKFIELD PROPERTY**	25.25	5.10%
29	BPS.PR.B	**BROOKFIELD PROPERTY**	25.30	5.00%
46	BRE	**BROOKFIELD REAL ESTA**	16.9	8.10%
17	BEP.PR.K	**BROOKFIELD RENEWAB**	22.01	5.60%
57	BEP.UN	**BROOKFIELD RENEWAB**	42.06	6.60%
17	BEP.PR.E	**BROOKFIELD RENEWAB**	21.6	6.50%
17	BEP.PR.M	**BROOKFIELD RENEWAB**	20.4	6.10%
17	BEP.PR.I	**BROOKFIELD RENEWAB**	25.34	5.70%
17	BEP.PR.G	**BROOKFIELD RENEWAB**	24.72	5.60%
22	BRF.PR.B	**BROOKFIELD RENEWAB**	15.75	6.70%
24	BRF.PR.C	**BROOKFIELD RENEWAB**	17.19	6.40%
27	BRF.PR.E	**BROOKFIELD RENEWAB**	19.69	6.30%
27	BRF.PR.F	**BROOKFIELD RENEWAB**	19.8	6.30%
30	BRF.PR.A	**BROOKFIELD RENEWAB**	15.58	5.40%

16	BSO.UN	**BROOKFIELD SELECT OP**	3.87	15%
24	HOM.U	**BSR REAL ESTATE INVES**	13.01	5.10%
54	BTB.UN	**BTB REAL ESTATE INVES**	4.85	9%
40	BCF	**BUILDERS CAPITAL MOR**	9.85	8%
30	CWL	**CALDWELL PARTNERS**	1.2	7.40%
53	CAL	**CALEDONIA MINING CO**	7.70	4.80%
8	CBL	**CALLIDUS CAPITAL COR**	0.67	185%
28	CF.PR.C	**CANACCORD GENUITY**	17.08	7.20%
16	BK	**CANADIAN BANC CORP**	11.32	9.50%
25	BK.PR.A	**CANADIAN BANC CORP**	10.40	5.20%
12	CCI.UN	**CANADIAN CONVERTIB**	4.97	13%
21	CIQ.UN	**CANADIAN HIGH INCOM**	7.57	8%
18	CM.PR.T	**CANADIAN IMP. BANK OF**	25.4	5.50%
17	CM.PR.S	**CANADIAN IMP. BANK OF**	20.59	5.50%
25	CM.PR.O	**CANADIAN IMP. BANK OF**	18.35	5.30%
25	CM.PR.P	**CANADIAN IMP. BANK OF**	17.77	5.30%
73	CM	**CANADIAN IMP. BANK OF**	113.00	5.00%
18	CM.PR.R	**CANADIAN IMP. BANK OF**	22.81	4.80%
24	CM.PR.Q	**CANADIAN IMP. BANK OF**	20.30	4.50%
24	LFE.PR.B	**CANADIAN LIFE CO**	10.04	6.50%
70	CNQ	**CANADIAN NATURAL RE**	37.68	3.70%
14	PFT.UN	**CANADIAN PREFERRED S**	8.04	5.00%
28	CU.PR.E	**CANADIAN UTILITIES LT**	22.77	5.40%
28	CU.PR.D	**CANADIAN UTILITIES LT**	22.9	5.40%

17	CU.PR.H	**CANADIAN UTILITIES LT**	24.6	5.30%
28	CU.PR.F	**CANADIAN UTILITIES LT**	21.2	5.30%
28	CU.PR.G	**CANADIAN UTILITIES LT**	21.15	5.30%
24	CU.PR.C	**CANADIAN UTILITIES LT**	18.20	4.70%
57	CU	**CANADIAN UTILITIES LT**	36.88	4.60%
50	CU.X	**CANADIAN UTILITIES LT**	36.90	4.60%
15	CU.PR.I	**CANADIAN UTILITIES LT**	26.01	4.30%
17	CWB.PR.C	**CANADIAN WESTERN BA**	25.81	6.10%
17	CWB.PR.D	**CANADIAN WESTERN BA**	25.75	5.90%
24	CWB.PR.B	**CANADIAN WESTERN BA**	18.57	5.80%
25	CF.PR.A	**CANNACORD GENUITY G**	14.1	6.90%
25	EIT.UN	**CANOE EIT INCOME FUN**	11.38	11%
17	EIT.PR.B	**CANOE EIT INCOME FUN**	25.10	4.80%
20	EIT.PR.A	**CANOE EIT INCOME FUN**	25.19	4.80%
36	CWX	**CANWEL BUILDING MAT**	4.81	11%
27	CPX.PR.X	**CAPITAL POWER CORP**	20.08	6.80%
27	CPX.PR.E	**CAPITAL POWER CORP**	19.73	6.60%
62	CPX	**CAPITAL POWER CORP**	30.23	5.90%
17	CPX.PR.G	**CAPITAL POWER CORP**	26.00	5.80%
17	CPX.PR.I	**CAPITAL POWER CORP**	25.25	5.70%
22	CPX.PR.A	**CAPITAL POWER CORP**	13.81	5.50%
26	CSE.PR.A	**CAPSTONE INFASTRUCT**	13.17	6.20%
54	CJ	**CARDINAL ENERGY LTD**	3.03	4.10%
44	CUP.U	**CARIBBEAN UTILITIES C**	20.80	4.50%

30	CEE	CENTAMIN PLC	1.59	4.40%
43	CSH.UN	CHARTWELL REITIREM	14.55	4.10%
36	CHE.UN	CHEMTRADE LOGISTICS	8.54	14%
43	CHW	CHESSWOOD GROUP LT	10.2	8.56%
32	CHP.UN	CHOICE PROP. REIT	13.4	5.50%
55	CHR	CHORUS AVIATION INC	7.58	6.30%
53	CIX	CI FINANCIAL CORP	19.35	3.70%
52	CGX	CINEPLEX INC	25.58	6.80%
33	KWH.UN	CIRUS ENERGY TRUST	8.69	9.60%
23	CLR	CLEARWATER SEAFOOD	4.95	4.00%
47	CUF.UN	COMINAR REIT	11.48	6.30%
25	YCM.PR.B	COMMERCE SPLIT CORP	5	7.50%
22	YCM.PR.A	COMMERCE SPLIT CORP	5.1	5.90%
42	CMG	COMPUTER MODELING	5.97	6.60%
48	CCS.PR.C	CO-OPERATORS GENER	23.74	5.30%
39	CSW.B	CORBY SPIRIT AND WINE	17.44	5.00%
40	CSW.A	CORBY SPIRIT AND WINE	17.99	4.90%
19	CDD.UN	CORE CANADIAN DIVIDEN	5.74	6.50%
59	CRR.UN	CROMBIE REAL ESTATE	14.42	6.20%
36	CRWN	CROWN CAPITAL PARTN	9.64	6.30%
57	CRT.UN	CT REAL ESTATE INVEST	13.89	5.40%
28	CIU.PR.A	CU INC	21.35	5.40%
20	CIU.PR.C	CU INC	13.62	4.10%
30	DE	DECISIVE DIVIDEND COR	4	9%
50	DIV	DIVERSIFIED REALTY	3.26	6.80%
21	DFN	DIVIDEND 15 SPLIT CORP	8.66	14%

26	DFN.PR.A	**DIVIDEND 15 SPLIT CORP**	10.09	5.20%
15	DF	**DIVIDEND 15 SPLIT CORP**	5.14	23%
25	DF.PR.A	**DIVIDEND 15 SPLIT CORP**	10.04	5.20%
16	DGS	**DIVIDEND GROWTH SPLI**	5.38	22%
24	DGS.PR.A	**DIVIDEND GROWTH SPLI**	10.12	5.20%
23	DS	**DIVIDEND SELECT 15 CO**	7.44	9.80%
61	UFS	**DOMTAR CORP**	63.31	3.70%
41	DII.B	**DOREL INDUSTRIES INC**	11.77	12%
39	DII.A	**DOREL INDUSTRIES INC**	12.51	11%
68	DRG.UN	**DREAM GLOBAL REAL E**	13.84	5.80%
30	DRA.UN	**DREAM HARD ASSET ALT**	7.56	5.20%
57	DIR.UN	**DREAM INDUSTRI REIT**	11.58	6.10%
63	D.UN	**DREAM OFFICE REIT**	23.51	4.30%
24	DRM.PR.A	**DREAM UNLIMITED CO**	7.49	6.80%
17	DC.PR.E	**DUNDEE CORP**	13.99	14%
17	DC.PR.D	**DUNDEE CORP**	12.57	11%
17	DC.PR.B	**DUNDEE CORP**	12.6	11%
18	ENS	**E SPLIT CORP**	14.75	10%
15	ENS.PR.A	**E SPLIT CORP**	10.19	5.10%
23	ECF.UN	**EAST COAST INVESTME**	9.20	5.20%
21	ERM	**ECLIPSE RESIDENTIAL M**	9.34	8%
17	ECN.PR.A	**ECN CAPITAL CORP**	21.95	7.40%
17	ECN.PR.A	**ECN CAPITAL CORP**	21.19	7.30%
28	ELF.PR.H	**E-L FINANCIAL COPR LT**	24.99	5.50%
28	ELF.PR.F	**E-L FINANCIAL COPR LT**	24.08	5.50%
28	ELF.PR.G	**E-L FINANCIAL COPR LT**	22.07	5.40%

33	EFN.PR.A	**ELEMENT FLEET MANAG**	21.57	8%
27	EFN.PR.E	**ELEMENT FLEET MANAG**	19.88	7.90%
30	EFN.PR.C	**ELEMENT FLEET MANAG**	20.4	7.90%
28	EFN.PR.G	**ELEMENT FLEET MANAG**	21.66	7.50%
17	EFN.PR.I	**ELEMENT FLEET MANAG**	20.1	7.10%
28	ELC	**ELYSEE DEVELOPMENT**	0.38	11%
24	EMA.PR.C	**EMERA INC**	20.2	5.80%
24	EMA.PR.F	**EMERA INC**	18.84	5.60%
28	EMA.PR.E	**EMERA INC**	20.48	5.50%
15	EMA.PR.B	**EMERA INC**	15.5	5.30%
17	EMA.PR.H	**EMERA INC**	23.70	5.20%
65	EMA	**EMERA INC**	50.31	4.70%
23	EMA.PR.A	**EMERA INC**	15.45	4.10%
30	ENB.PR.V	**ENBRIDGE INC**	29.02	6.90%
24	ENB.PR.H	**ENBRIDGE INC**	16.15	6.80%
27	ENB.PF.V	**ENBRIDGE INC**	26.94	6.70%
26	ENB.PF.N	**ENBRIDGE INC**	19.01	6.70%
27	ENB.PR.F	**ENBRIDGE INC**	17.61	6.70%
24	ENB.PR.D	**ENBRIDGE INC**	16.72	6.60%
24	ENB.PR.P	**ENBRIDGE INC**	16.95	6.50%
16	ENB.PR.C	**ENBRIDGE INC**	15.85	6.50%
28	ENB.PF.C	**ENBRIDGE INC**	17	6.40%
24	ENB.PR.J	**ENBRIDGE INC**	17.18	6.40%
24	ENB.PF.G	**ENBRIDGE INC**	17.15	6.40%
24	ENB.PF.A	**ENBRIDGE INC**	17.07	6.40%
24	ENB.PF.E	**ENBRIDGE INC**	17.15	6.40%
22	ENB.PR.Y	**ENBRIDGE INC**	15.71	6.40%
27	ENB.PF.U	**ENBRIDGE INC**	26.08	6.30%
27	ENB.PR.U	**ENBRIDGE INC**	26.23	6.30%
28	ENB.PR.T	**ENBRIDGE INC**	16.26	6.10%
60	ENB	**ENBRIDGE INC**	49.4	6.00%

28	ENB.PR.A	**ENBRIDGE INC**	24.69	5.60%
23	ENB.PR.B	**ENBRIDGE INC**	15.35	5.50%
17	ENB.PF.K	**ENBRIDGE INC**	22.89	5.30%
17	ENB.PR.I	**ENBRIDGE INC**	25.12	5.10%
26	ENI.UN	**ENERGY INCOME FUND**	1.82	6.60%
57	ESI	**ENSIGN ENERGY SERVIC**	5.33	9%
28	EQB.PR.C	**EQUTABLE GROUP INC**	24.74	6.40%
31	ERE.UN	**EUROPEAN RESID. REIT**	4.43	8%
49	ET	**EVERTZ TECHNOLOGIES**	17.00	4.20%
61	EIF	**EXCHANGE INCOME CO**	35.39	6.20%
42	XTC	**EXCO TECHNOLOGIES L**	8.93	4.00%
32	EXE	**EXTENDICARE INC**	7.94	5.90%
16	FFH.PR.H	**FAIRFAX FINANCIAL HO**	15.8	6.50%
24	FFH.PR.D	**FAIRFAX FINANCIAL HO**	18.1	6.50%
16	FFH.PR.J	**FAIRFAX FINANCIAL HO**	17.2	6.50%
25	FFH.PR.F	**FAIRFAX FINANCIAL HO**	14.69	6.30%
24	FFH.PR.C	**FAIRFAX FINANCIAL HO**	18.37	6.30%
24	FFH.PR.K	**FAIRFAX FINANCIAL HO**	19.33	5.90%
23	FFH.PR.I	**FAIRFAX FINANCIAL HO**	16.55	5.60%
23	FFH.PR.G	**FAIRFAX FINANCIAL HO**	15.49	5.40%
25	FFH.PR.M	**FAIRFAX FINANCIAL HO**	22.50	5.20%
22	FFH.PR.E	**FAIRFAX FINANCIAL HO**	14.20	5.10%
36	FSZ	**FIERA CAPITAL CORP**	12.33	6.80%
30	FTN	**FINANCIAL 15 SPLIT COR**	7.69	19%
23	FTN.PR.A	**FINANCIAL 15 SPLIT COR**	9.9	5.60%

40	FDI	**FINDEV INC**	0.46	6.50%
45	FCA	**FIRM CAPITAL AMERICA**	7.07	4.40%
50	FCA.U	**FIRM CAPITAL AMERICA**	9.40	4.40%
51	FC	**FIRM CAPITAL MORTGA**	13.48	7%
59	FCD	**FIRM CAPITAL PROPER**	6.31	7.50%
65	FCR	**FIRST CAPITAL REALTY**	21.48	4.00%
15	FN.PR.B	**FIRST NATIONAL FINAN**	13.68	6.80%
52	FN	**FIRST NATIONAL FINAN**	29.55	6.20%
24	FN.PR.A	**FIRST NATIONAL FINAN**	13.25	5.30%
30	FEC	**FONTERA ENERGY CORP**	11.93	4.10%
24	FTS.PR.G	**FORTIS INC**	19.10	5.80%
24	FTS.PR.K	**FORTIS INC**	17.67	5.50%
25	FTS.PR.J	**FORTIS INC**	21.93	5.50%
28	FTS.PR.F	**FORTIS INC**	22.65	5.40%
24	FTS.PR.M	**FORTIS INC**	19.18	5.30%
22	FTS.PR.I	**FORTIS INC**	14.3	5.30%
22	FTS.PR.H	**FORTIS INC**	14.51	4.30%
70	FTS	**FORTIS INC**	49.63	3.60%
43	FRU	**FREEHOLD ROYALTIES**	8.73	7.20%
32	FRO.UN	**FRONSAC REAL ESTATE**	0.62	3.60%
39	GH	**GAMEHOST INC**	9.92	6.90%
72	MIC	**GENWORTH MI CANADA I**	41.99	4.90%
29	WN.PR.A	**GEORGE WESTON LTD**	25.6	5.70%
28	WN.PR.D	**GEORGE WESTON LTD**	24.27	5.40%
28	WN.PR.C	**GEORGE WESTON LTD**	24.13	5.40%
29	WN.PR.E	**GEORGE WESTON LTD**	22.68	5.20%
47	GEI	**GIBSON ENERGY INC**	21.7	6.10%
9	GDV	**GLOBAL DIVIDEND GRO**	10.8	11%

15	GDV.PR.A	**GLOBAL DIVIDEND GRO**	10.23	4.90%
17	GRP.PR.A	**GLOBAL RESOURCE CHA**	25.49	6.10%
43	GS	**GLUSKIN SHEFF & ASSO**	14.46	6.90%
17	GMP.PR.C	**GMP CAPITAL INC**	11.15	10%
23	GMP.PR.B	**GMP CAPITAL INC**	11	8.56%
27	GMP	**GMP CAPITAL INC**	2.03	5.00%
22	GMN	**GOBIMI INC**	0.35	4.20%
41	GXO	**GRANITE OIL CORP**	0.92	13%
69	GRT.UN	**GRANITE REAL ESTATE I**	60.93	4.60%
29	GWO.PR.F	**GREAT-WEST LIFECO IN**	25.56	5.80%
20	GWO.PR.M	**GREAT-WEST LIFECO IN**	25.44	5.70%
33	GWO.PR.L	**GREAT-WEST LIFECO IN**	25.35	5.60%
28	GWO.PR.H	**GREAT-WEST LIFECO IN**	22.41	5.40%
28	GWO.PR.T	**GREAT-WEST LIFECO IN**	23.98	5.40%
28	GWO.PR.Q	**GREAT-WEST LIFECO IN**	23.97	5.40%
28	GWO.PR.G	**GREAT-WEST LIFECO IN**	24.16	5.40%
28	GWO.PR.P	**GREAT-WEST LIFECO IN**	24.97	5.40%
28	GWO.PR.R	**GREAT-WEST LIFECO IN**	22.50	5.30%
28	GWO.PR.S	**GREAT-WEST LIFECO IN**	24.73	5.30%
25	GWO.PR.I	**GREAT-WEST LIFECO IN**	21.13	5.30%
52	GWO	**GREAT-WEST LIFECO IN**	32.14	5.20%
15	GWO.PR.O	**GREAT-WEST LIFECO IN**	14.78	5.00%
20	GWO.PR.N	**GREAT-WEST LIFECO IN**	14.79	3.70%
61	HR.UN	**H&R REIT**	22.95	6.10%

46	HPS.A	**HAMMOND POWER SOLU**	7.70	3.60%
7	HFC	**HAMPTON FINANCIAL C**	0.2	400%
8	HFC.PR.A	**HAMPTON FINANCIAL C**	5.5	15%
41	HWO	**HIGH ARTIC ENERGY SE**	3.85	5.10%
44	HLF	**HIGH LINER FOODS INC**	7.8	7.40%
15	HSE.PR.B	**HUSKY ENERGY INC**	13.15	6.40%
24	HSE.PR.C	**HUSKY ENERGY INC**	18.96	6.00%
9	HSE.PR.G	**HUSKY ENERGY INC**	20.00	5.60%
24	HSE.PR.E	**HUSKY ENERGY INC**	20.7	5.50%
22	HSE.PR.A	**HUSKY ENERGY INC**	12.55	4.80%
34	H	**HYDRO ONE LTD**	21.75	4.20%
17	IAF.PR.I	**IA FINANCIAL CORP**	22.7	5.30%
28	IAF.PR.B	**IA FINANCIAL CORP**	22.10	5.20%
26	IAF.PR.G	**IA FINANCIAL CORP**	21.64	4.40%
50	IGM	**IGM FINANCIAL INC**	35.81	6.10%
57	IGM.PR.B	**IGM FINANCIAL INC**	24.99	5.90%
44	ISV	**INFORMATION SERVICES**	16.26	4.90%
32	INE.PR.C	**INNERGEX RENEWABLE**	22.82	6.30%
22	INE.PR.A	**INNERGEX RENEWABLE**	14.45	6.20%
48	INE	**INNERGEX RENEWABLE**	14.20	5.00%
65	INO.UN	**INOVALIS REIT**	10.33	8%
27	INP	**INPUT CAPITAL CORP**	0.69	5.70%
17	IFC.PR.G	**INTACT FINANCIAL COR**	20.56	6.00%
16	IFC.PR.D	**INTACT FINANCIAL COR**	18.43	5.80%
17	IFC.PR.F	**INTACT FINANCIAL COR**	24.49	5.40%
17	IFC.PR.E	**INTACT FINANCIAL COR**	24	5.40%
23	IFC.PR.A	**INTACT FINANCIAL COR**	15.8	5.40%

24	IFC.PR.C	INTACT FINANCIAL COR	18.40	4.50%
38	IAM	INTEGRATED ASSET MA	2.62	4.60%
62	IPL	INTER PIPELINE LTD	21.29	8.10%
46	ITP	INTERTAPE POLYMER G	18.13	4.10%
53	IVQ.U	INVESQUE INC	9.4	11%
22	IFB.UN	INVESTMENT GRADE INF	8.11	6.20%
20	ICL	ITASCA CAPITAL CORP	0.32	245%
22	JE	JUST ENERGY GROUP IN	4.94	10%
19	JE.PR.U	JUST ENERGY GROUP IN	29.23	9.80%
54	KEY	KEYERA COPR	30.6	5.90%
56	KMP.UN	KILLAM APART REIT	18.81	3.50%
17	KML.PR.C	KINDER MORGAN CANADA	23.67	5.50%
17	KML.PR.A	KINDER MORGAN CAN	23.83	5.50%
40	KML	KINDER MORGAN CAN	14.97	4.30%
35	KPT	KP INC	7.9	9%
24	LB.PR.H	LAURENTIAN BANK OF C	16.76	6.40%
63	LB	LAURENTIAN BANK OF C	42.78	6.10%
17	LB.PR.J	LAURENTIAN BANK OF C	25.79	5.70%
46	LNF	LEON'S FUNITURE LTD	14.22	3.90%
14	LBS	LIFE & BANC SPLIT CO	8.13	15%
26	LBS.PR.A	LIFE & BANC SPLIT COR	10.09	5.40%
28	L.PR.B	LOBLAWS COMPANIES L	24.94	5.30%
38	LUC	LUCARA DIAMOND COPR	1.61	6.30%
22	XMF.PR.C	M SPLIT CORP	5.23	7.30%
31	MKZ.UN	MACKENZIE MASTER LP	0.95	14%
24	MFC.PR.K	MANULIFE FINANCIAL C	19.16	5.80%

16	MFC.PR.Q	MANULIFE FINANCIAL C	20.70	5.70%
24	MFC.PR.J	MANULIFE FINANCIAL C	20.69	5.60%
24	MFC.PR.L	MANULIFE FINANCIAL C	17.62	5.60%
17	MFC.PR.O	MANULIFE FINANCIAL C	26.15	5.40%
28	MFC.PR.C	MANULIFE FINANCIAL C	21.01	5.30%
28	MFC.PR.B	MANULIFE FINANCIAL C	21.9	5.30%
24	MFC.PR.M	MANULIFE FINANCIAL C	18.47	5.30%
24	MFC.PR.N	MANULIFE FINANCIAL C	18.21	5.20%
24	MFC.PR.I	MANULIFE FINANCIAL C	21.21	5.10%
15	MFC.PR.B	MANULIFE FINANCIAL C	14.28	5.00%
17	MFC.PR.R	MANULIFE FINANCIAL C	25.12	4.80%
24	MFC.PR.H	MANULIFE FINANCIAL C	22.43	4.80%
33	MFC.PR.G	MANULIFE FINANCIAL C	20.74	4.70%
67	MFC	MANULIFE FINANCIAL C	24.64	4.00%
20	MFC.PR.F	MANULIFE FINANCIAL C	14.32	3.70%
22	MFR.UN	MANULIFE FLOATING R	7.63	9%
26	MBK.UN	MANULIFE US REGIONAL	11.57	4.30%
55	MBN	MBN CORP	6.65	4.80%
52	MKP	MCCAN MORTGAGE COR	15.76	8.1
23	MCS	MCCHIP RESOURCES INC	0.66	9%
40	MDF	MEDIAGRIF INTERACTI	10.09	4.00%
44	DR	MEDICAL FACILITIES CO	15.69	7%

51	MRD	MELCOR DEVELOPMENT	13.58	3.80%
47	MR.UN	MELCOR REAL ESTATE I	7.6	9%
43	RCO.UN	MIDDLEFIELD CAN GLO	12.25	5.30%
28	MID.UN	MINT INCOME FUND	6.66	7.20%
64	MRG.UN	MORGUARD NORTH AME	17.80	3.80%
58	MRT.UN	MORGUARD REAL ESTAT	12.3	7.80%
42	M	MOSAIC CAPITAL CORP	5.72	7.20%
35	MPVD	MOUNTAIN PROVINCE DI	1.42	11%
36	MTL	MULLEN GROUP LTD	9.75	6.10%
16	NA.PR.E	NATIONAL BANK OF CAN	20.35	5.70%
17	NA.PR.G	NATIONAL BANK OF CAN	21.85	5.70%
24	NA.PR.W	NATIONAL BANK OF CAN	17.61	5.50%
25	NA.PR.S	NATIONAL BANK OF CAN	18.51	5.50%
17	NA.PR.X	NATIONAL BANK OF CAN	26.04	5.40%
18	NA.PR.A	NATIONAL BANK OF CAN	25.85	5.20%
17	NA.PR.C	NATIONAL BANK OF CAN	22.65	4.90%
64	NA	NATIONAL BANK OF CAN	63.77	4.10%
28	NEW.PR.D	NEWGROWTH CORP	32.17	4.10%
41	NEXA	NEXA RESOURCES SA	13.83	4.90%
64	NXR.UN	NEXUS REAL ESTATE INV	2.01	8%
58	NFI	NFI GROUP INC	32.94	4.60%
45	OSB	NORBORD INC	33.52	4.70%
25	FFN.PR.A	NORTH AMERICAN FINA	10.04	5.50%
30	FFN	NORTH AMERICAN FINAN	6.56	18%

26	NPF.UN	**NORTH AMERICAN PREFE**	18.8	7.30%
16	NPI.PR.B	**NORTHLAND POWER INC**	16	6.80%
24	NPI.PR.C	**NORTHLAND POWER INC**	19.85	6.40%
26	NPI.PR.A	**NORTHLAND POWER INC**	15.85	5.50%
64	NPI	**NORTHLAND POWER INC**	23.83	5.00%
62	NVU.UN	**NORTHVIEW APAR. REIT**	28.26	5.80%
47	NWH.UN	**NORTHWEST HEALT REIT**	11.45	7%
48	OLY	**OLYMPIA FINANCIAL COR**	55.50	5.00%
26	PAR.UN	**PARTNERS REIT**	1.7	11%
16	PVF.PR.U	**PARTNERS VALUE INVESTMENTS LP**	26.19	5.80%
17	PVS.PR.E	**PARTNERS VALUE SPLIT C**	25.75	5.30%
28	PVS.PR.D	**PARTNERS VALUE SPLIT C**	25.58	4.40%
45	PSI	**PASON SYSTEMS INC**	20.48	3.50%
21	PCD.UN	**PATHFINDER INCOME FUN**	7.96	7.50%
44	PEGI	**PATTERN ENERGY GROUP**	30.93	7.30%
25	PPL.PR.A	**PEMBINA PIPELINE CORP**	17.59	7%
25	PPL.PR.E	**PEMBINA PIPELINE CORP**	18.77	6.70%
24	PPL.PR.C	**PEMBINA PIPELINE CORP**	17.42	6.40%
24	PPL.PR.G	**PEMBINA PIPELINE CORP**	17.76	6.30%
24	PPL.PR.O	**PEMBINA PIPELINE CORP**	17.75	6.30%
24	PPL.PR.Q	**PEMBINA PIPELINE CORP**	19.38	6.20%
25	PPL.PR.I	**PEMBINA PIPELINE CORP**	21.32	5.60%

17	PPL.PR.K	**PEMBINA PIPELINE CORP**	25.92	5.60%
17	PPL.PR.M	**PEMBINA PIPELINE CORP**	25.88	5.50%
18	PPL.PF.A	**PEMBINA PIPELINE CORP**	22.89	5.40%
26	PPL.PR.S	**PEMBINA PIPELINE CORP**	23.55	5.30%
67	PPL	**PEMBINA PIPELINE CORP**	47.53	5.10%
59	PEY	**PEYTO EXPLORATION & D**	5.82	4.20%
8	PT	**PINE TRAIL REIT**	0.13	6%
27	PL	**PINNACLE RENEWABLE EN**	12.12	5.20%
15	PTG	**PIVOT TECHNOLOGY SOLU**	1.28	13%
57	PZA	**PIZZA PIZZA ROYALTY C**	10.35	8.70%
49	PLZ.UN	**PLAZA RETAIL REIT**	4.13	6.70%
62	PIF	**POLARIS INFASTRUCTURE**	11.79	6.90%
29	POW.PR.C	**POWER CORPORATION OF**	25.55	5.70%
28	POW.PR.A	**POWER CORPORATION OF**	25.09	5.60%
28	POW.PR.D	**POWER CORPORATION OF**	22.65	5.50%
28	POW.PR.B	**POWER CORPORATION OF**	24.35	5.50%
29	POW.PR.G	**POWER CORPORATION OF**	25.5	5.50%
62	POW	**POWER CORPORATION OF**	30.40	5.00%
29	PWF.PR.I	**POWER FINANCIAL CORP**	25.8	5.80%
29	PWF.PR.G	**POWER FINANCIAL CORP**	25.50	5.80%
28	PWF.PR.O	**POWER FINANCIAL CORP**	25.53	5.70%
29	PWF.PR.H	**POWER FINANCIAL CORP**	25.47	5.60%

59	PWF	**POWER FINANCIAL CORP**	31.27	5.60%
28	PWF.PR.T	**POWER FINANCIAL CORP**	18.86	5.50%
28	PWF.PR.F	**POWER FINANCIAL CORP**	24.03	5.50%
28	PWF.PR.E	**POWER FINANCIAL CORP**	25.34	5.50%
27	PWF.PR.K	**POWER FINANCIAL CORP**	22.7	5.50%
17	PWF.PR.Z	**POWER FINANCIAL CORP**	23.62	5.40%
28	PWF.PR.L	**POWER FINANCIAL CORP**	23.48	5.40%
28	PWF.PR.S	**POWER FINANCIAL CORP**	22.11	5.40%
28	PWF.PR.R	**POWER FINANCIAL CORP**	25.65	5.40%
15	PWF.PR.Q	**POWER FINANCIAL CORP**	14.58	5.10%
22	PWF.PR.A	**POWER FINANCIAL CORP**	13.60	5.00%
23	PWF.PR.P	**POWER FINANCIAL CORP**	14.17	4.10%
47	PSK	**PRAIRIESKY ROYALTY L**	18.75	4.20%
19	MMP.UN	**PRECIOUS METALS AND MI**	1.33	9.20%
41	PIC.A	**PREMIUM INCOME CORP**	6.77	12%
25	PIC.PR.A	**PREMIUM INCOME CORP**	14.64	5.90%
18	PDV	**PRIME DIVIDEND CORP**	7.15	9.50%
25	PDV.PR.A	**PRIME DIVIDEND CORP**	10.2	6.10%
62	PRV.UN	**PRO REIT**	2.3	9%
60	RUF.U	**PURE MULTI-FAMILY REIT**	8.96	5.70%
28	RZE	**RAZOR ENERGY CORP**	2.71	5.40%
9	RE	**RE ROYALTIES LTD**	0.9	5.90%
36	RET	**REITMANS (CANADA) LTD**	3.21	6.10%

35	RET.A	**REITMANS (CANADA) LTD**	3.27	6.10%
64	REI.UN	**RIOCAN REIT**	25.96	5.60%
48	RME	**ROCKY MOUNTAIN DEAL**	8.73	5.60%
40	RSI	**ROGERS SUGAR INC**	5.93	6.10%
18	RY.PR.S	**ROYAL BANK OF CANADA**	21.6	5.60%
26	RY.PR.Z	**ROYAL BANK OF CANADA**	18.48	5.50%
18	RY.PR.Q	**ROYAL BANK OF CANADA**	25.92	5.30%
17	RY.PR.R	**ROYAL BANK OF CANADA**	26.05	5.30%
24	RY.PR.H	**ROYAL BANK OF CANADA**	18.80	5.20%
17	RY.PR.P	**ROYAL BANK OF CANADA**	25.25	5.20%
28	RY.PR.UN	**ROYAL BANK OF CANADA**	24.00	5.10%
15	RY.PR.O	**ROYAL BANK OF CANADA**	24.10	5.10%
28	RY.PR.W	**ROYAL BANK OF CANADA**	25.05	4.90%
28	RY.PR.C	**ROYAL BANK OF CANADA**	25.18	4.60%
24	BMO.PR.Y	**ROYAL BANK OF CANADA**	21.11	4.50%
27	RY.PR.E	**ROYAL BANK OF CANADA**	25.23	4.50%
26	RY.PR.G	**ROYAL BANK OF CANADA**	25.20	4.50%
26	RY.PR.F	**ROYAL BANK OF CANADA**	25.16	4.40%
24	RY.PR.A	**ROYAL BANK OF CANADA**	25.16	4.40%
24	RY.PR.M	**ROYAL BANK OF CANADA**	20.30	4.40%
16	RY.PR.J	**ROYAL BANK OF CANADA**	20.76	4.30%
76	RY	**ROYAL BANK OF CANADA**	107.00	3.80%
49	RUS	**RUSSEL METALS INC**	23.29	6.60%

25	SBN.PR.A	S SPLIT CORP	10.35	5.10%
37	SES	SECURE ENERGY SERVIC	7.56	3.60%
15	SJR.PR.B	SHAW COMMUNICATIONS	14.75	6.00%
23	SJR.PR.A	SHAW COMMUNICATIONS	14.40	4.90%
56	SJR.B	SHAW COMMUNICATIONS	27.12	4.40%
38	SJR.A	SHAW COMMUNICATIONS	28.80	4.20%
47	SIA	SIENNA SENIOR LIVING CO	18.52	5.00%
43	SRV.UN	SIR ROYALTY INCOME FU	16.36	7.70%
57	SOT.UN	SLATE OFFICE REIT	5.96	6.90%
25	SRT.U	SLATE RETAIL REIT	12.43	9%
50	SRT.UN	SLATE RETAIL REIT	12.44	9%
35	ZZZ	SLEEP COUNTRY CANADA	17.56	4.20%
59	SRU.UN	SMARTCENTRES REIT	33.76	5.30%
63	SNI.PR.A	SONOR INVESTMENTS LTD	8	9%
22	BSD.PR.A	SOUNDVEST SPLIT TRUST	9.52	6.30%
39	SPS.A	SPORTSCENE GROUP INC	6.80	4.60%
37	SIL	SPROTT INC	3.00	4.00%
14	STUS.U	STARLIGHT US MULTI-FA	12.17	7.20%
32	STUS.A	STARLIGHT US MULTI-FA	9.3	7%
27	RAY.A	STINGRAY GROUP INC	6.47	4.10%
19	RAY.B	STINGRAY GROUP INC	6.50	4.00%
34	SOX	STUART OLSON INC	4.50	5.30%
54	SMU.UN	SUMMIT INDUSTRIAL INC	12.05	4.30%
16	SLF.PR.K	SUN LIFE FINANCIAL INC	17.56	5.40%
28	SLF.PR.E	SUN LIFE FINANCIAL INC	21.10	5.30%

31	SLF.PR.A	SUN LIFE FINANCIAL INC	22.2	5.30%
28	SLF.PR.B	SUN LIFE FINANCIAL INC	22.65	5.30%
28	SLF.PR.C	SUN LIFE FINANCIAL INC	21.00	5.30%
28	SLF.PR.D	SUN LIFE FINANCIAL INC	21.00	5.30%
15	SLF.PR.J	SUN LIFE FINANCIAL INC	15.00	5.10%
24	SLF.PR.I	SUN LIFE FINANCIAL INC	20.63	4.60%
24	SLF.PR.H	SUN LIFE FINANCIAL INC	17.80	4.00%
20	SLF.PR.G	SUN LIFE FINANCIAL INC	15.00	3.80%
68	SLF	SUN LIFE FINANCIAL INC	55.41	3.60%
71	SU	SUNCOR ENERGY INC	43.11	3.90%
49	SPB	SUPERIOR PLUS CORP	11.42	6.30%
33	SXP	SUPREMEX INC	3.07	9%
47	SGY	SURGE ENERGY INC	1.39	7.10%
33	SWP	SWISS WATER DECAF COF	5.54	4.40%
28	XTD	TDB SPLIT CORP	6.29	9.60%
24	XTD.PR.A	TDB SPLIT CORP	10.06	5.20%
68	T	TELUS CORP	49.45	4.40%
40	EML.PR.A	THE EMPIRE LIFE INSUR	25.89	5.60%
49	KEG.UN	THE KEG ROYALTIES INC	17.49	6.50%
50	NWC	THE NORTH WEST CO INC	29.15	4.50%
17	TD.PF.J	THE TORONTO-DOM BANK	21.75	5.40%
24	TD.PF.A	THE TORONTO-DOM BANK	18.40	5.30%
32	TD.PF.G	THE TORONTO-DOM BANK	26.04	5.30%
25	TD.PF.B	THE TORONTO-DOM BANK	18.40	5.20%

17	TD.PF.F	THE TORONTO-DOM BANK	24.06	5.10%
24	TD.PF.C	THE TORONTO-DOM BANK	18.41	5.10%
17	TD.PF.I	THE TORONTO-DOM BANK	23.17	4.80%
17	TD.PF.H	THE TORONTO-DOM BANK	25.74	4.70%
18	TD.PF.D	THE TORONTO-DOM BANK	21.02	4.30%
24	TD.PF.E	THE TORONTO-DOM BANK	21.60	4.30%
74	TD	THE TORONTO-DOM BANK	76.38	3.90%
21	TRI.PR.B	THOMSON REUTERS CORP	13.08	5.10%
44	TF	TIMBERCREEK FINANCIAL	9.48	7.40%
20	TXT.UN	TOP 10 SPLIT TRUST	3.29	9%
49	TXT.PR.A	TOP 10 SPLIT TRUST	12.43	6.30%
47	TOG	TORC OIL & GAS LTD	4.66	5.70%
24	TS.B	TORSTAR CORP	0.73	14%
26	TA.PR.H	TRANSALTA CORP	18.5	7.10%
15	TA.PR.E	TRANSALTA CORP	13.02	7%
26	TA.PR.J	TRANSALTA CORP	19.11	6.90%
25	TA.PR.F	TRANSALTA CORP	15.83	6.40%
24	TA.PR.D	TRANSALTA CORP	12.28	5.60%
52	RNW	TRANSALTA RENEWABLES	13.89	6.80%
24	TRP.PR.E	TRANSCANADA CORP	16.75	6.30%
22	TRP.PR.F	TRANSCANADA CORP	14.86	6.10%
22	TRP.PR.H	TRANSCANADA CORP	12.32	6.00%
15	TRP.PR.I	TRANSCANADA CORP	13.83	5.70%
23	TRP.PR.D	TRANSCANADA CORP	17.03	5.70%
22	TRP.PR.A	TRANSCANADA CORP	15.10	5.40%
17	TRP.PR.J	TRANSCANADA CORP	26.07	5.30%
24	TRP.PR.G	TRANSCANADA CORP	19.21	5.00%
18	TRP.PR.K	TRANSCANADA CORP	25.51	4.80%

75	TRP	**TRANSCANADA CORP**	63.07	4.80%
21	TRP.PR.B	**TRANSCANADA CORP**	12.35	4.30%
22	TRP.PR.C	**TRANSCANADA CORP**	13.13	4.30%
47	TCL.B	**TRANSCONTINENTAL INC**	15.77	5.60%
46	TCL.A	**TRANSCONTINENTAL INC**	15.71	5.60%
51	TGL	**TRANSGLOBE ENERGY CO**	2.5	7.40%
21	TSL	**TREE ISLAND STEEL LTD**	2.06	3.90%
56	TNT.UN	**TRUE NORTH COM. REIT**	6.63	9%
20	FTU.PR.B	**US FINANCIAL 15 SPLIT CO**	7.89	10%
19	USF.UN	**US FINANCIALS INCOME F**	7.23	6.90%
30	VNR.PR.A	**VALENER INC**	25.00	4.60%
54	VNR	**VALENER INC**	26.12	4.60%
66	VET	**VERMILLION ENERGY INC**	32.03	9%
25	VB.PR.A	**VERSABANK**	10.1	6.90%
24	VB.PR.B	**VERSABANK**	10.22	6.50%
46	WJX	**WAJAX CORP**	15.82	6.40%
44	WFC	**WALL FINANCIAL CORP**	24.50	4.10%
20	WBE	**WESTBOND ENTERPRISED**	0.18	5.70%
17	W.PR.K	**WESTCOAST ENERGY IN**	25.60	5.10%
18	W.PR.N	**WESTCOAST ENERGY IN**	25.73	5.00%
38	WEF	**WESTERN FOREST PROD**	1.80	5.00%
50	WCP	**WHITRCAP RESOURCES I**	5.11	6.70%
23	WFS.PR.A	**WORLD FINANCIAL SPLIT**	9.95	5.30%
57	WIR.U	**WPT INDUSTRIAL REAL ES**	18.59	5.40%

CHAPTER 15

The 654 By Dividend Percent

(Data Extracted May 6, 2019)

Following are the 654 stocks that paid a dividend of 3.5% or more on the Toronto Stock Exchange. In this chapter the sort is in descending order by the annual **dividend** percent, which is the dividend amount paid, calculated as a percentage of the company's common share price.

In the final Chapter, that follows, you will find the same information sorted in descending order by the company's share price. The four sorts of the 654 stocks will help you find the 20 stocks that you would want to add to your portfolio.

Before you make a decision on buying a stock based on the sorting of this data be sure to recalculate the score. Dividend percentages and the scores can change daily with fluctuations in stock prices and volume of shares being traded.

A high dividend does not make a desirable stock, as you can see by the first stock on this list. Hampton Financial Corp's score is 7 even though their dividend percentage is the highest of the 654 stocks. This is the lowest score I have ever encountered.

The highest score is a bank scoring 76. You will see banks towards the bottom of this list. They do not pay the highest dividends. You need more than banks to give you a steady dividend income of 6% of the value of your portfolio. The objective is not only good income but also a portfolio that never stops growing.

The first company in this sort that has a score over 50 is IVQ.U. It is paying a dividend of 11%.

The lateral order of this display is: (1) SCORE (2) STOCK SYMBOL (3) COMPANY NAME (4) STOCK PRICE (5) DIVIDEND %

7	HFC	HAMPTON FINANCIAL CO	0.2	400%
20	ICL	ITASCA CAPITAL CORP	0.32	245%
8	CBL	CALLIDUS CAPITAL CORP	0.67	185%
10	OSP	BROMPTON OIL SPLIT COR	2.85	42%
15	DF	DIVIDEND 15 SPLIT	5.14	23%
16	DGS	DIVIDEND GROWTH SPLIT	5.38	22%
30	FTN	FINANCIAL 15 SPLIT CORP	7.69	19%
30	FFN	NORTH AMERICAN FIN S	6.56	18%
18	SAT	ASIAN TELEVISION NET	0.11	18%
12	LCS	BROMPTON LIFECO SPLIT	4.8	18%
38	AFCC	AUTOMOTIVE FINCO CO	1.34	16%
16	BSO.UN	BROOKFIELD SLECT OP	3.87	15%
14	LBS	LIFE & BANC SPLIT CORP	8.13	15%
8	HFC.PR.A	HAMPTON FINANCIAL C	8.54	14%
36	CHE.UN	CHEMTRADE LOGISTICS	8.54	14%
24	TS.B	TORSTAR CORP	0.73	14%

16	BSO.UN	BROOKFIELD SELECT OPP. IN	3.87	**15%**
14	LBS	LIFE & BANC SPLIT CORP	8.13	**15%**
8	HFC.PR.A		5.5	**15%**
21	DFN	DIVIDEND 15 SPLIT CORP	8.66	**14%**
31	MKZ.UN	MACKENZIE MASTER LP	0.95	**14%**
17	DC.PR.E	DUNDEE CORP	13.99	**14%**
41	GXO	GRANITE OIL CORP	0.92	**13%**
12	CCI.UN	CANADIAN CONVERTIBLES P	4.97	**13%**
15	PTG	PIVOT TECHNOLOGY SOL. INC	1.28	**13%**
28	HOT.U	AMERICAN HOTEL INCOME P	6.91	**12%**
38	HOT.UN	AMERICAN HOTEL INC REIT	6.89	**12%**
41	PIC.A	PREMIUM INCOME CORP	6.77	**12%**
41	DII.B	DOREL INDUSTRIES INC	11.77	**12%**
36	CWX	CANWEL BUILDING MATER	4.81	**11%**
35	MPVD	MOUNTAIN PROVINCE DIAM	1.42	**11%**
17	DC.PR.D	DUNDEE CORP	12.57	**11%**
28	AKT.A	AKITA DRILLING LTD	2.98	**11%**
17	DC.PR.B	DUNDEE CORP	12.6	**11%**
9	GDV	GLOBAL DIVIDEND GROWTH	10.8	**11%**
26	PAR.UN	PARTNERS RE INVESTMENT T	1.7	**11%**
39	DII.A	DOREL INDUSTRIES INC	12.51	**11%**
53	IVQ.U	INVESQUE INC	9.4	**11%**

25	EIT.UN	CANOE EIT INCOME FUND	11.38	11%
28	ELC	ELYSEE DEVELOPMENT CORP	0.38	11%
18	ENS	E SPLIT CORP	14.75	10%
20	FTU.PR.B	US FINANCIAL 15 SPLIT CORP	7.89	10%
17	GMP.PR.C	GMP CAPITAL INC	11.15	10%
22	JE	JUST ENERGY GROUP INC	4.94	10%
17	PRM	BIG PHARMA SPLIT CORP	12.2	10%
34	FAP	ABERDEEN ASIA-PACIFIC INC	3.83	10%
23	DS	DIVIDEND SELECT 15 CORP	7.44	9.80%
19	JE.PR.U	JUST ENERGY GROUP INC	29.23	9.80%
33	KWH.UN	CIRUS ENERGY TRUST	8.69	9.60%
28	XTD	TDB SPLIT CORP	6.29	9.60%
16	BK	CANADIAN BANC CORP	11.32	9.50%
18	PDV	PRIME DIVIDEND CORP	7.15	9.50%
19	MMP.UN	PRECIOUS METALS AND MINI	1.33	9.20%
25	SRT.U	SLATE RETAIL REIT	12.43	9%
50	SRT.UN	SLATE RETAIL REIT	12.44	9%
62	PRV.UN	PRO REAL ESTATE INVESTMENT TR	2.3	9%
58	AD	ALARIS ROYALTY CORP	18.07	9%
23	MCS	MCCHIP RESOURCES INC	0.66	9%
36	SBC	BROMPTON SPLIT BANC CORP	12.37	9%
26	BGI.UN	BROOKFIELD GLOBAL INFA. S	6.72	9%
57	ESI	ENSIGN ENERGY SERVICES I	5.33	9%
35	KPT	KP TISSUE INC	7.9	9%
56	TNT.UN	TRUE NORTH COMMERCIALREIT	6.63	9%
22	MFR.UN	MANULIFE FLTING RATE SENI	7.63	9%
21	BBD.PR.B	BOMBARDIER INC	11.3	9%
47	MR.UN	MELCOR REIT	7.6	9%

30	DE	DECISIVE DIVIDEND CORP	4	**9%**
54	BTB.UN	BTB REIT	4.85	**9%**
29	BBD.PR.D	BOMBARDIER INC	11.57	**9%**
63	SNI.PR.A	SONOR INVESTMENTS LTD	8	**9%**
66	VET	VERMILLION ENERGY INC	32.03	**9%**
25	AKT.B	AKITA DRILLING LTD	4	**9%**
33	SXP	SUPREMEX INC	3.07	**9%**
20	TXT.UN	TOP 10 SPLIT TRUST	3.29	**9%**
57	PZA	PIZZA PIZZA ROYALTY CORP	10.35	**8.70%**
43	CHW	CHESSWOOD GROUP LTD	10.2	**8.56%**
23	GMP.PR.B	GMP CAPITAL INC	11	**8.56%**
32	BIR.PR.A	BIRCHCLIFF ENERGY LTD	25.42	**8.20%**
46	BRE	BROOKFIELD REAL ESTATE S	16.9	**8.10%**
52	MKP	MCCAN MORTGAGE CORP	15.76	**8.1**
62	IPL	INTER PIPELINE LTD	21.29	**8.10%**
31	ERE.UN	EUROPEAN RESIDENTIA REIT	4.43	**8%**
40	BCF	BUILDERS CAPITAL MORTG	9.85	**8%**
21	CIQ.UN	CANADIAN HIGH INCOME EQ	7.57	**8%**
21	ERM	ECLIPSE RES. MORTGAGE IN	9.34	**8%**
33	EFN.PR.A	ELEMENT FLEET MANAGEMENT CO	21.57	**8%**
65	INO.UN	INOVALIS REIT	10.33	**8%**
64	NXR.UN	NEXUS REIT	2.01	**8%**
31	AZP.PR.A	ATLANTIC POWER PREFER	15.48	**8%**
27	EFN.PR.E	ELEMENT FLEET MANAGEM	19.88	**7.90%**
30	EFN.PR.C	ELEMENT FLEET MANAGEM	20.4	**7.90%**
48	BPF.UN	BOSTON PIZZA ROYALTIES IN	17.56	**7.80%**
58	MRT.UN	MORGUARD REIT	12.3	**7.80%**

43	SRV.UN	SIR ROYALTY INCOME FUNE	16.36	**7.70%**
59	APR.UN	AUTOMOTIVE PROPERTIES RE	10.58	**7.60%**
31	AZP.PR.B	ATLANTIC POWER PREFERR	18.48	**7.50%**
21	PCD.UN	PATHFINDER INCOME FUND	7.96	**7.50%**
32	BBD.PR.C	BOMBARDIER INC	20.75	**7.50%**
25	YCM.PR.B	COMMERCE SPLIT CORP	5	**7.50%**
59	FCD	FIRM CAPITAL PROPERTY TR	6.31	**7.50%**
28	EFN.PR.G	ELEMENT FLEET MANAGEM	21.66	**7.50%**
31	AZP.PR.C	ATLANTIC POWER PREFERRE	18.52	**7.40%**
36	ALA.PR.B	ALTAGAS LTD	14.61	**7.40%**
17	ECN.PR.A	ECN CAPITAL CORP	21.95	**7.40%**
65	ARX	ARC RESOURGES LTD	8.06	**7.40%**
51	TGL	TRANSGLOBE ENERGY CORP	2.5	**7.40%**
30	CWL	CALDWELL PARTNERS INTE	1.2	**7.40%**
44	HLF	HIGH LINER FOODS INC	7.8	**7.40%**
44	TF	TIMBERCREEK FINANCIAL CO	9.48	**7.40%**
22	XMF.PR.C	M SPLIT CORP	5.23	**7.30%**
17	ECN.PR.A	ECN CAPITAL CORP	21.19	**7.30%**
26	NPF.UN	NORTH AMERICAN PREFERR	18.8	**7.30%**
44	PEGI	PATTERN ENERGY GROUP INC	30.93	**7.30%**
24	ALA.PR.G	ALTAGAS LTD	16.58	**7.20%**
25	RBN.UN	BLUE RIBBON INCOME FUND	8.27	**7.20%**
28	MID.UN	MINT INCOME FUND	6.66	**7.20%**
43	FRU	FREEHOLD ROYALTIES LTD	8.73	**7.20%**
14	STUS.U	STARLIGHT US MULTI-FAMILY (NO5)	12.17	**7.20%**

28	CF.PR.C	CANACCORD GENUITY GROU	17.08	**7.20%**
42	M	MOSAIC CAPITAL CORP	5.72	**7.20%**
47	SGY	SURGE ENERGY INC	1.39	**7.10%**
24	BPO.PR.T	BROOKFIELD OFFICE PROPE	18.9	**7.10%**
17	EFN.PR.I	ELEMENT FLEET MANAGEM	20.1	**7.10%**
24	ALA.PR.E	ALTAGAS LTD	19.09	**7.10%**
26	TA.PR.H	TRANSALTA CORP	18.5	**7.10%**
29	BIR.PR.C	BIRCHCLIFF ENERGY LTD	25.08	**7%**
24	BPO.PR.A	BROOKFIELD OFFICE PROPE	16.9	**7%**
44	DR	MEDICAL FACILITIES CORP	15.69	**7%**
47	NWH.UN	NORTHWEST HEALTHCARE P	11.45	**7%**
15	TA.PR.E	TRANSALTA CORP	13.02	**7%**
32	STUS.A	STARLIGHT US MULTI-FAMI	9.3	**7%**
51	FC	FIRM CAPITAL MORTGAGE IN	13.48	**7%**
25	PPL.PR.A	PEMBINA PIPELINE CORP	17.59	**7%**
43	GS	GLUSKIN SHEFF & ASSOCIAT	14.46	**6.90%**
62	PIF	POLARIS INFASTRUCTURE I	11.79	**6.90%**
25	VB.PR.A	VERSABANK	10.1	**6.90%**
51	AND	ACADIAN TIMBER CORP	16.7	**6.90%**
39	GH	GAMEHOST INC	9.92	**6.90%**
30	ENB.PR.V	ENBRIDGE INC	29.02	**6.90%**
26	TA.PR.J	TRANSALTA CORP	19.11	**6.90%**
19	USF.UN	US FINANCIALS INCOME FU	7.23	**6.90%**
25	CF.PR.A	CANNACORD GENUITY GROU	14.1	**6.90%**
57	SOT.UN	SLATE OFFICE REIT	5.96	**6.90%**
36	FSZ	FIERA CAPITAL CORP	12.33	**6.80%**
52	CGX	CINEPLEX INC	25.58	**6.80%**

280

50	DIV	DIVERSIFIED REALTY CORP	3.26	**6.80%**
24	DRM.PR.A	DREAM UNLIMITED CORP	7.49	**6.80%**
24	ENB.PR.H	ENBRIDGE INC	16.15	**6.80%**
15	FN.PR.B	FIRST NATIONAL FINANCIAL	13.68	**6.80%**
27	CPX.PR.X	CAPITAL POWER CORP	20.08	**6.80%**
52	RNW	TRANSALTA RENEWABLES IN	13.89	**6.80%**
21	CLIQ	ALCANNA INC	26.1	**6.80%**
24	ALA.PR.U	ALTAGAS LTD	26.1	**6.80%**
31	AX.PR.E	ARTIS REIT	20.36	**6.80%**
16	NPI.PR.B	NORTHLAND POWER INC	16	**6.80%**
49	PLZ.UN	PLAZA RETAIL REIT	4.13	**6.70%**
55	AI	ATRIUM MORTGAGE INVES	13.36	**6.70%**
25	PPL.PR.E	PEMBINA PIPELINE CORP	18.77	**6.70%**
27	ENB.PF.V	ENBRIDGE INC	26.94	**6.70%**
26	ENB.PF.N	ENBRIDGE INC	19.01	**6.70%**
22	BRF.PR.B	BROOKFIELD RENEWABLE P	15.75	**6.70%**
27	ENB.PR.F	ENBRIDGE INC	17.61	**6.70%**
50	WCP	WHITRCAP RESOURCES INC	5.11	**6.70%**
24	BPO.PR.P	BROOKFIELD OFFICE PROPE	15.71	**6.70%**
27	BCE.PR.C	BCE INC	16.65	**6.70%**
24	ENB.PR.D	ENBRIDGE INC	16.72	**6.60%**
57	BEP.UN	BROOKFIELD RENEWABLE P	42.06	**6.60%**
27	CPX.PR.E	CAPITAL POWER CORP	19.73	**6.60%**
26	ENI.UN	ENERGY INCOME FUND	1.82	**6.60%**
16	BCE.PR.R	BCE INC	15.7	**6.60%**
42	CMG	COMPUTER MODELING GRO	5.97	**6.60%**
49	RUS	RUSSEL METALS INC	23.29	**6.60%**
27	AQN.PR.A	ALGONQUIN POWER UTILITIE	19.75	**6.50%**

16	FFH.PR.H	FAIRFAX FINANCIAL HOLDI	15.8	**6.50%**
49	KEG.UN	THE KEG ROYALTIES INCOME	17.49	**6.50%**
16	AX.PR.A	ARTIS REIT	21.89	**6.50%**
40	FDI	FINDEV INC	0.46	**6.50%**
24	FFH.PR.D	FAIRFAX FINANCIAL HOLDI	18.1	**6.50%**
24	LFE.PR.B	CANADIAN LIFE COMPANIES S	10.04	**6.50%**
24	VB.PR.B	VERSABANK	10.22	**6.50%**
19	CDD.UN	CORE CANADIAN DIVIDEND T	5.74	**6.50%**
16	FFH.PR.J	FAIRFAX FINANCIAL HOLDI	17.2	**6.50%**
17	BEP.PR.E	BROOKFIELD RENEWA PART	21.6	**6.50%**
24	ENB.PR.P	ENBRIDGE INC	16.95	**6.50%**
16	ENB.PR.C	ENBRIDGE INC	15.85	**6.50%**
28	ENB.PF.C	ENBRIDGE INC	17	**6.40%**
24	ENB.PR.J	ENBRIDGE INC	17.18	**6.40%**
24	ENB.PF.G	ENBRIDGE INC	17.15	**6.40%**
28	EQB.PR.C	EQUTABLE GROUP INC	24.74	**6.40%**
24	LB.PR.H	LAURENTIAN BANK OF CANADA	16.76	**6.40%**
24	PPL.PR.C	PEMBINA PIPELINE CORP	17.42	**6.40%**
24	ENB.PF.A	ENBRIDGE INC	17.07	**6.40%**
24	BRF.PR.C	BROOKFIELD RENEW. POWER	17.19	**6.40%**
15	HSE.PR.B	HUSKY ENERGY INC	13.15	**6.40%**
46	WJX	WAJAX CORP	15.82	**6.40%**
24	ENB.PF.E	ENBRIDGE INC	17.15	**6.40%**
23	BCE.PR.J	BCE INC	15.58	**6.40%**
24	NPI.PR.C	NORTHLAND POWER INC	19.85	**6.40%**
15	BCE.PR.N	BCE INC	14.71	**6.40%**
22	ENB.PR.Y	ENBRIDGE INC	15.71	**6.40%**
25	TA.PR.F	TRANSALTA CORP	15.83	**6.40%**
23	BCE.PR.B	BCE INC	15.65	**6.40%**

24	BCE.PR.Y	BCE INC	15.53	**6.40%**
21	BPO.PR.W	BROOKFIELD OFFICE PROPE	10.68	**6.40%**
23	BCE.PR.S	BCE INC	15.65	**6.40%**
23	BCE.PR.E	BCE INC	15.6	**6.30%**
27	ENB.PF.U	ENBRIDGE INC	26.08	**6.30%**
23	BCE.PR.H	BCE INC	15.59	**6.30%**
24	TRP.PR.E.	TRANSCANADA CORP	16.75	**6.30%**
23	BCE.PR.D	BCE INC	15.59	**6.30%**
21	BPO.PR.Y	BROOKFIELD OFFICE PROPE	10.76	**6.30%**
55	CHR	CHORUS AVIATION INC	7.58	**6.30%**
47	CUF.UN	COMINAR REIT	11.48	**6.30%**
22	BSD.PR.A	SOUNDVEST SPLIT TRUST	9.52	**6.30%**
25	FFH.PR.F	FAIRFAX FINANCIAL HOLDI	14.69	**6.30%**
24	PPL.PR.G	PEMBINA PIPELINE CORP	17.76	**6.30%**
59	BPY.UN	BROOKFIELD PROP. PARTN	28.06	**6.30%**
32	INE.PR.C	INNERGEX RENEWABLE ENE	22.82	**6.30%**
24	PPL.PR.O	PEMBINA PIPELINE CORP	17.75	**6.30%**
49	SPB	SUPERIOR PLUS CORP	11.42	**6.30%**
49	TXT.PR.A	TOP 10 SPLIT TRUST	12.43	**6.30%**
27	BRF.PR.E	BROOKFIELD RENEW. POWER	19.69	**6.30%**
24	FFH.PR.C	FAIRFAX FINANCIAL HOLDIN	18.37	**6.30%**
27	BRF.PR.F	BROOKFIELD RE PREF. EQUI	19.8	**6.30%**
27	ENB.PR.U	ENBRIDGE INC	26.23	**6.30%**
15	BCE.PR.L	BCE INC	14.17	**6.30%**
36	CRWN	CROWN CAPITAL PARTNERS	9.64	**6.30%**
38	LUC	LUCARA DIAMOND COPR	1.61	**6.30%**
26	CSE.PR.A	CAPSTONE INFASTRUCTURE C	13.17	**6.20%**
24	PPL.PR.Q	PEMBINA PIPELINE CORP	19.38	**6.20%**

24	LCS.PR.A	BROMPTON LIFECO SPLIT CO	10.04	**6.20%**
24	BAM.PF.E	BROOKFIELD ASSET MANAGE	17.9	**6.20%**
22	INE.PR.A	INNERGEX RENEWABLE ENE	14.45	**6.20%**
22	IFB.UN	INVESTMENT GRADE INFAST	8.11	**6.20%**
23	BCE.PR.Z	BCE INC	15.65	**6.20%**
61	EIF	EXCHANGE INCOME CORP	35.39	**6.20%**
59	CRR.UN	CROMBIE REIT	14.42	**6.20%**
52	FN	FIRST NATIONAL FINANCIAL	29.55	**6.20%**
17	GRP.PR.A	GLOBAL RESOURCE CHAMPIO	25.49	**6.10%**
36	MTL	MULLEN GROUP LTD	9.75	**6.10%**
25	PDV.PR.A	PRIME DIVIDEND CO	10.2	**6.10%**
36	RET	REITMANS (CANADA) LTD	3.21	**6.10%**
16	BAM.PR.S	BROOKFIELD ASSET MANA	16.15	**6.10%**
35	RET.A	REITMANS (CANADA) LTD	3.27	**6.10%**
21	BPO.PR.X	BROOKFIELD OFFICE PROPE	10.75	**6.10%**
17	BEP.PR.M	BROOKFIELD RENEWABLE PA	20.4	**6.10%**
28	ENB.PR.T	ENBRIDGE INC	16.26	**6.10%**
24	BPO.PR.N	BROOKFIELD OFFICE PROPE	15.74	**6.10%**
50	IGM	IGM FINANCIAL INC	35.81	**6.10%**
22	TRP.PR.F	TRANSCANADA CORP	14.86	**6.10%**
24	BAM.PF.A	BROOKFIELD ASSET MANAGE	20.74	**6.10%**
63	LB	LAURENTIAN BANK OF CAN	42.78	**6.10%**
40	RSI	ROGERS SUGAR INC	5.93	**6.10%**
17	CWB.PR.C	CANADIAN WESTERN BANK	25.81	**6.10%**
47	GEI	GIBSON ENERGY INC	21.7	**6.10%**
61	HR.UN	H&R REIT	22.95	**6.10%**

17	AX.PR.I	ARTIS REIT	24.69	**6.10%**
24	BCE.PR.Q	BCE INC	19.85	**6.10%**
57	DIR.UN	DREAM INDUSTRIAL REITT	11.58	**6.10%**
17	ALA.PR.K	ALTAGAS LTD	20.54	**6%**
24	BPO.PR.R	BROOKFIELD OFFICE PROPES I	17.3	**6.00%**
15	SJR.PR.B	SHAW COMMUNICATIONS INC	14.75	**6.00%**
47	AGF.B	AGF MANAGEMENT LTD	5.24	**6.00%**
60	ENB	ENBRIDGE INC	49.4	**6.00%**
8	PT	PINE TRAIL REIT	0.13	**6%**
22	TRP.PR.H	TRANSCANADA CORP	12.32	**6.00%**
24	HSE.PR.C	HUSKY ENERGY INC	18.96	**6.00%**
17	IFC.PR.G	INTACT FINANCIAL CORP	20.56	**6.00%**
17	CWB.PR.D	CANADIAN WESTERN BANK	25.75	**5.90%**
32	EXE	EXTENDICARE INC	7.94	**5.90%**
9	RE	RE ROYALTIES LTD	0.9	**5.90%**
62	CPX	CAPITAL POWER CORP	30.23	**5.90%**
33	HRR.UN	AUSTRALIAN REIT INCOME	11.01	**5.90%**
57	IGM.PR.B	IGM FINANCIAL INC	24.99	**5.90%**
54	KEY	KEYERA COPR	30.6	**5.90%**
24	BAM.PF.G	BROOKFIELD ASSET MANAGEM	19.14	**5.90%**
22	YCM.PR.A	COMMERCE SPLIT CORP	5.1	**5.90%**
25	PIC.PR.A	PREMIUM INCOME CORP	14.64	**5.90%**
25	AQN.PR.D	ALGONQUIN POWER UTILITI	21.32	**5.90%**
24	FFH.PR.K	FAIRFAX FINANCIAL HOLDIN	19.33	**5.90%**
22	ALA.PR.A	ALTAGAS LTD	14.42	**5.90%**
23	BAM.PR.E	BROOKFIELD ASSET MANAGE	16.9	**5.80%**
24	CWB.PR.B	CANADIAN WESTERN BANK	18.57	**5.80%**
24	EMA.PR.C	EMERA INC	20.2	**5.80%**

62	NVU.UN	NORTHVIEW APARTMENT R	28.26	**5.80%**
29	PWF.PR.I	POWER FINANCIAL CORP	25.8	**5.80%**
16	BAM.PF.F	BROOKFIELD ASSET MANAGE	19.4	**5.80%**
21	BAM.PF.Z	BROOKFIELD ASSET MANAG	20.00	**5.80%**
20	BPO.PR.C	BROOKFIELD OFFICE PROPE	25.78	**5.80%**
68	DRG.UN	DREAM GLOBAL REIT	13.84	**5.80%**
29	PWF.PR.G	POWER FINANCIAL CORP	25.50	**5.80%**
16	IFC.PR.D	INTACT FINANCIAL CORP	18.43	**5.80%**
25	BAM.PR.N	BROOKFIELD ASSET MANAG	20.5	**5.80%**
28	BAM.PF.C	BROOKFIELD ASSET MANAGE	21.07	**5.80%**
17	CPX.PR.G	CAPITAL POWER CORP	26.00	**5.80%**
16	PVF.PR.U	PARTNERS VALUE INVESTME	26.19	**5.80%**
21	BAM.PR.K	BROOKFIELD ASSET MANAG	11.64	**5.80%**
24	FTS.PR.G	FORTIS INC	19.10	**5.80%**
29	GWO.PR.F	GREAT-WEST LIFECO INC	25.56	**5.80%**
25	BAM.PR.M	BROOKFIELD ASSET MANAG	20.67	**5.80%**
24	MFC.PR.K	MANULIFE FINANCIAL CORP	19.16	**5.80%**
15	TRP.PR.I	TRANSCANADA CORP	13.83	**5.70%**
23	TRP.PR.D	TRANSCANADA CORP	17.03	**5.70%**
31	AX.PR.G	ARTIS REIT	21.75	**5.70%**
47	TOG	TORC OIL & GAS LTD	4.66	**5.70%**
21	BAM.PR.C	BROOKFIELD ASSET MANA	11.67	**5.70%**
27	INP	INPUT CAPITAL CORP	0.69	**5.70%**
20	WBE	WESTBOND ENTERPRISED C	0.18	**5.70%**
22	BAM.PR.B	BROOKFIELD ASSET MANAGE	11.68	**5.70%**
17	CPX.PR.I	CAPITAL POWER CORP	25.25	**5.70%**

29	POW.PR.C	POWER CORPORATION OF CA	25.55	**5.70%**
26	BCE.PR.A	BCE INC	15.9	**5.70%**
20	GWO.PR.M	GREAT-WEST LIFECO INC	25.44	**5.70%**
28	PWF.PR.O	POWER FINANCIAL CORP	25.53	**5.70%**
52	BEK.A	BECKER MILK CO LTD	14.10	**5.70%**
30	BPS.PR.A	BROOKFIELD PROPERTY SPL	25.35	**5.70%**
17	BEP.PR.I	BROOKFIELD RENEWABLE PA	25.34	**5.70%**
17	LB.PR.J	LAURENTIAN BANK OF CAN	25.79	**5.70%**
16	MFC.PR.Q	MANULIFE FINANCIAL CORP	20.70	**5.70%**
16	NA.PR.E	NATIONAL BANK OF CANADA	20.35	**5.70%**
17	NA.PR.G	NATIONAL BANK OF CANADA	21.85	**5.70%**
60	RUF.U	PURE MULTI-FAMILY REIT LP	8.96	**5.70%**
17	ALA.PR.I	ALTAGAS LTD	22.96	**5.70%**
29	WN.PR.A	GEORGE WESTON LTD	25.6	**5.70%**
25	BAM.PF.D	BROOKFIELD ASSET MANGNT	21.5	**5.70%**
24	EMA.PR.F	EMERA INC	18.84	**5.60%**
9	HSE.PR.G	HUSKY ENERGY INC	20.00	**5.60%**
29	PWF.PR.H	POWER FINANCIAL CORP	25.47	**5.60%**
48	RME	ROCKY MOUNTAIN DEALER	8.73	**5.60%**
17	BIP.PR.E	BROOKFIELD INFASTRUCTU	21.99	**5.60%**
24	MFC.PR.J	MANULIFE FINANCIAL CORP	20.69	**5.60%**
24	BAM.PF.B	BROOKFIELD ASSET MANAGE	18.50	**5.60%**
17	BEP.PR.K	BROOKFIELD RENEWABEL PA	22.01	**5.60%**
23	FFH.PR.I	FAIRFAX FINANCIAL HOLDI	16.55	**5.60%**
59	PWF	POWER FINANCIAL CORP	31.27	**5.60%**
64	REI.UN	RIOCAN REIT	25.96	**5.60%**

33	GWO.PR.L	GREAT-WEST LIFECO INC	25.35	**5.60%**
25	PPL.PR.I	PEMBINA PIPELINE CORP	21.32	**5.60%**
28	POW.PR.A	POWER CORPORATION OF CA	25.09	**5.60%**
18	RY.PR.S	ROYAL BANK OF CANADA	21.6	**5.60%**
47	TCL.B	TRANSCONTINENTAL INC	15.77	**5.60%**
28	ENB.PR.A	ENBRIDGE INC	24.69	**5.60%**
24	TA.PR.D	TRANSALTA CORP	12.28	**5.60%**
17	BEP.PR.G	BROOKFIELD RENEWABLE PA	24.72	**5.60%**
23	FTN.PR.A	FINANCIAL 15 SPLIT CORP	9.9	**5.60%**
17	PPL.PR.K	PEMBINA PIPELINE CORP	25.92	**5.60%**
46	TCL.A	TRANSCONTINENTAL INC	15.71	**5.60%**
24	MFC.PR.L	MANULIFE FINANCIAL CORP	17.62	**5.60%**
40	EML.PR.A	THE EMPIRE LIFE INSURANCE	25.89	**5.60%**
24	NA.PR.W	NATIONAL BANK OF CANADA	17.61	**5.50%**
17	PPL.PR.M	PEMBINA PIPELINE CORP	25.88	**5.50%**
24	FTS.PR.K	FORTIS INC	17.67	**5.50%**
28	POW.PR.D	POWER CORPORATION OF CA	22.65	**5.50%**
28	EMA.PR.E	EMERA INC	20.48	**5.50%**
25	NA.PR.S	NATIONAL BANK OF CANADA	18.51	**5.50%**
26	NPI.PR.A	NORTHLAND POWER INC	15.85	**5.50%**
28	POW.PR.B	POWER CORPORATION OF CA	24.35	**5.50%**
28	PWF.PR.T	POWER FINANCIAL CORP	18.86	**5.50%**
23	ENB.PR.B	ENBRIDGE INC	15.35	**5.50%**
18	CM.PR.T	CANADIAN IMPERIAL BANK O	25.4	**5.50%**
22	CPX.PR.A	CAPITAL POWER CORP	13.81	**5.50%**
29	POW.PR.G	POWER CORPORATION OF CA	25.5	**5.50%**
28	ELF.PR.H	E-L FINANCIAL COPR LTD	24.99	**5.50%**

17	KML.PR.C	KINDER MORGAN CANADA L	23.67	**5.50%**
17	KML.PR.A	KINDER MORGAN CANADA L	23.83	**5.50%**
17	BIP.PR.B	BROOKFIELD INFASTRUCTUR	25.13	**5.50%**
32	CHP.UN	CHOICE PROPERTIES REIT	13.4	**5.50%**
28	ELF.PR.F	E-L FINANCIAL COPR LTD	24.08	**5.50%**
28	PWF.PR.F	POWER FINANCIAL CORP	24.03	**5.50%**
28	PWF.PR.E	POWER FINANCIAL CORP	25.34	**5.50%**
24	BIP.PR.A	BROOKFIELD INFASTRUCTUR	20.59	**5.50%**
25	FFN.PR.A	NORTH AMERICAN FINANC. 15	10.04	**5.50%**
17	CM.PR.S	CANADIAN IMPERIAL BANK O	20.59	**5.50%**
25	FTS.PR.J	FORTIS INC	21.93	**5.50%**
27	PWF.PR.K	POWER FINANCIAL CORP	22.7	**5.50%**
26	RY.PR.Z	ROYAL BANK OF CANADA	18.48	**5.50%**
24	HSE.PR.E	HUSKY ENERGY INC	20.7	**5.50%**
17	IFC.PR.F	INTACT FINANCIAL CORP	24.49	**5.40%**
17	PWF.PR.Z	POWER FINANCIAL CORP	23.62	**5.40%**
28	PWF.PR.L	POWER FINANCIAL CORP	23.48	**5.40%**
16	SLF.PR.K	SUN LIFE FINANCIAL INC	17.56	**5.40%**
57	WIR.U	WPT INDUSTRIAL REIT	18.59	**5.40%**
28	PWF.PR.S	POWER FINANCIAL CORP	22.11	**5.40%**
17	BMO.PR.E	BANK OF MONTREAL	22.33	**5.40%**
57	CRT.UN	CT REIT	13.89	**5.40%**
17	IFC.PR.E	INTACT FINANCIAL CORP	24	**5.40%**
28	RZE	RAZOR ENERGY CORP	2.71	**5.40%**
23	BAM.PR.T	BROOKFIELD ASSET MANAG	15.6	**5.40%**
17	BIR.PR.D	BROOKFIELD INFASTRUC	22.65	**5.40%**
28	FTS.PR.F	FORTIS INC	22.65	**5.40%**
22	TRP.PR.A	TRANSCANADA CORP	15.10	**5.40%**
28	GWO.PR.H	GREAT-WEST LIFECO INC	22.41	**5.40%**
28	GWO.PR.T	GREAT-WEST LIFECO INC	23.98	**5.40%**

26	LBS.PR.A	LIFE & BANC SPLIT CORP	10.09	**5.40%**
17	TD.PF.J	THE TORONTO-DOMINION BANK	21.75	**5.40%**
28	WN.PR.D	GEORGE WESTON LTD	24.27	**5.40%**
28	GWO.PR.Q	GREAT-WEST LIFECO INC	23.97	**5.40%**
18	BNS.PR.I	BANK OF NOVA SCOTIA	22.60	**5.40%**
28	CU.PR.E	CANADIAN UTILITIES LTD	22.77	**5.40%**
28	GWO.PR.G	GREAT-WEST LIFECO INC	24.16	**5.40%**
28	GWO.PR.P	GREAT-WEST LIFECO INC	24.97	**5.40%**
17	NA.PR.X	NATIONAL BANK OF CANADA	26.04	**5.40%**
24	BMO.PR.T	BANK OF MONTREAL	18.15	**5.40%**
28	CU.PR.D	CANADIAN UTILITIES LTD	22.9	**5.40%**
28	ELF.PR.G	E-L FINANCIAL COPR LTD	22.07	**5.40%**
23	FFH.PR.G	FAIRFAX FINANCIAL HOLDINGS LTD	15.49	**5.40%**
28	WN.PR.C	GEORGE WESTON LTD	24.13	**5.40%**
23	IFC.PR.A	INTACT FINANCIAL CORP	15.8	**5.40%**
28	PWF.PR.R	POWER FINANCIAL CORP	25.65	**5.40%**
30	BRF.PR.A	BROOKFIELD RENEW. POWER	15.58	**5.40%**
28	CIU.PR.A	CU INC	21.35	**5.40%**
17	MFC.PR.O	MANULIFE FINANCIAL CORP	26.15	**5.40%**
18	PPL.PF.A	PEMBINA PIPELINE CORP	22.89	**5.40%**
59	SRU.UN	SMARTCENTRES REIT	33.76	**5.30%**
24	BMO.PR.S	BANK OF MONTREAL	18.75	**5.30%**
17	BIP.PR.C	BROOKFIELD INFASTRUCTU	25.00	**5.30%**
24	FTS.PR.M	FORTIS INC	19.18	**5.30%**
25	CM.PR.O	CANADIAN IMPERIAL BANK O	18.35	**5.30%**
17	CU.PR.H	CANADIAN UTILITIES LTD	24.6	**5.30%**
28	CU.PR.F	CANADIAN UTILITIES LTD	21.2	**5.30%**
28	MFC.PR.C	MANULIFE FINANCIAL CORP	21.01	**5.30%**
28	SLF.PR.E	SUN LIFE FINANCIAL INC	21.10	**5.30%**
28	CU.PR.G	CANADIAN UTILITIES LTD	21.15	**5.30%**

15	EMA.PR.B	EMERA INC	15.5	5.30%
28	MFC.PR.B	MANULIFE FINANCIAL CORP	21.9	5.30%
48	CCS.PR.C	CO-OPERATORS GENERAL INS	23.74	5.30%
22	FTS.PR.I	FORTIS INC	14.3	5.30%
28	L.PR.B	LOBLAWS COMPANIES LTD	24.94	5.30%
69	BCE	BCE INC	59.69	5.30%
17	ENB.PF.K	ENBRIDGE INC	22.89	5.30%
28	GWO.PR.R	GREAT-WEST LIFECO INC	22.50	5.30%
28	GWO.PR.S	GREAT-WEST LIFECO INC	24.73	5.30%
43	RCO.UN	MIDDLEFIELD CAN GLBAL REI	12.25	5.30%
24	TD.PF.A	THE TORONTO-DOMINION B	18.40	5.30%
17	BNS.PR.E	BANK OF NOVA SCOTIA	29.52	5.30%
25	GWO.PR.I	GREAT-WEST LIFECO INC	21.13	5.30%
17	PVS.PR.E	PARTNERS VALUE SPLIT CORP	25.75	5.30%
34	SOX	STUART OLSON INC	4.50	5.30%
31	SLF.PR.A	SUN LIFE FINANCIAL INC	22.2	5.30%
28	SLF.PR.B	SUN LIFE FINANCIAL INC	22.65	5.30%
17	IAF.PR.I	IA FINANCIAL CORP	22.7	5.30%
18	RY.PR.Q	ROYAL BANK OF CANADA	25.92	5.30%
28	SLF.PR.C	SUN LIFE FINANCIAL INC	21.00	5.30%
28	SLF.PR.D	SUN LIFE FINANCIAL INC	21.00	5.30%
32	TD.PF.G	THE TORONTO-DOMINION BA	26.04	5.30%
23	WFS.PR.A	WORLD FINANCIAL SPLIT COR	9.95	5.30%
26	PPL.PR.S	PEMBINA PIPELINE CORP	23.55	5.30%
17	BNS.PR.G	BANK OF NOVA SCOTIA	26.15	5.30%
25	CM.PR.P	CANADIAN IMPERIAL BANK O	17.77	5.30%
24	FN.PR.A	FIRST NATIONAL FINANCIAL	13.25	5.30%

24	MFC.PR.M	MANULIFE FINANCIAL CORP	18.47	**5.30%**
17	RY.PR.R	ROYAL BANK OF CANADA	26.05	**5.30%**
17	TRP.PR.J	TRANSCANADA CORP	26.07	**5.30%**
25	BMO.PR.W	BANK OF MONTREAL	18.10	**5.20%**
30	DRA.UN	DREAM HARD ASSET ALTERN	7.56	**5.20%**
25	FFH.PR.M	FAIRFAX FINANCIAL HOLDI	22.50	**5.20%**
24	RY.PR.H	ROYAL BANK OF CANADA	18.80	**5.20%**
26	BCE.PR.K	BCE INC	14.03	**5.20%**
25	DF.PR.A	DIVIDEND 15 SPLIT CORP II	10.04	**5.20%**
23	ECF.UN	EAST COAST INVESTMENT GR	9.20	**5.20%**
25	BK.PR.A	CANADIAN BANC CORP	10.40	**5.20%**
28	IAF.PR.B	IA FINANCIAL CORP	22.10	**5.20%**
24	MFC.PR.N	MANULIFE FINANCIAL CORP	18.21	**5.20%**
18	NA.PR.A	NATIONAL BANK OF CANADA	25.85	**5.20%**
24	XTD.PR.A	TDB SPLIT CORP	10.06	**5.20%**
26	DFN.PR.A	DIVIDEND 15 SPLIT CORP	10.09	**5.20%**
17	RY.PR.P	ROYAL BANK OF CANADA	25.25	**5.20%**
24	DGS.PR.A	DIVIDEND GROWTH SPLIT CO	10.12	**5.20%**
52	GWO	GREAT-WEST LIFECO INC	32.14	**5.20%**
25	BCE.PR.O	BCE INC	20.49	**5.20%**
27	PL	PINNACLE RENEWABLE ENERGY INC	12.12	**5.20%**
29	WN.PR.E	GEORGE WESTON LTD	22.68	**5.20%**
25	TD.PF.B	THE TORONTO-DOMINION BA	18.40	**5.20%**
17	EMA.PR.H	EMERA INC	23.70	**5.20%**
23	OSP.PR.A	BROMPTON OIL SPLIT CORP	9.71	**5.10%**
30	BPS.PR.C	BROOKFIELD PROPERTY SPL	25.25	**5.10%**

15	ENS.PR.A	E SPLIT CORP	10.19	**5.10%**
15	PWF.PR.Q	POWER FINANCIAL CORP	14.58	**5.10%**
21	TRI.PR.B	THOMSON REUTERS CORP	13.08	**5.10%**
58	ALA	ALTAGAS LTD	18.79	**5.10%**
24	HOM.U	BSR REIT	13.01	**5.10%**
41	HWO	HIGH ARTIC ENERGY SERVICE	3.85	**5.10%**
24	MFC.PR.I	MANULIFE FINANCIAL CORP	21.21	**5.10%**
17	W.PR.K	WESTCOAST ENERGY IN	25.60	**5.10%**
15	SLF.PR.J	SUN LIFE FINANCIAL INC	15.00	**5.10%**
55	AX.UN	ARTIS REIT	10.56	**5.10%**
30	BPS.PR.U	BROOKFIELD OFFICE PROPE	34.50	**5.10%**
17	ENB.PR.I	ENBRIDGE INC	25.12	**5.10%**
27	BDT	BIRD CONSTRUCTION INC	7.55	**5.10%**
28	RY.PR.UN	ROYAL BANK OF CANADA	24.00	**5.10%**
22	FFH.PR.E	FAIRFAX FINANCIAL HOLDINGS LTD	14.20	**5.10%**
15	RY.PR.O	ROYAL BANK OF CANADA	24.10	**5.10%**
17	TD.PF.F	THE TORONTO-DOMINION BA	24.06	**5.10%**
18	BAM.PF.J	BROOKFIELD ASSET MANAG	23.03	**5.10%**
25	SBN.PR.A	S SPLIT CORP	10.35	**5.10%**
24	TD.PF.C	THE TORONTO-DOMINION BA	18.41	**5.10%**
22	BCE.PR.F	BCE INC	15.30	**5.10%**
67	PPL	PEMBINA PIPELINE CORP	47.53	**5.10%**
64	NPI	NORTHLAND POWER INC	23.83	**5.00%**
18	W.PR.N	WESTCOAST ENERGY IN	25.73	**5.00%**
15	GWO.PR.O	GREAT-WEST LIFECO INC	14.78	**5.00%**
62	POW	POWER CORPORATION OF CA	30.40	**5.00%**
22	PWF.PR.A	POWER FINANCIAL CORP	13.60	**5.00%**
47	SIA	SIENNA SENIOR LIVING CORP	18.52	**5.00%**

22	BCE.PR.T	BCE INC	15.12	**5.00%**
39	CSW.B	CORBY SPIRIT AND WINE LTD	17.44	**5.00%**
27	GMP	GMP CAPITAL INC	2.03	**5.00%**
18	BMO.PR.Z	BANK OF MONTREAL	24.79	**5.00%**
14	PFT.UN	CANADIAN PREFERRED SHAR	8.04	**5.00%**
38	WEF	WESTERN FOREST PRODUCTS	1.80	**5.00%**
29	BPS.PR.B	BROOKFIELD PROPERTY SPL	25.30	**5.00%**
73	CM	CANADIAN IMPERIAL BANK O	113.00	**5.00%**
48	INE	INNERGEX RENEWABLE ENER	14.20	**5.00%**
15	MFC.PR.B	MANULIFE FINANCIAL CORP	14.28	**5.00%**
48	OLY	OLYMPIA FINANCIAL CORP I	55.50	**5.00%**
24	TRP.PR.G	TRANSCANADA CORP	19.21	**5.00%**
44	ISV	INFORMATION SERVICES COR	16.26	**4.90%**
17	BAM.PF.I	BROOKFIELD ASSET MANAGE	24.55	**4.90%**
40	CSW.A	CORBY SPIRIT AND WINE LTD	17.99	**4.90%**
18	BMO.PR.D	BANK OF MONTREAL	22.50	**4.90%**
15	GDV.PR.A	GLOBAL DIVIDEND GROWTH	10.23	**4.90%**
28	RY.PR.W	ROYAL BANK OF CANADA	25.05	**4.90%**
72	MIC	GENWORTH MI CANADA INC	41.99	**4.90%**
41	NEXA	NEXA RESOURCES SA	13.83	**4.90%**
24	BAM.PF.H	BROOKFIELD ASSET MANAG	25.60	**4.90%**
17	NA.PR.C	NATIONAL BANK OF CANADA	22.65	**4.90%**
15	PRM.PR.A	BIG PHARMA SPLIT CORP	10.28	**4.90%**
27	SBC.PR.A	BROMPTON SPLIT BANC CORP	10.28	**4.90%**

23	SJR.PR.A	SHAW COMMUNICATIONS INC	14.40	**4.90%**
17	TD.PF.I	THE TORONTO-DOMINION BA	23.17	**4.80%**
17	MFC.PR.R	MANULIFE FINANCIAL CORP	25.12	**4.80%**
56	BIP.UN	BROOKFIELD INFASTRUCT	55.96	**4.80%**
55	MBN	MBN CORP	6.65	**4.80%**
17	EIT.PR.B	CANOE EIT INCOME FUND	25.10	**4.80%**
24	MFC.PR.H	MANULIFE FINANCIAL CORP	22.43	**4.80%**
18	TRP.PR.K	TRANSCANADA CORP	25.51	**4.80%**
53	CAL	CALEDONIA MINING CORP PLC	7.70	**4.80%**
22	HSE.PR.A	HUSKY ENERGY INC	12.55	**4.80%**
75	TRP	TRANSCANADA CORP	63.07	**4.80%**
23	BAM.PR.X	BROOKFIELD ASSET MANAGEMENT I	14.05	**4.80%**
20	EIT.PR.A	CANOE EIT INCOME FUND	25.19	**4.80%**
22	BCE.PR.M	BCE INC	14.48	**4.80%**
18	CM.PR.R	CANADIAN IMPERIAL BANK OF COM	22.81	**4.80%**
74	BNS	BANK OF NOVA SCOTIA	73.46	**4.70%**
18	BMO.PR.C	BANK OF MONTREAL	23.79	**4.70%**
17	TD.PF.H	THE TORONTO-DOMINION BANK	25.74	**4.70%**
17	BMO.PR.B	BANK OF MONTREAL	25.75	**4.70%**
24	CU.PR.C	CANADIAN UTILITIES LTD	18.20	**4.70%**
45	OSB	NORBORD INC	33.52	**4.70%**
17	BNS.PR.H	BANK OF NOVA SCOTIA	25.80	**4.70%**
33	MFC.PR.G	MANULIFE FINANCIAL CORP	20.74	**4.70%**
23	BAM.PR.R	BROOKFIELD ASSET MANA	16.01	**4.70%**
65	EMA	EMERA INC	50.31	**4.70%**
22	BCE.PR.G	BCE INC	15.10	**4.60%**
30	VNR.PR.A	VALENER INC	25.00	**4.60%**
39	SPS.A	SPORTSCENE GROUP INC	6.80	**4.60%**

69	GRT.UN	GRANITE REIT	60.93	**4.60%**
58	NFI	NFI GROUP INC	32.94	**4.60%**
17	ALB.PR.C	ALLBANC SPLIT CORP II	26.50	**4.60%**
54	VNR	VALENER INC	26.12	**4.60%**
57	CU	CANADIAN UTILITIES LTD	36.88	**4.60%**
50	CU.X	CANADIAN UTILITIES LTD	36.90	**4.60%**
38	IAM	INTEGRATED ASSET MANAGEMENT	2.62	**4.60%**
24	SLF.PR.I	SUN LIFE FINANCIAL INC	20.63	**4.60%**
28	RY.PR.C	ROYAL BANK OF CANADA	25.18	**4.60%**
39	AWI	ADVENT-AWI HOLDINGS INC	1.10	**4.50%**
22	BCE.PR.I	BCE INC	15.14	**4.50%**
50	NWC	THE NORTH WEST CO INC	29.15	**4.50%**
44	CUP.U	CARIBBEAN UTILITIES CO L	20.80	**4.50%**
59	AQN	ALGONQUIN POWER UTILITI	15.20	**4.50%**
43	BNP	BONAVISTA ENERGY CORP	0.85	**4.50%**
24	CM.PR.Q	CANADIAN IMPERIAL BANK O	20.30	**4.50%**
24	IFC.PR.C	INTACT FINANCIAL CORP	18.40	**4.50%**
24	BMO.PR.Y	ROYAL BANK OF CANADA	21.11	**4.50%**
27	RY.PR.E	ROYAL BANK OF CANADA	25.23	**4.50%**
26	RY.PR.G	ROYAL BANK OF CANADA	25.20	**4.50%**
30	CEE	CENTAMIN PLC	1.59	**4.40%**
45	FCA	FIRM CAPITAL AMERICAN REALTY P	7.07	**4.40%**
50	FCA.U	FIRM CAPITAL AMERICAN REALTY P	9.40	**4.40%**
26	RY.PR.F	ROYAL BANK OF CANADA	25.16	**4.40%**
33	SWP	SWISS WATER DECAF COFFEE	5.54	**4.40%**
28	PVS.PR.D	PARTNERS VALUE SPLIT CORP	25.58	**4.40%**

24	RY.PR.A	ROYAL BANK OF CANADA	25.16	**4.40%**
24	RY.PR.M	ROYAL BANK OF CANADA	20.30	**4.40%**
68	T	TELUS CORP	49.45	**4.40%**
56	SJR.B	SHAW COMMUNICATIONS INC	27.12	**4.40%**
26	IAF.PR.G	IA FINANCIAL CORP	21.64	**4.40%**
40	KML	KINDER MORGAN CANADA LTD	14.97	**4.30%**
15	CU.PR.I	CANADIAN UTILITIES LTD	26.01	**4.30%**
16	RY.PR.J	ROYAL BANK OF CANADA	20.76	**4.30%**
26	MBK.UN	MANULIFE US REGIONAL BANK TRUS	11.57	**4.30%**
22	FTS.PR.H	FORTIS INC	14.51	**4.30%**
54	SMU.UN	SUMMIT INDUSTRIAL INCOME REIT	12.05	**4.30%**
21	TRP.PR.B	TRANSCANADA CORP	12.35	**4.30%**
22	TRP.PR.C	TRANSCANADA CORP	13.13	**4.30%**
53	AW.UN	A&W REVENUE ROYALTIES INCOM	43.68	**4.30%**
63	D.UN	DREAM OFFICE REIT	23.51	**4.30%**
18	TD.PF.D	THE TORONTO-DOMINION B	21.02	**4.30%**
24	TD.PF.E	THE TORONTO-DOMINION B	21.60	**4.30%**
49	ET	EVERTZ TECHNOLOGIES LTD	17.00	**4.20%**
34	H	HYDRO ONE LTD	21.75	**4.20%**
38	SJR.A	SHAW COMMUNICATIONS INC	28.80	**4.20%**
35	ZZZ	SLEEP COUNTRY CANADA HO	17.56	**4.20%**
59	PEY	PEYTO EXPLORATION & DEV	5.82	**4.20%**
47	PSK	PRAIRIESKY ROYALTY LTD	18.75	**4.20%**
57	AFN	AG GROWTH INTERNATIONAL	57.74	**4.20%**
22	GMN	GOBIMI INC	0.35	**4.20%**

22	BAM.PR.G	BROOKFIELD ASSET MANAGE	16.54	**4.20%**
28	NEW.PR.D	NEWGROWTH CORP	32.17	**4.10%**
43	CSH.UN	CHARTWELL REITIREMENT R	14.55	**4.10%**
20	CIU.PR.C	CU INC	13.62	**4.10%**
23	EMA.PR.A	EMERA INC	15.45	**4.10%**
23	PWF.PR.P	POWER FINANCIAL CORP	14.17	**4.10%**
27	RAY.A	STINGRAY GROUP INC	6.47	**4.10%**
30	FEC	FONTERA ENERGY CORP	11.93	**4.10%**
54	CJ	CARDINAL ENERGY LTD	3.03	**4.10%**
44	WFC	WALL FINANCIAL CORP	24.50	**4.10%**
46	ITP	INTERTAPE POLYMER GROUP	18.13	**4.10%**
64	NA	NATIONAL BANK OF CANADA	63.77	**4.10%**
23	CLR	CLEARWATER SEAFOODS INC	4.95	**4.00%**
67	MFC	MANULIFE FINANCIAL CORP	24.64	**4.00%**
65	FCR	FIRST CAPITAL REALTY INC	21.48	**4.00%**
37	SIL	SPROTT INC	3.00	**4.00%**
19	RAY.B	STINGRAY GROUP INC	6.50	**4.00%**
40	MDF	MEDIAGRIF INTERACTIVE TE	10.09	**4.00%**
42	XTC	EXCO TECHNOLOGIES LTD	8.93	**4.00%**
24	SLF.PR.H	SUN LIFE FINANCIAL INC	17.80	**4.00%**
21	TSL	TREE ISLAND STEEL LTD	2.06	**3.90%**
14	BSC.PR.C	BNS SPLIT CORP II	20.18	**3.90%**
46	LNF	LEON'S FUNITURE LTD	14.22	**3.90%**
74	TD	THE TORONTO-DOMINION BA	76.38	**3.90%**
71	SU	SUNCOR ENERGY INC	43.11	**3.90%**
64	MRG.UN	MORGUARD NORTH AMERICA	17.80	**3.80%**
76	RY	ROYAL BANK OF CANADA	107.00	**3.80%**

20	SLF.PR.G	SUN LIFE FINANCIAL INC	15.00	**3.80%**
51	MRD	MELCOR DEVELOPMENTS LT	13.58	**3.80%**
74	BMO	BANK OF MONTREAL	106.00	**3.80%**
53	CIX	CI FINANCIAL CORP	19.35	**3.70%**
20	MFC.PR.F	MANULIFE FINANCIAL CORP	14.32	**3.70%**
42	ACQ	AUTOCANADA INC	10.67	**3.70%**
61	UFS	DOMTAR CORP	63.31	**3.70%**
70	CNQ	CANADIAN NATURAL RESOURCES L	37.68	**3.70%**
20	GWO.PR.N	GREAT-WEST LIFECO INC	14.79	**3.70%**
32	FRO.UN	FRONSAC REAL ESTATE INVESTMEN	0.62	**3.60%**
70	FTS	FORTIS INC	49.63	**3.60%**
46	BLX	BORALEX INC	18.31	**3.60%**
68	SLF	SUN LIFE FINANCIAL INC	55.41	**3.60%**
40	ACI	ALTAGAS CANADA INC	19.35	**3.60%**
46	HPS.A	HAMMOND POWER SOLUTIONS INC	7.70	**3.60%**
37	SES	SECURE ENERGY SERVICES IN	7.56	**3.60%**
30	ABT	ABSOLUTE SOFTWARE CORP	8.98	**3.60%**
55	ACO.Y	ATCO LTD	45.50	**3.60%**
62	ACO.X	ATCO LTD	45.14	**3.50%**
56	KMP.UN	KILLAM APARTMENT REIT	18.81	**3.50%**
45	PSI	PASON SYSTEMS INC	20.48	**3.50%**
43	ACD	ACCORD FINANCIAL CORP	10.25	**3.50%**

dividend income of 6% of the value of your portfolio. The objective is not only a good income but also a portfolio that never stops growing.

The first company in the following sort that has a score over 50 is IVQ.U. It is paying a dividend of 11%.

The order of this Stock Dividend Percentage, in descending order, display is

#1 = Score

#2 = Stock Symbol

#3 = Company Name

#4 = Stock Price

#5 = Stock's Dividend %

CHAPTER 16

The 654 By Descending Price

(Data Extracted May 6, 2019)

Following are the 654 stocks that paid a dividend of 3.5% or more on the Toronto Stock Exchange. The sort in this chapter is descending order by **share price**. The four sorts of the 654 stocks will help you find the 20 stocks that you would add to your portfolio. This sort is a quick way to find a stock in a certain price range to substitute for a stock you now own whose score is now too low or it is not now paying a high enough dividend.

Before you decide on buying a stock based on the sorting of this data be sure to recalculate the score. Dividend percentages and the scores can change daily with fluctuations in stock prices and volume of shares being traded.

The five largest Canadian banks have the highest price per share. They also have the highest scores. Although banks do not appear to pay high dividends, this is misleading. Their profits keep rising almost in tandem with their share price. As the share price increases, they pay higher dividend amounts to keep the dividend percentage stable. Thus, even though 10 years ago you may have been receiving the same 3.80% dividend rate, the amount of money you are now receiving may be double what it was then.

It is interesting to go to the bottom of this list and review the stocks trading for less than a dollar a share. A few have a score over 40 and may be worth closer inspection. There are many affordable shares with scores over 50.

The order of this Stock Price in Descending Order display is

#1 = Score

#2 = Stock Symbol

#3 = Company Name

#4 = Stock Price

#5 = Stock's Dividend %

#1	#1	#3	#4	#5
73	CM	CANADIAN IMPERIAL BANK	113.00	5.00%
76	RY	ROYAL BANK OF CANADA	107.00	3.80%
74	BMO	BANK OF MONTREAL	106.00	3.80%
74	TD	THE TORONTO-DOMINION B	76.38	3.90%
74	BNS	BANK OF NOVA SCOTIA	73.46	4.70%
64	NA	NATIONAL BANK OF CANAD	63.77	4.10%
61	UFS	DOMTAR CORP	63.31	3.70%

75	TRP	TRANSCANADA CORP	63.07	4.80%
69	GRT.UN	GRANITE REIT	60.93	4.60%
69	BCE	BCE INC	59.69	5.30%
57	AFN	AG GROWTH INTERNATION	57.74	4.20%
56	BIP.UN	BROOKFIELD INFASTRUCTU	55.96	4.80%
48	OLY	OLYMPIA FINANCIAL CORP	55.50	5.00%
68	SLF	SUN LIFE FINANCIAL INC	55.41	3.60%
65	EMA	EMERA INC	50.31	4.70%
70	FTS	FORTIS INC	49.63	3.60%
68	T	TELUS CORP	49.45	4.40%
60	ENB	ENBRIDGE INC	49.4	6.00%
67	PPL	PEMBINA PIPELINE CORP	47.53	5.10%
55	ACO.Y	ATCO LTD	45.50	3.60%
62	ACO.X	ATCO LTD	45.14	3.50%
53	AW.UN	A&W REVENUE ROYALTIES I	43.68	4.30%
71	SU	SUNCOR ENERGY INC	43.11	3.90%
63	LB	LAURENTIAN BANK OF CAN	42.78	6.10%
57	BEP.UN	BROOKFIELD RENEWABLE P	42.06	6.60%
72	MIC	GENWORTH MI CANADA INC	41.99	4.90%
70	CNQ	CANADIAN NATURAL RES	37.68	3.70%
50	CU.X	CANADIAN UTILITIES LTD	36.90	4.60%
57	CU	CANADIAN UTILITIES LTD	36.88	4.60%
50	IGM	IGM FINANCIAL INC	35.81	6.10%
61	EIF	EXCHANGE INCOME CORP	35.39	6.20%
30	BPS.PR.U	BROOKFIELD OFFICE PROPE	34.50	5.10%
59	SRU.UN	SMARTCENTRES REIT	33.76	5.30%
45	OSB	NORBORD INC	33.52	4.70%
58	NFI	NFI GROUP INC	32.94	4.60%
28	NEW.PR.D	NEWGROWTH CORP	32.17	4.10%
52	GWO	GREAT-WEST LIFECO INC	32.14	5.20%
66	VET	VERMILLION ENERGY INC	32.03	9%
59	PWF	POWER FINANCIAL CORP	31.27	5.60%
44	PEGI	PATTERN ENERGY GROUP IN	30.93	7.30%
54	KEY	KEYERA COPR	30.6	5.90%

62	POW	POWER CORPORATION OF C	30.40	5.00%
62	CPX	CAPITAL POWER CORP	30.23	5.90%
52	FN	FIRST NATIONAL FINANCIAL	29.55	6.20%
17	BNS.PR.E	BANK OF NOVA SCOTIA	29.52	5.30%
19	JE.PR.U	JUST ENERGY GROUP INC	29.23	9.80%
50	NWC	THE NORTH WEST CO INC	29.15	4.50%
30	ENB.PR.V	ENBRIDGE INC	29.02	6.90%
38	SJR.A	SHAW COMMUNICATIONS I	28.80	4.20%
62	NVU.UN	NORTHVIEW APARTMENT R	28.26	5.80%
59	BPY.UN	BROOKFIELD PROPERTY PA	28.06	6.30%
56	SJR.B	SHAW COMMUNICATIONS IN	27.12	4.40%
27	ENB.PF.V	ENBRIDGE INC	26.94	6.70%
17	ALB.PR.C	ALLBANC SPLIT CORP II	26.50	4.60%
27	ENB.PR.U	ENBRIDGE INC	26.23	6.30%
16	PVF.PR.U	PARTNERS VALUE INVEST	26.19	5.80%
17	BNS.PR.G	BANK OF NOVA SCOTIA	26.15	5.30%
17	MFC.PR.O	MANULIFE FINANCIAL CORP	26.15	5.40%
54	VNR	VALENER INC	26.12	4.60%
24	ALA.PR.U	ALTAGAS LTD	26.1	6.80%
21	CLIQ	ALCANNA INC	26.1	6.80%
27	ENB.PF.U	ENBRIDGE INC	26.08	6.30%
17	TRP.PR.J	TRANSCANADA CORP	26.07	5.30%
17	RY.PR.R	ROYAL BANK OF CANADA	26.05	5.30%
32	TD.PF.G	THE TORONTO-DOMINION B	26.04	5.30%
17	NA.PR.X	NATIONAL BANK OF CANA	26.04	5.40%
15	CU.PR.I	CANADIAN UTILITIES LTD	26.01	4.30%
17	CPX.PR.G	CAPITAL POWER CORP	26.00	5.80%
64	REI.UN	RIOCAN REIT	25.96	5.60%
18	RY.PR.Q	ROYAL BANK OF CANADA	25.92	5.30%
17	PPL.PR.K	PEMBINA PIPELINE CORP	25.92	5.60%
40	EML.PR.A	THE EMPIRE LIFE INSURANC	25.89	5.60%
17	PPL.PR.M	PEMBINA PIPELINE CORP	25.88	5.50%
18	NA.PR.A	NATIONAL BANK OF CANAD	25.85	5.20%
17	CWB.PR.C	CANADIAN WESTERN BANK	25.81	6.10%

29	PWF.PR.I	POWER FINANCIAL CORP	25.8	5.80%
17	BNS.PR.H	BANK OF NOVA SCOTIA	25.80	4.70%
17	LB.PR.J	LAURENTIAN BANK OF CAN	25.79	5.70%
20	BPO.PR.C	BROOKFIELD OFFICE PROP	25.78	5.80%
17	BMO.PR.B	BANK OF MONTREAL	25.75	4.70%
17	CWB.PR.D	CANADIAN WESTERN BANK	25.75	5.90%
17	PVS.PR.E	PARTNERS VALUE SPLIT CO	25.75	5.30%
17	TD.PF.H	THE TORONTO-DOMINION B	25.74	4.70%
18	W.PR.N	WESTCOAST ENERGY IN	25.73	5.00%
28	PWF.PR.R	POWER FINANCIAL CORP	25.65	5.40%
29	WN.PR.A	GEORGE WESTON LTD	25.6	5.70%
24	BAM.PF.H	BROOKFIELD ASSET MANAGEMENT INC	25.60	4.90%
17	W.PR.K	WESTCOAST ENERGY IN	25.60	5.10%
52	CGX	CINEPLEX INC	25.58	6.80%
28	PVS.PR.D	PARTNERS VALUE SPLIT CO	25.58	4.40%
29	GWO.PR.F	GREAT-WEST LIFECO INC	25.56	5.80%
29	POW.PR.C	POWER CORPORATION OF C	25.55	5.70%
28	PWF.PR.O	POWER FINANCIAL CORP	25.53	5.70%
18	TRP.PR.K	TRANSCANADA CORP	25.51	4.80%
29	POW.PR.G	POWER CORPORATION OF C	25.5	5.50%
29	PWF.PR.G	POWER FINANCIAL CORP	25.50	5.80%
17	GRP.PR.A	GLOBAL RESOURCE CHAMP	25.49	6.10%
29	PWF.PR.H	POWER FINANCIAL CORP	25.47	5.60%
20	GWO.PR.M	GREAT-WEST LIFECO INC	25.44	5.70%
32	BIR.PR.A	BIRCHCLIFF ENERGY LTD	25.42	8.20%
18	CM.PR.T	CANADIAN IMPERIAL BANK	25.4	5.50%
33	GWO.PR.L	GREAT-WEST LIFECO INC	25.35	5.60%
30	BPS.PR.A	BROOKFIELD PROPERTY SPL	25.35	5.70%
28	PWF.PR.E	POWER FINANCIAL CORP	25.34	5.50%
17	BEP.PR.I	BROOKFIELD RENEWABLE P	25.34	5.70%
29	BPS.PR.B	BROOKFIELD PROPERTY SP	25.30	5.00%
30	BPS.PR.C	BROOKFIELD PROPERTY SP	25.25	5.10%
17	CPX.PR.I	CAPITAL POWER CORP	25.25	5.70%
17	RY.PR.P	ROYAL BANK OF CANADA	25.25	5.20%

27	RY.PR.E	ROYAL BANK OF CANADA	**25.23**	4.50%
26	RY.PR.G	ROYAL BANK OF CANADA	**25.20**	4.50%
20	EIT.PR.A	CANOE EIT INCOME FUND	**25.19**	4.80%
28	RY.PR.C	ROYAL BANK OF CANADA	**25.18**	4.60%
26	RY.PR.F	ROYAL BANK OF CANADA	**25.16**	4.40%
24	RY.PR.A	ROYAL BANK OF CANADA	**25.16**	4.40%
17	BIP.PR.B	BROOKFIELD INFASTRUC	**25.13**	5.50%
17	ENB.PR.I	ENBRIDGE INC	**25.12**	5.10%
17	MFC.PR.R	MANULIFE FINANCIAL CORP	**25.12**	4.80%
17	EIT.PR.B	CANOE EIT INCOME FUND	**25.10**	4.80%
28	POW.PR.A	POWER CORPORATION OF C	**25.09**	5.60%
29	BIR.PR.C	BIRCHCLIFF ENERGY LTD	**25.08**	7%
28	RY.PR.W	ROYAL BANK OF CANADA	**25.05**	4.90%
30	VNR.PR.A	VALENER INC	**25.00**	4.60%
17	BIP.PR.C	BROOKFIELD INFASTRUCTU	**25.00**	5.30%
57	IGM.PR.B	IGM FINANCIAL INC	**24.99**	5.90%
28	ELF.PR.H	E-L FINANCIAL COPR LTD	**24.99**	5.50%
28	GWO.PR.P	GREAT-WEST LIFECO INC	**24.97**	5.40%
28	L.PR.B	LOBLAWS COMPANIES LTD	**24.94**	5.30%
18	BMO.PR.Z	BANK OF MONTREAL	**24.79**	5.00%
28	EQB.PR.C	EQUTABLE GROUP INC	**24.74**	6.40%
28	GWO.PR.S	GREAT-WEST LIFECO INC	**24.73**	5.30%
17	BEP.PR.G	BROOKFIELD RENEWABLE P	**24.72**	5.60%
28	ENB.PR.A	ENBRIDGE INC	**24.69**	5.60%
17	AX.PR.I	ARTIS REAL ESTAT INVEST	**24.69**	6.10%
67	MFC	MANULIFE FINANCIAL CORP	**24.64**	4.00%
17	CU.PR.H	CANADIAN UTILITIES LTD	**24.6**	5.30%
17	BAM.PF.I	BROOKFIELD ASSET MANAG	**24.55**	4.90%
44	WFC	WALL FINANCIAL CORP	**24.50**	4.10%
17	IFC.PR.F	INTACT FINANCIAL CORP	**24.49**	5.40%
28	POW.PR.B	POWER CORPORATION OF C	**24.35**	5.50%
28	WN.PR.D	GEORGE WESTON LTD	**24.27**	5.40%
28	GWO.PR.G	GREAT-WEST LIFECO INC	**24.16**	5.40%
28	WN.PR.C	GEORGE WESTON LTD	**24.13**	5.40%

15	RY.PR.O	ROYAL BANK OF CANADA	24.10	5.10%
28	ELF.PR.F	E-L FINANCIAL COPR LTD	24.08	5.50%
17	TD.PF.F	THE TORONTO-DOMINION B	24.06	5.10%
28	PWF.PR.F	POWER FINANCIAL CORP	24.03	5.50%
28	RY.PR.UN	ROYAL BANK OF CANADA	24.00	5.10%
17	IFC.PR.E	INTACT FINANCIAL CORP	24	5.40%
28	GWO.PR.T	GREAT-WEST LIFECO INC	23.98	5.40%
28	GWO.PR.Q	GREAT-WEST LIFECO INC	23.97	5.40%
64	NPI	NORTHLAND POWER INC	23.83	5.00%
17	KML.PR.A	KINDER MORGAN CANADA	23.83	5.50%
18	BMO.PR.C	BANK OF MONTREAL	23.79	4.70%
48	CCS.PR.C	CO-OPERATORS GENERAL IN	23.74	5.30%
17	EMA.PR.H	EMERA INC	23.70	5.20%
17	KML.PR.C	KINDER MORGAN CANADA	23.67	5.50%
17	PWF.PR.Z	POWER FINANCIAL CORP	23.62	5.40%
26	PPL.PR.S	PEMBINA PIPELINE CORP	23.55	5.30%
63	D.UN	DREAM OFFICE REIT	23.51	4.30%
28	PWF.PR.L	POWER FINANCIAL CORP	23.48	5.40%
49	RUS	RUSSEL METALS INC	23.29	6.60%
17	TD.PF.I	THE TORONTO-DOMINION B	23.17	4.80%
18	BAM.PF.J	BROOKFIELD ASSET MANA	23.03	5.10%
17	ALA.PR.I	ALTAGAS LTD	22.96	5.70%
61	HR.UN	H&R REAL ESTATE INVEST	22.95	6.10%
28	CU.PR.D	CANADIAN UTILITIES LTD	22.9	5.40%
18	PPL.PF.A	PEMBINA PIPELINE CORP	22.89	5.40%
17	ENB.PF.K	ENBRIDGE INC	22.89	5.30%
32	INE.PR.C	INNERGEX RENEWABLE ENE	22.82	6.30%
18	CM.PR.R	CANADIAN IMPERIAL BANK	22.81	4.80%
28	CU.PR.E	CANADIAN UTILITIES LTD	22.77	5.40%
27	PWF.PR.K	POWER FINANCIAL CORP	22.7	5.50%
17	IAF.PR.I	IA FINANCIAL CORP	22.7	5.30%
29	WN.PR.E	GEORGE WESTON LTD	22.68	5.20%
28	FTS.PR.F	FORTIS INC	22.65	5.40%
28	POW.PR.D	POWER CORPORATION OF C	22.65	5.50%

28	SLF.PR.B	SUN LIFE FINANCIAL INC	22.65	5.30%
17	BIR.PR.D	BROOKFIELD INFASTRUCT	22.65	5.40%
17	NA.PR.C	NATIONAL BANK OF CANA	22.65	4.90%
18	BNS.PR.I	BANK OF NOVA SCOTIA	22.60	5.40%
28	GWO.PR.R	GREAT-WEST LIFECO INC	22.50	5.30%
25	FFH.PR.M	FAIRFAX FINANCIAL HOLD	22.50	5.20%
18	BMO.PR.D	BANK OF MONTREAL	22.50	4.90%
24	MFC.PR.H	MANULIFE FINANCIAL CORP	22.43	4.80%
28	GWO.PR.H	GREAT-WEST LIFECO INC	22.41	5.40%
17	BMO.PR.E	BANK OF MONTREAL	22.33	5.40%
31	SLF.PR.A	SUN LIFE FINANCIAL INC	22.2	5.30%
28	PWF.PR.S	POWER FINANCIAL CORP	22.11	5.40%
28	IAF.PR.B	IA FINANCIAL CORP	22.10	5.20%
28	ELF.PR.G	E-L FINANCIAL COPR LTD	22.07	5.40%
17	BEP.PR.K	BROOKFIELD RENEWABEL P	22.01	5.60%
17	BIP.PR.E	BROOKFIELD INFASTRUC	21.99	5.60%
17	ECN.PR.A	ECN CAPITAL CORP	21.95	7.40%
25	FTS.PR.J	FORTIS INC	21.93	5.50%
28	MFC.PR.B	MANULIFE FINANCIAL CORP	21.9	5.30%
16	AX.PR.A	ARTIS REAL ESTAT INVEST	21.89	6.50%
17	NA.PR.G	NATIONAL BANK OF CANA	21.85	5.70%
34	H	HYDRO ONE LTD	21.75	4.20%
31	AX.PR.G	ARTIS REAL ESTAT INVEST	21.75	5.70%
17	TD.PF.J	THE TORONTO-DOMINION B	21.75	5.40%
47	GEI	GIBSON ENERGY INC	21.7	6.10%
28	EFN.PR.G	ELEMENT FLEET MANAGE	21.66	7.50%
26	IAF.PR.G	IA FINANCIAL CORP	21.64	4.40%
24	TD.PF.E	THE TORONTO-DOMINION B	21.60	4.30%
18	RY.PR.S	ROYAL BANK OF CANADA	21.6	5.60%
17	BEP.PR.E	BROOKFIELD RENEWABLE	21.6	6.50%
33	EFN.PR.A	ELEMENT FLEET MANAG	21.57	8%
25	BAM.PF.D	BROOKFIELD ASSET MANAG	21.5	5.70%
65	FCR	FIRST CAPITAL REALTY INC	21.48	4.00%
28	CIU.PR.A	CU INC	21.35	5.40%

25	AQN.PR.D	ALGONQUIN POWER UTILITI	21.32	5.90%
25	PPL.PR.I	PEMBINA PIPELINE CORP	21.32	5.60%
62	IPL	INTER PIPELINE LTD	21.29	8.10%
24	MFC.PR.I	MANULIFE FINANCIAL CORP	21.21	5.10%
28	CU.PR.F	CANADIAN UTILITIES LTD	21.2	5.30%
17	ECN.PR.A	ECN CAPITAL CORP	21.19	7.30%
28	CU.PR.G	CANADIAN UTILITIES LTD	21.15	5.30%
25	GWO.PR.I	GREAT-WEST LIFECO INC	21.13	5.30%
24	BMO.PR.Y	ROYAL BANK OF CANADA	21.11	4.50%
28	SLF.PR.E	SUN LIFE FINANCIAL INC	21.10	5.30%
28	BAM.PF.C	BROOKFIELD ASSET MANAG	21.07	5.80%
18	TD.PF.D	THE TORONTO-DOMINION B	21.02	4.30%
28	MFC.PR.C	MANULIFE FINANCIAL CORP	21.01	5.30%
28	SLF.PR.C	SUN LIFE FINANCIAL INC	21.00	5.30%
28	SLF.PR.D	SUN LIFE FINANCIAL INC	21.00	5.30%
44	CUP.U	CARIBBEAN UTILITIES CO L	20.80	4.50%
16	RY.PR.J	ROYAL BANK OF CANADA	20.76	4.30%
32	BBD.PR.C	BOMBARDIER INC	20.75	7.50%
33	MFC.PR.G	MANULIFE FINANCIAL CORP	20.74	4.70%
24	BAM.PF.A	BROOKFIELD ASSET MANAG	20.74	6.10%
24	HSE.PR.E	HUSKY ENERGY INC	20.7	5.50%
16	MFC.PR.Q	MANULIFE FINANCIAL CORP	20.70	5.70%
24	MFC.PR.J	MANULIFE FINANCIAL CORP	20.69	5.60%
25	BAM.PR.M	BROOKFIELD ASSET MANAG	20.67	5.80%
24	SLF.PR.I	SUN LIFE FINANCIAL INC	20.63	4.60%
24	BIP.PR.A	BROOKFIELD INFASTRUCT	20.59	5.50%
17	CM.PR.S	CANADIAN IMPERIAL BANK	20.59	5.50%
17	IFC.PR.G	INTACT FINANCIAL CORP	20.56	6.00%
17	ALA.PR.K	ALTAGAS LTD	20.54	6%
25	BAM.PR.N	BROOKFIELD ASSET MAN	20.5	5.80%
25	BCE.PR.O	BCE INC	20.49	5.20%
45	PSI	PASON SYSTEMS INC	20.48	3.50%
28	EMA.PR.E	EMERA INC	20.48	5.50%
30	EFN.PR.C	ELEMENT FLEET MANAGEM	20.4	7.90%

17	BEP.PR.M	BROOKFIELD RENEWABLE P	**20.4**	6.10%
31	AX.PR.E	ARTIS REAL ESTAT INVEST	**20.36**	6.80%
16	NA.PR.E	NATIONAL BANK OF CANA	**20.35**	5.70%
24	CM.PR.Q	CANADIAN IMPERIAL BANK	**20.30**	4.50%
24	RY.PR.M	ROYAL BANK OF CANADA	**20.30**	4.40%
24	EMA.PR.C	EMERA INC	**20.2**	5.80%
14	BSC.PR.C	BNS SPLIT CORP II	**20.18**	3.90%
17	EFN.PR.I	ELEMENT FLEET	**20.1**	7.10%
27	CPX.PR,X	CAPITAL POWER CORP	**20.08**	6.80%
21	BAM.PF.Z	BROOKFIELD ASSET MANA	**20.00**	5.80%
9	HSE.PR.G	HUSKY ENERGY INC	**20.00**	5.60%
27	EFN.PR.E	ELEMENT FLEET MANAGE	**19.88**	7.90%
24	BCE.PR.Q	BCE INC	**19.85**	6.10%
24	NPI.PR.C	NORTHLAND POWER INC	**19.85**	6.40%
27	BRF.PR.F	BROOKFIELD RENEWABLE P	**19.8**	6.30%
27	AQN,PR.A	ALGONQUIN POWER UTILIT	**19.75**	6.50%
27	CPX.PR.E	CAPITAL POWER CORP	**19.73**	6.60%
27	BRF.PR.E	BROOKFIELD RENEWABLE P	**19.69**	6.30%
16	BAM.PF.F	BROOKFIELD ASSET MANAG	**19.4**	5.80%
24	PPL.PR.Q	PEMBINA PIPELINE CORP	**19.38**	6.20%
53	CIX	CI FINANCIAL CORP	**19.35**	3.70%
40	ACI	ALTAGAS CANADA INC	**19.35**	3.60%
24	FFH.PR.K	FAIRFAX FINANCIAL HOLDINGS LTD	**19.33**	5.90%
24	TRP.PR.G	TRANSCANADA CORP	**19.21**	5.00%
24	FTS.PR.M	FORTIS INC	**19.18**	5.30%
24	MFC.PR.K	MANULIFE FINANCIAL CORP	**19.16**	5.80%
24	BAM.PF.G	BROOKFIELD ASSET MANAG	**19.14**	5.90%
26	TA.PR.J	TRANSALTA CORP	**19.11**	6.90%
24	FTS.PR.G	FORTIS INC	**19.10**	5.80%
24	ALA.PR.E	ALTAGAS LTD	**19.09**	7.10%
26	ENB.PF.N	ENBRIDGE INC	**19.01**	6.70%
24	HSE.PR.C	HUSKY ENERGY INC	**18.96**	6.00%
24	BPO.PR.T	BROOKFIELD OFFICE PROPE	**18.9**	7.10%
28	PWF.PR.T	POWER FINANCIAL CORP	**18.86**	5.50%

24	EMA.PR.F	EMERA INC	**18.84**	5.60%
56	KMP.UN	KILLAM APARTMENT REIT	**18.81**	3.50%
26	NPF.UN	NORTH AMERICAN PREFER	**18.8**	7.30%
24	RY.PR.H	ROYAL BANK OF CANADA	**18.80**	5.20%
58	ALA	ALTAGAS LTD	**18.79**	5.10%
25	PPL.PR.E	PEMBINA PIPELINE CORP	**18.77**	6.70%
47	PSK	PRAIRIESKY ROYALTY LTD	**18.75**	4.20%
24	BMO.PR.S	BANK OF MONTREAL	**18.75**	5.30%
57	WIR.U	WPT INDUSTRIAL REIT	**18.59**	5.40%
24	CWB.PR.B	CANADIAN WESTERN BANK	**18.57**	5.80%
47	SIA	SIENNA SENIOR LIVING CO	**18.52**	5.00%
31	AZP.PR.C	ATLANTIC POWER PREFER	**18.52**	7.40%
25	NA.PR.S	NATIONAL BANK OF CANA	**18.51**	5.50%
26	TA.PR.H	TRANSALTA CORP	**18.5**	7.10%
24	BAM.PF.B	BROOKFIELD ASSET MANAG	**18.50**	5.60%
31	AZP.PR.B	ATLANTIC POWER PREFERR	**18.48**	7.50%
26	RY.PR.Z	ROYAL BANK OF CANADA	**18.48**	5.50%
24	MFC.PR.M	MANULIFE FINANCIAL CORP	**18.47**	5.30%
16	IFC.PR.D	INTACT FINANCIAL CORP	**18.43**	5.80%
24	TD.PF.C	THE TORONTO-DOMINION B	**18.41**	5.10%
25	TD.PF.B	THE TORONTO-DOMINION B	**18.40**	5.20%
24	IFC.PR.C	INTACT FINANCIAL CO	**18.40**	4.50%
24	TD.PF.A	THE TORONTO-DOMINION B	**18.40**	5.30%
24	FFH.PR.C	FAIRFAX FINANCIAL HOLDI	**18.37**	6.30%
25	CM.PR.O	CANADIAN IMPERIAL BANK	**18.35**	5.30%
46	BLX	BORALEX INC	**18.31**	3.60%
24	MFC.PR.N	MANULIFE FINANCIAL CORP	**18.21**	5.20%
24	CU.PR.C	CANADIAN UTILITIES LTD	**18.20**	4.70%
24	BMO.PR.T	BANK OF MONTREAL	**18.15**	5.40%
46	ITP	INTERTAPE POLYMER GRO	**18.13**	4.10%
25	BMO.PR.W	BANK OF MONTREAL	**18.10**	5.20%
24	FFH.PR.D	FAIRFAX FINANCIAL HOLDI	**18.1**	6.50%
58	AD	ALARIS ROYALTY CORP	**18.07**	9%
40	CSW.A	CORBY SPIRIT AND WINE L	**17.99**	4.90%

24	BAM.PF.E	BROOKFIELD ASSET MANAG	17.9	6.20%
64	MRG.UN	MORGUARD NORTH AMERI	17.80	3.80%
24	SLF.PR.H	SUN LIFE FINANCIAL INC	17.80	4.00%
25	CM.PR.P	CANADIAN IMPERIAL BANK	17.77	5.30%
24	PPL.PR.G	PEMBINA PIPELINE CORP	17.76	6.30%
24	PPL.PR.O	PEMBINA PIPELINE CORP	17.75	6.30%
24	FTS.PR.K	FORTIS INC	17.67	5.50%
24	MFC.PR.L	MANULIFE FINANCIAL CORP	17.62	5.60%
27	ENB.PR.F	ENBRIDGE INC	17.61	6.70%
24	NA.PR.W	NATIONAL BANK OF CAN	17.61	5.50%
25	PPL.PR.A	PEMBINA PIPELINE CORP	17.59	7%
48	BPF.UN	BOSTON PIZZA ROYALTIES	17.56	7.80%
35	ZZZ	SLEEP COUNTRY CANADA HOLDINGS IN	17.56	4.20%
16	SLF.PR.K	SUN LIFE FINANCIAL INC	17.56	5.40%
49	KEG.UN	THE KEG ROYALTIES INCOME FUND	17.49	6.50%
39	CSW.B	CORBY SPIRIT AND WINE LTD	17.44	5.00%
24	PPL.PR.C	PEMBINA PIPELINE CORP	17.42	6.40%
24	BPO.PR.R	BROOKFIELD OFFICE PROPERTIES INC	17.3	6.00%
16	FFH.PR.J	FAIRFAX FINANCIAL HOLDINGS LTD	17.2	6.50%
24	BRF.PR.C	BROOKFIELD RENEWABLE POWER PREF.	17.19	6.40%
24	ENB.PR.J	ENBRIDGE INC	17.18	6.40%
24	ENB.PF.G	ENBRIDGE INC	17.15	6.40%
24	ENB.PF.E	ENBRIDGE INC	17.15	6.40%
28	CF.PR.C	CANACCORD GENUITY GROUP INC	17.08	7.20%
24	ENB.PF.A	ENBRIDGE INC	17.07	6.40%
23	TRP.PR.D	TRANSCANADA CORP	17.03	5.70%
49	ET	EVERTZ TECHNOLOGIES LTD	17.00	4.20%
28	ENB.PF.C	ENBRIDGE INC	17	6.40%
24	ENB.PR.P	ENBRIDGE INC	16.95	6.50%

46	BRE	BROOKFIELD REAL ESTATE SERVICES I	16.9	8.10%
24	BPO.PR.A	BROOKFIELD OFFICE PROPERTIES INC	16.9	7%
23	BAM.PR.E	BROOKFIELD ASSET MANAGEMENT INC	16.9	5.80%
24	LB.PR.H	LAURENTIAN BANK OF CANADA	16.76	6.40%
24	TRP.PR.E.	TRANSCANADA CORP	16.75	6.30%
24	ENB.PR.D	ENBRIDGE INC	16.72	6.60%
51	I	ACADIAN TIMBER CORP	16.7	6.90%
27	BCE.PR.C	BCE INC	16.65	6.70%
24	ALA.PR.G	ALTAGAS LTD	16.58	7.20%
23	FFH.PR.I	FAIRFAX FINANCIAL HOLDINGS LTD	16.55	5.60%
22	BAM.PR.G	BROOKFIELD ASSET MANAGEMENT INC	16.54	4.20%
43	SRV.UN	SIR ROYALTY INCOME FUNE	16.36	7.70%
44	ISV	INFORMATION SERVICES CORP	16.26	4.90%
28	ENB.PR.T	ENBRIDGE INC	16.26	6.10%
24	ENB.PR.H	ENBRIDGE INC	16.15	6.80%
16	BAM.PR.S	BROOKFIELD ASSET MANAGEMENT INC	16.15	6.10%
23	BAM.PR.R	BROOKFIELD ASSET MANAGEMENT INC	16.01	4.70%
16	NPI.PR.B	NORTHLAND POWER INC	16	6.80%
26	BCE.PR.A	BCE INC	15.9	5.70%
26	NPI.PR.A	NORTHLAND POWER INC	15.85	5.50%
16	ENB.PR.C	ENBRIDGE INC	15.85	6.50%
25	TA.PR.F	TRANSALTA CORP	15.83	6.40%
46	WJX	WAJAX CORP	15.82	6.40%
23	IFC.PR.A	INTACT FINANCIAL CORP	15.8	5.40%
16	FFH.PR.H	FAIRFAX FINANCIAL HOLD	15.8	6.50%
47	TCL.B	TRANSCONTINENTAL INC	15.77	5.60%
52	MKP	MCCAN MORTGAGE CORP	15.76	8.1
22	BRF.PR.B	BROOKFIELD RENEWABLE P	15.75	6.70%
24	BPO.PR.N	BROOKFIELD OFFICE PROP	15.74	6.10%

46	TCL.A	TRANSCONTINENTAL INC	15.71	5.60%
24	BPO.PR.P	BROOKFIELD OFFICE PROPE	15.71	6.70%
22	ENB.PR.Y	ENBRIDGE INC	15.71	6.40%
16	BCE.PR.R	BCE INC	15.7	6.60%
44	DR	MEDICAL FACILITIES CORP	15.69	7%
23	BCE.PR.B	BCE INC	15.65	6.40%
23	BCE.PR.S	BCE INC	15.65	6.40%
23	BCE.PR.Z	BCE INC	15.65	6.20%
23	BCE.PR.E	BCE INC	15.6	6.30%
23	BAM.PR.T	BROOKFIELD ASSET MANA	15.6	5.40%
23	BCE.PR.H	BCE INC	15.59	6.30%
23	BCE.PR.D	BCE INC	15.59	6.30%
30	BRF.PR.A	BROOKFIELD RENEWABLE P	15.58	5.40%
23	BCE.PR.J	BCE INC	15.58	6.40%
24	BCE.PR.Y	BCE INC	15.53	6.40%
15	EMA.PR.B	EMERA INC	15.5	5.30%
23	FFH.PR.G	FAIRFAX FINANCIAL HOLD	15.49	5.40%
31	AZP.PR.A	ATLANTIC POWER PREFER	15.48	8%
23	EMA.PR.A	EMERA INC	15.45	4.10%
23	ENB.PR.B	ENBRIDGE INC	15.35	5.50%
22	BCE.PR.F	BCE INC	15.30	5.10%
59	AQN	ALGONQUIN POWER UTILIT	15.20	4.50%
22	BCE.PR.I	BCE INC	15.14	4.50%
22	BCE.PR.T	BCE INC	15.12	5.00%
22	BCE.PR.G	BCE INC	15.10	4.60%
22	TRP.PR.A	TRANSCANADA CORP	15.10	5.40%
20	SLF.PR.G	SUN LIFE FINANCIAL INC	15.00	3.80%
15	SLF.PR.J	SUN LIFE FINANCIAL INC	15.00	5.10%
40	KML	KINDER MORGAN CANADA	14.97	4.30%
22	TRP.PR.F	TRANSCANADA CORP	14.86	6.10%
20	GWO.PR.N	GREAT-WEST LIFECO INC	14.79	3.70%
15	GWO.PR.O	GREAT-WEST LIFECO INC	14.78	5.00%
18	ENS	E SPLIT CORP	14.75	10%
15	SJR.PR.B	SHAW COMMUNICATIONS I	14.75	6.00%

15	BCE.PR.N	BCE INC	14.71	6.40%
25	FFH.PR.F	FAIRFAX FINANCIAL HOLDI	14.69	6.30%
25	PIC.PR.A	PREMIUM INCOME CORP	14.64	5.90%
36	ALA.PR.B	ALTAGAS LTD	14.61	7.40%
15	PWF.PR.Q	POWER FINANCIAL CORP	14.58	5.10%
43	CSH.UN	CHARTWELL REITIREMENT	14.55	4.10%
22	FTS.PR.H	FORTIS INC	14.51	4.30%
22	BCE.PR.M	BCE INC	14.48	4.80%
43	GS	GLUSKIN SHEFF & ASSOCIA	14.46	6.90%
22	INE.PR.A	INNERGEX RENEWABLE ENE	14.45	6.20%
59	CRR.UN	CROMBIE REIT	14.42	6.20%
22	ALA.PR.A	ALTAGAS LTD	14.42	5.90%
23	SJR.PR.A	SHAW COMMUNICATIONS I	14.40	4.90%
20	MFC.PR.F	MANULIFE FINANCIAL CORP	14.32	3.70%
22	FTS.PR.I	FORTIS INC	14.3	5.30%
15	MFC.PR.B	MANULIFE FINANCIAL CORP	14.28	5.00%
46	LNF	LEON'S FUNITURE LTD	14.22	3.90%
48	INE	INNERGEX RENEWABLE E	14.20	5.00%
22	FFH.PR.E	FAIRFAX FINANCIAL HOLDINGS LTD	14.20	5.10%
23	PWF.PR.P	POWER FINANCIAL CORP	14.17	4.10%
15	BCE.PR.L	BCE INC	14.17	6.30%
52	BEK.A	BECKER MILK CO LTD	14.10	5.70%
25	CF.PR.A	CANNACORD GENUITY GROUP INC	14.1	6.90%
23	BAM.PR.X	BROOKFIELD ASSET MANAGEMENT INC	14.05	4.80%
26	BCE.PR.K	BCE INC	14.03	5.20%
17	DC.PR.E	DUNDEE CORP	13.99	14%
57	CRT.UN	CT REAL ESTATE INVESTME	13.89	5.40%
52	RNW	TRANSALTA RENEWABLES I	13.89	6.80%
68	DRG.UN	DREAM GLOBAL REIT	13.84	5.80%
41	NEXA	NEXA RESOURCES SA	13.83	4.90%
15	TRP.PR.I	TRANSCANADA CORP	13.83	5.70%
22	CPX.PR.A	CAPITAL POWER CORP	13.81	5.50%
15	FN.PR.B	FIRST NATIONAL FINANCIAL	13.68	6.80%

20	CIU.PR.C	CU INC	13.62	4.10%
22	PWF.PR.A	POWER FINANCIAL CORP	13.60	5.00%
51	MRD	MELCOR DEVELOPMENTS L	13.58	3.80%
51	FC	FIRM CAPITAL MORTGAGE I	13.48	7%
32	CHP.UN	CHOICE PROPERTIES REIT	13.4	5.50%
55	AI	ATRIUM MORTGAGE INVES	13.36	6.70%
24	FN.PR.A	FIRST NATIONAL FINANCIAL	13.25	5.30%
26	CSE.PR.A	CAPSTONE INFASTRUCTURE	13.17	6.20%
15	HSE.PR.B	HUSKY ENERGY INC	13.15	6.40%
22	TRP.PR.C	TRANSCANADA CORP	13.13	4.30%
21	TRI.PR.B	THOMSON REUTERS CORP	13.08	5.10%
15	TA.PR.E	TRANSALTA CORP	13.02	7%
24	HOM.U	BSR REAL ESTATE INVE	13.01	5.10%
17	DC.PR.B	DUNDEE CORP	12.6	11%
17	DC.PR.D	DUNDEE CORP	12.57	11%
22	HSE.PR.A	HUSKY ENERGY INC	12.55	4.80%
39	DII.A	DOREL INDUSTRIES INC	12.51	11%
50	SRT.UN	SLATE RETAIL REIT	12.44	9%
49	TXT.PR.A	TOP 10 SPLIT TRUST	12.43	6.30%
25	SRT.U	SLATE RETAIL REIT	12.43	9%
36	SBC	BROMPTON SPLIT BANC CO	12.37	9%
21	TRP.PR.B	TRANSCANADA CORP	12.35	4.30%
36	FSZ	FIERA CAPITAL CORP	12.33	6.80%
22	TRP.PR.H	TRANSCANADA CORP	12.32	6.00%
58	MRT.UN	MORGUARD REIT	12.3	7.80%
24	TA.PR.D	TRANSALTA CORP	12.28	5.60%
43	RCO.UN	MIDDLEFIELD CAN GLOBAL	12.25	5.30%
17	PRM	BIG PHARMA SPLIT CORP	12.2	10%
14	STUS.U	STARLIGHT US MULTI-FAM	12.17	7.20%
27	PL	PINNACLE RENEWABLE ENE	12.12	5.20%
54	SMU.UN	SUMMIT INDUSTRIAL INCO	12.05	4.30%
30	FEC	FONTERA ENERGY CORP	11.93	4.10%
62	PIF	POLARIS INFASTRUCTURE I	11.79	6.90%
41	DII.B	DOREL INDUSTRIES INC	11.77	12%

22	BAM.PR.B	BROOKFIELD ASSET MANAG	11.68	5.70%
21	BAM.PR.C	BROOKFIELD ASSET MAN	11.67	5.70%
21	BAM.PR.K	BROOKFIELD ASSET MANAGEMENT INC	11.64	5.80%
57	DIR.UN	DREAM INDUSTRIAL REIT	11.58	6.10%
29	BBD.PR.D	BOMBARDIER INC	11.57	9%
26	MBK.UN	MANULIFE US REGIONAL BA	11.57	4.30%
47	CUF.UN	COMINAR REIT	11.48	6.30%
47	NWH.UN	NORTHWEST HEALTHCARE	11.45	7%
49	SPB	SUPERIOR PLUS CORP	11.42	6.30%
25	EIT.UN	CANOE EIT INCOME FUND	11.38	11%
16	BK	CANADIAN BANC CORP	11.32	9.50%
21	BBD.PR.B	BOMBARDIER INC	11.3	9%
17	GMP.PR.C	GMP CAPITAL INC	11.15	10%
33	HRR.UN	AUSTRALIAN REIT INCOME	11.01	5.90%
23	GMP.PR.B	GMP CAPITAL INC	11	8.56%
9	GDV	GLOBAL DIVIDEND GROWTH	10.8	11%
21	BPO.PR.Y	BROOKFIELD OFFICE PROPE	10.76	6.30%
21	BPO.PR.X	BROOKFIELD OFFICE PROP	10.75	6.10%
21	BPO.PR.W	BROOKFIELD OFFICE PROP	10.68	6.40%
42	ACQ	AUTOCANADA INC	10.67	3.70%
59	APR.UN	AUTOMOTIVE PROPERTIES	10.58	7.60%
55	AX.UN	ARTIS REAL ESTAT INVEST	10.56	5.10%
25	BK.PR.A	CANADIAN BANC CORP	10.40	5.20%
57	PZA	PIZZA PIZZA ROYALTY CORP	10.35	8.70%
25	SBN.PR.A	S SPLIT CORP	10.35	5.10%
65	INO.UN	INOVALIS REIT	10.33	8%
27	SBC.PR.A	BROMPTON SPLIT BANC COR	10.28	4.90%
15	PRM.PR.A	BIG PHARMA SPLIT CORP	10.28	4.90%
43	ACD	ACCORD FINANCIAL CORP	10.25	3.50%
15	GDV.PR.A	GLOBAL DIVIDEND GROWTH	10.23	4.90%
24	VB.PR.B	VERSABANK	10.22	6.50%

43	CHW	CHESSWOOD GROUP LTD	**10.2**	8.56%
25	PDV.PR.A	PRIME DIVIDEND CORP	**10.2**	6.10%
15	ENS.PR.A	E SPLIT CORP	**10.19**	5.10%
24	DGS.PR.A	DIVIDEND GROWTH SPLIT C	**10.12**	5.20%
25	VB.PR.A	VERSABANK	**10.1**	6.90%
40	MDF	MEDIAGRIF INTERACTIVE T	**10.09**	4.00%
26	DFN.PR.A	DIVIDEND 15 SPLIT CORP	**10.09**	5.20%
26	LBS.PR.A	LIFE & BANC SPLIT CORP	**10.09**	5.40%
24	XTD.PR.A	TDB SPLIT CORP	**10.06**	5.20%
25	DF.PR.A	DIVIDEND 15 SPLIT CORP II	**10.04**	5.20%
25	FFN.PR.A	NORTH AMERICAN FINA	**10.04**	5.50%
24	LCS.PR.A	BROMPTON LIFECO SPLIT C	**10.04**	6.20%
24	LFE.PR.B	CANADIAN LIFE COMPANIES	**10.04**	6.50%
23	WFS.PR.A	WORLD FINANCIAL SPLIT C	**9.95**	5.30%
39	GH	GAMEHOST INC	**9.92**	6.90%
23	FTN.PR.A	FINANCIAL 15 SPLIT CORP	**9.9**	5.60%
40	BCF	BUILDERS CAPITAL MOR	**9.85**	8%
36	MTL	MULLEN GROUP LTD	**9.75**	6.10%
23	OSP.PR.A	BROMPTON OIL SPLIT CORP	**9.71**	5.10%
36	CRWN	CROWN CAPITAL PARTNERS	**9.64**	6.30%
22	BSD.PR.A	SOUNDVEST SPLIT TRUST	**9.52**	6.30%
44	TF	TIMBERCREEK FINANCIAL C	**9.48**	7.40%
53	IVQ.U	INVESQUE INC	**9.4**	11%
50	FCA.U	FIRM CAPITAL AMERICAN R	**9.40**	4.40%
21	ERM	ECLIPSE RESIDENTIAL MORT	**9.34**	8%
32	STUS.A	STARLIGHT US MULTI-FAMI	**9.3**	7%
23	ECF.UN	EAST COAST INVESTMENT G	**9.20**	5.20%
30	ABT	ABSOLUTE SOFTWARE CORP	**8.98**	3.60%
60	RUF.U	PURE MULTI-FAMILY REIT L	**8.96**	5.70%
42	XTC	EXCO TECHNOLOGIES LTD	**8.93**	4.00%
48	RME	ROCKY MOUNTAIN DEALE	**8.73**	5.60%
43	FRU	FREEHOLD ROYALTIES LTD	**8.73**	7.20%
33	KWH.UN	CIRUS ENERGY TRUST	**8.69**	9.60%
21	DFN	DIVIDEND 15 SPLIT CORP	**8.66**	14%

36	CHE.UN	CHEMTRADE LOGISTICS INC	8.54	14%
25	RBN.UN	BLUE RIBBON INCOME FUND	8.27	7.20%
14	LBS	LIFE & BANC SPLIT CORP	8.13	15%
22	IFB.UN	INVESTMENT GRADE INFAS	8.11	6.20%
65	ARX	ARC RESOURGES LTD	8.06	7.40%
14	PFT.UN	CANADIAN PREFERRED SHA	8.04	5.00%
63	SNI.PR.A	SONOR INVESTMENTS LTD	8	9%
21	PCD.UN	PATHFINDER INCOME FUND	7.96	7.50%
32	EXE	EXTENDICARE INC	7.94	5.90%
35	KPT	KP TISSUE INC	7.9	9%
20	FTU.PR.B	US FINANCIAL 15 SPLIT COR	7.89	10%
44	HLF	HIGH LINER FOODS INC	7.8	7.40%
53	CAL	CALEDONIA MINING CORP P	7.70	4.80%
46	HPS.A	HAMMOND POWER SOLUTI	7.70	3.60%
30	FTN	FINANCIAL 15 SPLIT CORP	7.69	19%
22	MFR.UN	MANULIFE FLOATING RATE	7.63	9%
47	MR.UN	MELCOR REIT	7.6	9%
55	CHR	CHORUS AVIATION INC	7.58	6.30%
21	CIQ.UN	CANADIAN HIGH INCOME EQ	7.57	8%
37	SES	SECURE ENERGY SERVICES	7.56	3.60%
30	DRA.UN	DREAM HARD ASSET ALTE	7.56	5.20%
27	BDT	BIRD CONSTRUCTION INC	7.55	5.10%
24	DRM.PR.A	DREAM UNLIMITED CORP	7.49	6.80%
23	DS	DIVIDEND SELECT 15 CORP	7.44	9.80%
19	USF.UN	US FINANCIALS INCOME F	7.23	6.90%
18	PDV	PRIME DIVIDEND CORP	7.15	9.50%
45	FCA	FIRM CAPITAL AMERICAN R	7.07	4.40%
28	HOT.U	AMERICAN HOTEL INCOME	6.91	12%
38	HOT.UN	AMERICAN HOTEL INCOME	6.89	12%
39	SPS.A	SPORTSCENE GROUP INC	6.80	4.60%
41	PIC.A	PREMIUM INCOME CORP	6.77	12%
26	BGI.UN	BROOKFIELD GLOBAL INFA.	6.72	9%
28	MID.UN	MINT INCOME FUND	6.66	7.20%

55	MBN	MBN CORP	**6.65**	4.80%
56	TNT.UN	TRUE NORTH COMMERCIAL	**6.63**	9%
30	FFN	NORTH AMERICAN FINANCIAL SPLIT CO	**6.56**	18%
19	RAY.B	STINGRAY GROUP INC	**6.50**	4.00%
27	RAY.A	STINGRAY GROUP INC	**6.47**	4.10%
59	FCD	FIRM CAPITAL PROPERTY TR	**6.31**	7.50%
28	XTD	TDB SPLIT CORP	**6.29**	9.60%
42	CMG	COMPUTER MODELING GRO	**5.97**	6.60%
57	SOT.UN	SLATE OFFICE REIT	**5.96**	6.90%
40	RSI	ROGERS SUGAR INC	**5.93**	6.10%
59	PEY	PEYTO EXPLORATION & DEVELOPMENT	**5.82**	4.20%
19	CDD.UN	CORE CANADIAN DIVIDEND	**5.74**	6.50%
42	M	MOSAIC CAPITAL CORP	**5.72**	7.20%
33	SWP	SWISS WATER DE COFFEE	**5.54**	4.40%
8	HFC.PR.A	HAMPTON FINANCIAL CORP	**5.5**	15%
16	DGS	DIVIDEND GROWTH SPLIT C	**5.38**	22%
57	ESI	ENSIGN ENERGY SERVICES I	**5.33**	9%
47	AGF.B	AGF MANAGEMENT LTD	**5.24**	6.00%
22	XMF.PR.C	M SPLIT CORP	**5.23**	7.30%
15	DF	DIVIDEND 15 SPLIT CORP II	**5.14**	23%
50	WCP	WHITRCAP RESOURCES INC	**5.11**	6.70%
22	YCM.PR.A	COMMERCE SPLIT CORP	**5.1**	5.90%
25	YCM.PR.B	COMMERCE SPLIT CORP	**5**	7.50%
12	CCI.UN	CANADIAN CONVERTIBLES	**4.97**	13%
23	CLR	CLEARWATER SEAFOODS I	**4.95**	4.00%
22	JE	JUST ENERGY GROUP INC	**4.94**	10%
54	BTB.UN	BTB REAL ESTATE INVEST	**4.85**	9%
36	CWX	CANWEL BUILDING MATER	**4.81**	11%
12	LCS	BROMPTON LIFECO SPLIT C	**4.8**	18%
47	TOG	TORC OIL & GAS LTD	**4.66**	5.70%
34	SOX	STUART OLSON INC	**4.50**	5.30%
31	ERE.UN	EUROPEAN RESIDENTIAL RE	**4.43**	8%
49	PLZ.UN	PLAZA RETAIL REIT	**4.13**	6.70%

30	DE	DECISIVE DIVIDEND CORP	**4**	9%
25	AKT.B	AKITA DRILLING LTD	**4**	9%
16	BSO.UN	BROOKFIELD SELECT OPP. I	**3.87**	15%
41	HWO	HIGH ARTIC ENERGY SERVI	**3.85**	5.10%
34	FAP	ABERDEEN ASIA-PACIFIC	**3.83**	10%
20	TXT.UN	TOP 10 SPLIT TRUST	**3.29**	9%
35	RET.A	REITMANS (CANADA) LTD	**3.27**	6.10%
50	DIV	DIVERSIFIED REALTY CORP	**3.26**	6.80%
36	RET	REITMANS (CANADA) LTD	**3.21**	6.10%
33	SXP	SUPREMEX INC	**3.07**	9%
54	CJ	CARDINAL ENERGY LTD	**3.03**	4.10%
37	SIL	SPROTT INC	**3.00**	4.00%
28	AKT.A	AKITA DRILLING LTD	**2.98**	11%
10	0SP	BROMPTON OIL SPLIT CORP	**2.85**	42%
28	RZE	RAZOR ENERGY CORP	**2.71**	5.40%
38	IAM	INTEGRATED ASSET MANAGEMENT CO	**2.62**	4.60%
51	TGL	TRANSGLOBE ENERGY CORP	**2.5**	7.40%
62	PRV.UN	PRO REAL ESTATE INVESTMENT TRUST	**2.3**	9%
21	TSL	TREE ISLAND STEEL LTD	**2.06**	3.90%
27	GMP	GMP CAPITAL INC	**2.03**	5.00%
64	NXR.UN	NEXUS REIT	**2.01**	8%
26	ENI.UN	ENERGY INCOME FUND	**1.82**	6.60%
38	WEF	WESTERN FOREST PRODU	**1.80**	5.00%
26	PAR.UN	PARTNERS REIT	**1.7**	11%
38	LUC	LUCARA DIAMOND COPR	**1.61**	6.30%
30	CEE	CENTAMIN PLC	**1.59**	4.40%
35	MPVD	MOUNTAIN PROVINCE DIAM	**1.42**	11%
47	SGY	SURGE ENERGY INC	**1.39**	7.10%
38	AFCC	AUTOMOTIVE FINCO CORP	**1.34**	16%
19	MMP.UN	PRECIOUS METALS AND MINING TRUST	**1.33**	9.20%
15	PTG	PIVOT TECHNOLOGY SOLUTI	**1.28**	13%
30	CWL	CALDWELL PARTNERS INTE	**1.2**	7.40%

39	AWI	ADVENT-AWI HOLDINGS INC	**1.10**	4.50%
31	MKZ.UN	MACKENZIE MASTER LP	**0.95**	14%
41	GXO	GRANITE OIL CORP	**0.92**	13%
9	RE	RE ROYALTIES LTD	**0.9**	5.90%
43	BNP	BONAVISTA ENERGY CORP	**0.85**	4.50%
24	TS.B	TORSTAR CORP	**0.73**	14%
27	INP	INPUT CAPITAL CORP	**0.69**	5.70%
8	CBL	CALLIDUS CAPITAL CORP	**0.67**	185%
23	MCS	MCCHIP RESOURCES INC	**0.66**	9%
32	FRO.UN	FRONSAC REAL ESTATE INV	**0.62**	3.60%
40	FDI	FINDEV INC	**0.46**	6.50%
28	ELC	ELYSEE DEVELOPMENT CO	**0.38**	11%
22	GMN	GOBIMI INC	**0.35**	4.20%
20	ICL	ITASCA CAPITAL CORP	**0.32**	245%
7	HFC	HAMPTON FINANCIAL CORP	**0.2**	400%
20	WBE	WESTBOND ENTERPRISED C	**0.18**	5.70%
8	PT	PINE TRAIL REIT	**0.13**	6%
18	SAT	ASIAN TELEVISION NETWOR	**0.11**	18%

THE FINAL WORD

On July 20, 2019 I received the following message from Ms. Innocence. It illustrates just how far Ms. Innocence had progressed in her investing and how her speculative thinking lingers on:

"I forgot to mention: one of my investments is with BMO. Somewhere around $30,000. The interest I get from BMO is just about 4%. I feel like selling it and re-investing in BCE

*or PZA or even Scotiabank. I would gain 1% or even a bit
more. What do you think?*

*And PIF is doing great. Now when you talk about making
money also with the company, did you mean the actual
shares and the amount it shows? Like I made $22,000 with
Royal Bank so far. Should I cash some of it? Or leave it?
What happens AFTER you have invested?"*

The following was my reply:

"Bank stocks have the top scores. With bank stocks it isn't
the dividend percentage that is important, it is the actual
dollar amount being paid out in dividends. While today the
dividend percentage may be 4% on a $100 stock, which
means you are getting $4.000 on 1,000 shares, next year the
dividend will still be 4% but the stock could double to $200
and the amount being paid out in dividends would then be
$8,000.

 Before it would get to $200 a share the bank would likely
split the shares. This means the 1,000 shares worth $100
each would be split and become 2,000 shares worth $50
each. An example of this happening in the past was in
January 2014 when the TD Bank share price rose to $86.45.
It was split and the shares then had a new price of $45.33.
Since 2014 the TD Bank stock has risen and on July 24,
2019 it was worth $77.45. This is a capital gain of $32.12
per share or gain of 71 %.   For the last five years this is an
average capital gain of 14.26 % per year which greatly
exceeds the 2 or 3 percent in additional dividend income

which would have been realized by purchasing a stock, such as BCE that pays a higher dividend.

Banks split shares because they think a lower price for their shares makes the shares more attractive to investors to buy. An increased volume of shares purchased keeps their share price increasing, This, is an important objective for the bank's executives.

When you see a capital gain of $22,000 with the Royal Bank that is interesting but all it is, is interesting. It means the share price has gone up. To keep their dividend at 4% the Royal Bank is now going to have start paying out more dollars in dividends because if they didn't the dividend percentage would drop. They don't want it to drop because it would become a less attractive stock to own than those of other banks.

A growing portfolio is like having an income insurance policy. You don't live on the money invested in the shares in your portfolio, you are living on the dividend income being generated from the shares in the portfolio. As the share price increases, your net worth is increasing but not your monthly dividend income. If you ever needed more money, in an emergency, then you can always sell off a few shares in one of your stocks. The value of your portfolio would drop down immediately, but still be ahead of where you were when you first established your portfolio. With the continued capital gain in your stocks, the dollars you took out would soon be recovered in your portfolio.

If you don't have an emergency, and you don't need any more money than what you are receiving from your dividend income, than don't meddle in your portfolio. Just leave it alone. You picked good stocks that will grow your portfolio. Interestingly even your dividend income will increase because the companies will increase the dollar amounts, they pay out in dividends.

You don't need to do anything. Relax.

THE END

THREE NOVELS
by
IAN DUNCAN
MACDONALD

Now for something different. You may enjoy Ian MacDonald's novel, *BEWARE THE ABANDONED.*

It is a strange story about a New Mexico based capitalist sect that recruits clever, abandoned children off the world's streets. They turn them into successful capitalists. The sect is then rewarded with a percentage of their graduates' income and wealth.

The action takes place in Paris, Las Vegas, Philadelphia and Delaware. Both the mob and the FBI are seeking the sect's graduate who forcefully retrieved the millions the mob stole from him. Can murders be justified if they help the sect save thousand of abandoned children who might die in the streets? You may have a hard time putting this novel down.

BEWARE THE ABANDONED can be purchased from Amazon. Go to:

https://www.amazon.ca/BEWARE-ABANDONED-IAN-DUNCAN-MACDONALD/dp/0991931793

***

Ian's earlier novel, *USING DROUGHT USA,* follows Rob Lyons, a Secretary of State employee, assigned to solving the South West's drought by getting separatist in Quebec and Alberta to step aside, while the US invades Ontario and diverts its waters to the Colorado River. It is an election year. The president wants to win the votes in California, New Mexico, Arizona and Nevada. A greedy lobbyist, a native chief out for revenge and a love interest make this a page turner.

USING DROUGHT USA can be purchased from Amazon. Go to:

https://www.amazon.ca/USING-DROUGHT-USA-DUNCAN-MACDONALD/dp/0991931769

***

Ian's first novel, *DUEL*, follows Rob Lyons, a Secretary of State employee, sent to St Matts, an island in the Caribbean, to prevent the People's Republic of China from leasing an abandoned naval base. It would confirm China's dominance in the region, to the detriment of the USA. Assassination, a threat of nuclear war, an evacuation and a romance make this an interesting, thoughtful read.

DUEL can be purchased from Amazon. Go to:

https://www.amazon.ca/DUEL-Threatening-Massive-Nuclear.../dp/0991931750

***

Manufactured by Amazon.ca
Bolton, ON